POEMS TEACHERS ASK FOR

BOOK ONE

Selected by

READERS OF "NORMAL INSTRUCTOR-PRIMARY PLANS"

COMPRISING THE POEMS MOST FREQUENTLY REQUESTED FOR PUBLICATION IN THAT MAGAZINE ON THE PAGE "POEMS OUR READERS HAVE ASKED FOR"

Granger Poetry Library

GRANGER BOOK CO., INC.
Great Neck, NY

First Published 1925
Reprinted 1979

INTERNATIONAL STANDARD BOOK NUMBER
0-89609-122-8

LIBRARY OF CONGRESS CATALOG NUMBER
78-73496

PRINTED IN THE UNITED STATES OF AMERICA

INDEX

INDEX

INDEX

PREFACE

Seldom does a book of poems appear that is definitely a response to demand and a reflection of readers' preferences. Of this collection that can properly be claimed. For a decade NORMAL INSTRUCTOR-PRIMARY PLANS has carried monthly a page entitled "Poems Our Readers Have Asked For." The interest in this page has been, and is, phenomenal. Occasionally space considerations or copyright restrictions have prevented compliance with requests, but so far as practicable poems asked for have been printed. Because it has become impossible to furnish many of the earlier issues of the magazine, the publishers decided to select the poems most often requested and, carefully revising these for possible errors, to include them in the present collection. In some cases the desired poems are old favorite dramatic recitations, but many of them are poems that are required or recommended for memorizing in state courses of study. This latter feature will of itself make the book extremely valuable to teachers throughout the country. We are glad to offer here certain poems, often requested, but too long for insertion on our magazine Poetry Page. We are pleased also to be able to include a number of popular copyright poems. Special permission to use these has been granted through arrangement with the authorized publishers, whose courtesy is acknowledged below in detail:

THE BOBBS-MERRILL COMPANY—*The Raggedy Man,* from "The Biographical Edition of the Complete Works of James Whitcomb Riley," copyright 1913.

CHARLES SCRIBNER'S SONS—*Seein' Things* and *Little Boy Blue,* by Eugene Field; *Gradatim* and *Give Us Men,* from "The Poetical Works of J. G. Holland"; and *You and You,* by Edith Wharton, copyright 1919.

HARPER AND BROTHERS—*Over the Hill to the Poor-House, The Ride of Jennie M'Neal, The Little Black-Eyed Rebel,* and *The First Settler's Story,* by Will Carleton.

THE DODGE PUBLISHING COMPANY—*The Moo Cow Moo* and *The Young Man Waited,* by Edmund Vance Cooke.

LOTHROP, LEE AND SHEPARD COMPANY—*The House by the Side of the Road* and *The Calf Path,* by Sam Walter Foss.

LITTLE, BROWN AND COMPANY—*October's Bright Blue Weather,* by Helen Hunt Jackson.

HOUGHTON MIFFLIN COMPANY—Poems by John G. Whittier, Alice Cary, Phoebe Cary, James T. Fields, and Lucy Larcom.

THE PUBLISHERS.

POEMS TEACHERS ASK FOR

O Captain! My Captain!

(*This poem was written in memory of Abraham Lincoln.*)

O Captain! My Captain! our fearful
 trip is done,
The ship has weathered every rack, the
 prize we sought is won;
The port is near, the bells I hear, the
 people all exulting,
While follow eyes the steady keel, the
 vessel grim and daring;
 But, O heart! heart! heart!
  O the bleeding drops of red,
 Where on the deck my Captain lies,
  Fallen, cold and dead.

O Captain! My Captain! rise up and
 hear the bells;
Rise up—for you the flag is flung—for
 you the bugle trills,
For you bouquets and ribboned wreaths
 —for you the shores a-crowding,
For you they call, the swaying mass,
 their eager faces turning;
 Here, Captain! dear father!
  This arm beneath your head!
 It is some dream that on the deck
  You've fallen cold and dead.

My Captain does not answer, his lips
 are pale and still;
My father does not feel my arm, he
 has no pulse nor will;
The ship is anchored safe and sound,
 its voyage closed and done;
From fearful trip the victor ship comes
 in with object won;
 Exult, O shores! and ring, O bells!
  But I, with mournful tread,
 Walk the deck my Captain lies,
  Fallen, cold and dead.

Walt Whitman.

A Poet's Prophecy

For I dipt into the future, far as hu-
 man eye could see,
Saw the Vision of the world, and all
 the wonder that would be;
Saw the heavens fill with commerce, ar-
 gosies of magic sails,
Pilots of the purple twilight, dropping
 down with costly bales;
Heard the heavens fill with shouting,
 and there rained a ghastly dew
From the nations' airy navies grap-
 pling in the central blue;
Far along the world-wide whisper of
 the south-wind rushing warm,
With the standards of the peoples
 plunging through the thunder-
 storm;
Till the war-drum throbb'd no longer,
 and the battleflags were furl'd
In the Parliament of man, the Federa-
 tion of the world.
There the common sense of most shall
 hold a fretful realm in awe,
And the kindly earth shall slumber,
 lapt in universal law.

Tennyson, "Locksley Hall," 1842.

The Landing of the Pilgrims

The breaking waves dashed high
On a stern and rock-bound coast,
And the woods against a stormy sky
Their giant branches tossed;

And the heavy night hung dark
The hills and waters o'er,
When a band of exiles moored their bark
On the wild New England shore.

Not as the conqueror comes,
They, the true-hearted, came,—
Not with the roll of the stirring drums,
And the trumpet that sings of fame;

Not as the flying come,
In silence and in fear;
They shook the depths of the desert's gloom
With their hymns of lofty cheer.

Amidst the storms they sang;
And the stars heard, and the sea;
And the sounding aisles of the dim woods rang
To the anthem of the free.

The ocean eagle soared
From his nest by the white wave's foam;
And the rocking pines of the forest roared—
This was their welcome home!

There were men with hoary hair
Amidst that pilgrim band;
Why had they come to wither there
Away from their childhood's land?

There was woman's fearless eye,
Lit by her deep love's truth;
There was manhood's brow serenely high,
And the fiery heart of youth.

What sought they thus afar?
Bright jewels of the mine?
The wealth of seas, the spoils of war?—
They sought a faith's pure shrine.

Ay, call it holy ground,—
The soil where first they trod!
They have left unstained what there they found—
Freedom to worship God!

Felicia Hemans.

Bobby Shaftoe

"Marie, will you marry me?
For you know how I love thee!
Tell me, darling, will you be
The wife of Bobby Shaftoe?"

"Bobby, pray don't ask me more,
For you've asked me twice before;
Let us be good friends, no more,
No more, Bobby Shaftoe."

"If you will not marry me,
I will go away to sea;
And you ne'er again shall be
A friend of Bobby Shaftoe."

"Oh, you will not go away
For you've said so twice to-day.
Stop! He's gone! Dear Bobby, stay!
Dearest Bobby Shaftoe!

"Bobby Shaftoe's gone to sea,
Silver buckles on his knee,
But he'll come back and marry me,
Pretty Bobby Shaftoe.

"He will soon come back to me,
And how happy I shall be,
He'll come back and marry me,
Dearest Bobby Shaftoe."

"Bobby Shaftoe's lost at sea,
He cannot come back to thee.
And you ne'er again will see
Your dear Bobby Shaftoe.

"Oh, we sadly mourn for thee,
And regret we ne'er shall see
Our friend Bobby, true and free,
Dearest Bobby Shaftoe."

"Bobby Shaftoe's lost at sea.
And can ne'er come back to me,
But I'll ever faithful be,
True to Bobby Shaftoe."

"Darling, I've come home from sea,
I've come back to marry thee,
For I know you're true to me,
True to Bobby Shaftoe."

"Yes, I always cared for thee,
And now you've come back to me,
And we will always happy be,
Dearest Bobby Shaftoe."

"Bobby Shaftoe's come from sea,
And we will united be,
Heart and hand in unity,
Mr. and Mrs. Shaftoe."

The Overworked Elocutionist

(Or "ROBERT REESE")

Once there was a little boy
Whose name was Robert Reese,
And every Friday afternoon
He had to speak a piece.

So many poems thus he learned
That soon he had a store
Of recitations in his head
And still kept learning more.

Now this it is what happened:
He was called upon one week
And totally forgot the piece
He was about to speak.

His brain he vainly cudgeled
But no word was in his head,
And so he spoke at random,
And this is what he said:

My beautiful, my beautiful,
Who standest proudly by,
It was the schooner Hesperus
The breaking waves dashed high.

Why is the Forum crowded?
What means this stir in Rome?
Under a spreading chestnut tree
There is no place like home.

When Freedom from her mountain height
Cried, "Twinkle, little star,"
Shoot if you must this old gray head,
King Henry of Navarre.

If you're waking, call me early
To be or not to be,
Curfew must not ring to-night,
Oh, woodman, spare that tree.

Charge, Chester, Charge! On, Stanley, on!
And let who will be clever,
The boy stood on the burning deck
But I go on for ever.

The Kid Has Gone to the Colors

The Kid has gone to the Colors
And we don't know what to say;
The Kid we have loved and cuddled
Stepped out for the Flag to-day.
We thought him a child, a baby
With never a care at all,
But his country called him man-size
And the Kid has heard the call.

He paused to watch the recruiting,
Where, fired by the fife and drum,
He bowed his head to Old Glory
And thought that it whispered: "Come!"
The Kid, not being a slacker,
Stood forth with patriot-joy
To add his name to the roster—
And God, we're proud of the boy!

The Kid has gone to the Colors;
It seems but a little while
Since he drilled a schoolboy army
In a truly martial style.
But now he's a man, a soldier,
And we lend him a listening ear,
For his heart is a heart all loyal,
Unscourged by the curse of fear.

His dad, when he told him, shuddered,
His mother—God bless her!—cried;
Yet, blest with a mother-nature,
She wept with a mother-pride.
But he whose old shoulders straightened
Was Granddad—for memory ran
To years when he, too, a youngster,
Was changed by the Flag to a man!

W. M. Herschell.

Kentucky Belle

Summer of 'sixty-three, sir, and Conrad was gone away—
Gone to the county-town, sir, to sell our first load of hay—
We lived in the log house yonder, poor as ever you've seen;
Roschen there was a baby, and I was only nineteen.

Conrad, he took the oxen, but he left Kentucky Belle.
How much we thought of Kentuck, I couldn't begin to tell—
Came from the Blue-Grass country; my father gave her to me
When I rode north with Conrad, away from the Tennessee.

Conrad lived in Ohio—a German he is, you know—
The house stood in broad cornfields, stretching on, row after row.
The old folks made me welcome; they were kind as kind could be;
But I kept longing, longing, for the hills of the Tennessee.

Oh, for a sight of water, the shadowed slope of a hill!
Clouds that hang on the summit, a wind that never is still!
But the level land went stretching away to meet the sky—
Never a rise, from north to south, to rest the weary eye!

From east to west, no river to shine out under the moon,
Nothing to make a shadow in the yellow afternoon:
Only the breathless sunshine, as I looked out, all forlorn;
Only the rustle, rustle, as I walked among the corn.

When I fell sick with pining, we didn't wait any more,
But moved away from the cornlands, out to this river shore—
The Tuscarawas it's called, sir—off there's a hill, you see—
And now I've grown to like it next best to the Tennessee.

I was at work that morning. Some one came riding like mad
Over the bridge and up the road—Farmer Rouf's little lad.
Bareback he rode; he had no hat; he hardly stopped to say,
"Morgan's men are coming, Frau; they're galloping on this way.

"I'm sent to warn the neighbors. He isn't a mile behind;
He sweeps up all the horses—every horse that he can find.
Morgan, Morgan the raider, and Morgan's terrible men,
With bowie knives and pistols, are galloping up the glen!"

The lad rode down the valley, and I stood still at the door;

The baby laughed and prattled, playing with spools on the floor;
Kentuck was out in the pasture; Conrad, my man, was gone.
Nearer, nearer, Morgan's men were galloping, galloping on!

Sudden I picked up baby, and ran to the pasture bar.
"Kentuck!" I called—"Kentucky!" She knew me ever so far!
I led her down the gully that turns off there to the right,
And tied her to the bushes; her head was just out of sight.

As I ran back to the log house, at once there came a sound—
The ring of hoofs, galloping hoofs, trembling over the ground—
Coming into the turnpike out from the White Woman Glen—
Morgan, Morgan the raider, and Morgan's terrible men.

As near they drew and nearer, my heart beat fast in alarm;
But still I stood in the doorway with baby on my arm.
They came, they passed; with spur and whip in haste they sped along—
Morgan, Morgan the raider, and his band, six hundred strong.

Weary they looked and jaded, riding through night and through day;
Pushing on east to the river, many long miles away,
To the border strip where Virginia runs up into the West,
And fording the Upper Ohio before they could stop to rest.

On like the wind they hurried, and Morgan rode in advance;
Bright were his eyes like live coals, as he gave me a sideways glance.
And I was just breathing freely, after my choking pain,
When the last one of the troopers suddenly drew his rein.

Frightened I was to death, sir; I scarce dared look in his face,
As he asked for a drink of water, and glanced around the place.
I gave him a cup, and he smiled—'twas only a boy, you see;
Faint and worn, with dim blue eyes; and he'd sailed on the Tennessee.

Only sixteen he was, sir—a fond mother's only son—
Off and away with Morgan before his life had begun!
The damp drops stood on his temples; drawn was the boyish mouth;
And I thought me of the mother waiting down in the South.

Oh! pluck was he to the backbone, and clear grit through and through;
Boasted and bragged like a trooper; but the big words wouldn't do;—
The boy was dying, sir, dying as plain as plain could be,
Worn out by his ride with Morgan up from the Tennessee.

But when I told the laddie that I too was from the South,
Water came in his dim eyes, and quivers around his mouth.
"Do you know the Blue-Grass country?" he wistful began to say;
Then swayed like a willow sapling, and fainted dead away.

I had him into the log house, and worked and brought him to;
I fed him, and I coaxed him, as I thought his mother'd do;
And when the lad got better, and the noise in his head was gone,

Morgan's men were miles away, galloping, galloping on.

"Oh, I must go," he muttered; "I must be up and away!
Morgan—Morgan is waiting for me; Oh, what will Morgan say?"
But I heard a sound of tramping and kept him back from the door—
The ringing sound of horses' hoofs that I had heard before.

And on, on, came the soldiers—the Michigan cavalry—
And fast they rode, and black they looked, galloping rapidly,—
They had followed hard on Morgan's track; they had followed day and night;
But of Morgan and Morgan's raiders they had never caught a sight.

And rich Ohio sat startled through all those summer days;
For strange, wild men were galloping over her broad highways—
Now here, now there, now seen, now gone, now north, now east, now west,
Through river-valleys and cornland farms, sweeping away her best.

A bold ride and a long ride; but they were taken at last.
They almost reached the river by galloping hard and fast;
But the boys in blue were upon them ere ever they gained the ford,
And Morgan, Morgan the raider, laid down his terrible sword.

Well, I kept the boy till evening—kept him against his will—
But he was too weak to follow, and sat there pale and still.
When it was cool and dusky—you'll wonder to hear me tell—
But I stole down to that gully, and brought up Kentucky Belle.

I kissed the star on her forehead—my pretty gentle lass—
But I knew that she'd be happy back in the old Blue-Grass.
A suit of clothes of Conrad's, with all the money I had,
And Kentuck, pretty Kentuck, I gave to the worn-out lad.

I guided him to the southward as well as I know how;
The boy rode off with many thanks, and many a backward bow;
And then the glow it faded, and my heart began to swell,
As down the glen away she went, my lost Kentucky Belle!

When Conrad came in the evening, the moon was shining high;
Baby and I were both crying—I couldn't tell him why—
But a battered suit of rebel gray was hanging on the wall,
And a thin old horse, with drooping head, stood in Kentucky's stall.

Well, he was kind, and never once said a hard word to me;
He knew I couldn't help it—'twas all for the Tennessee.
But, after the war was over, just think what came to pass—
A letter, sir; and the two were safe back in the old Blue-Grass.

The lad had got across the border, riding Kentucky Belle;
And Kentuck, she was thriving, and fat, and hearty, and well;
He cared for her, and kept her, nor touched her with whip or spur.
Ah! we've had many horses since, but never a horse like her!

Constance F. Woolson.

An Inventor's Wife

I remember it all so very well, the first of my married life,
That I can't believe it was years ago—it doesn't seem true at all;
Why, I just can *see* the little church where they made us man and wife,
And the merry glow of the first wood-fire that danced on our cottage wall.

We were happy? Yes; and we prospered, too; the house belonged to Joe,
And then, he worked in the planing mill, and drew the best of pay;
And our cup was full when Joey came,—our baby-boy, you know;
So, all went well till that mill burned down and the owner moved away.

It wasn't long till Joe found work, but 'twas never quite the same,—
Never steady, with smaller pay; so to make the two ends meet
He fell to inventin' some machine—I don't recall the name,
But he'd sit for hours in his little shop that opens toward the street,—

Sit for hours, bent over his work, his tools all strewn about.
I used to want to go in there to dust and sweep the floor,
But 'twas just as if 'twas the parson there, writing his sermon out;
Even the baby—bless the child!—learned never to slam that door!

People called him a clever man, and folks from the city came
To look at his new invention and wish my Joe success;
And Joe would say, "Little woman,"—for that was my old pet-name,—
"If my plan succeeds, you shall have a coach and pair, and a fine silk dress!"

I didn't want 'em, the grand new things, but it made the big tears start
To see my Joe with his restless eyes, his fingers worn away
To the skin and bone, for he wouldn't eat; and it almost broke my heart
When he tossed at night from side to side, till the dawning of the day.

Of course, with it all he lost his place. I couldn't blame the man,
The foreman there at the factory, for losing faith in Joe,
For his mind was never upon his work, but on some invention-plan,
As with folded arms and his head bent down he wandered to and fro.

Yet, he kept on workin' at various things, till our little money went
For wheels and screws and metal casts and things I had never seen;
And I ceased to ask, "Any pay, my dear?" with the answer, "Not a cent!"
When his lock and his patent-saw had failed, he clung to that great machine.

I remember one special thing that year. He had bought some costly tool,
When we wanted our boy to learn to read—he was five years old, you know;
He went to his class with cold, bare feet, till at last he came from school
And gravely said, "Don't send me back; the children tease me so!"

I hadn't the heart to cross the child, so, while I sat and sewed

He would rock his little sister in the cradle at my side;
And when the struggle was hardest and I felt keen hunger's goad
Driving me almost to despair—the little baby died.

Her father came to the cradle-side, as she lay, so small and white;
"Maggie," he said, "I have killed this child, and now I am killing you!
I swear by heaven, I will give it up!" Yet, like a thief, that night
He stole to the shop and worked; his brow all wet with a clammy dew.

I cannot tell how I lived that week, my little boy and I,
Too proud to beg; too weak to work; and the weather cold and wild.
I can only think of one dark night when the rain poured from the sky,
And the wind went wailing round the house, like the ghost of my buried child.

Joe still toiled in the little shop. Somebody clicked the gate;
A neighbor-lad brought in the mail and laid it on the floor,
But I sat half-stunned by my heavy grief crouched over the empty grate,
Till I heard—the crack of a pistol-shot; and I sprang to the workshop door.

That door was locked and the bolt shut fast. I could not cry, nor speak,
But I snatched my boy from the corner there, sick with a sudden dread,
And carried him out through the garden plot, forgetting my arms were weak,
Forgetting the rainy torrent that beat on my bare young head.

The front door yielded to my touch. I staggered faintly in,
Fearing—*what?* He stood unharmed, though the wall showed a jagged hole.
In his trembling hand, his aim had failed, and the great and deadly sin
Of his own life's blood was not yet laid on the poor man's tortured soul.

But the pistol held another charge, I knew; and like something mad
I shook my fist in my poor man's face, and shrieked at him, fierce and wild,
"How can you dare to rob us so?"—and I seized the little lad;
"How can you dare to rob your wife and your little helpless child?"

All of a sudden, he bowed his head, while from his nerveless hand
That hung so limp, I almost feared to see the pistol fall.
"Maggie," he said in a low, low voice, "you see me as I stand
A hopeless man. My plan has failed. That letter tells you all."

Then for a moment the house was still as ever the house of death;
Only the drip of the rain outside, for the storm was almost o'er;
But no;—there followed another sound, and I started, caught my breath,
As a stalwart man with a heavy step came in at the open door.

I shall always think him an angel sent from heaven in a human guise;
He must have guessed our awful state; he couldn't help but see
There was something wrong; but never a word, never a look in his eyes
Told what he thought, as in kindly way he talked to Joe and me.

He was come from a thriving city firm, and they'd sent him here to say
That *one* of Joe's inventions was a great, successful thing;
And which do you think? His window-catch that he'd tinkered up one day;
And we were to have a good per cent on the sum that each would bring.

And then the pleasant stranger went, and we wakened as from a dream.
My man bent down his head and said, "Little woman, you've saved my life!"
The worn look gone from his dear gray eyes, and in its place, a gleam
From the sun that has shone so brightly since, on Joe and his happy wife!

Jeannie Pendleton Ewing.

The Two Glasses

There sat two glasses filled to the brim
On a rich man's table, rim to rim,
One was ruddy and red as blood,
And one was clear as the crystal flood.

Said the Glass of Wine to his paler brother:
"Let us tell tales of the past to each other;
I can tell of banquet and revel and mirth,
Where I was king, for I ruled in might;
For the proudest and grandest souls of earth
Fell under my touch, as though struck with blight.
From the heads of kings I have torn the crown;
From the heights of fame I have hurled men down.
I have blasted many an honored name;
I have taken virtue and given shame;
I have tempted youth with a sip, a taste,
That has made his future a barren waste.
Far greater than any king am I,
Or than any army beneath the sky.
I have made the arm of the driver fail;
And sent the train from the iron rail.
I have made good ships go down at sea,
And the shrieks of the lost were sweet to me.
Fame, strength, wealth, genius before me fall;
And my might and power are over all!
Ho, ho, pale brother," said the Wine,
"Can you boast of deeds as great as mine?"

Said the Water Glass: "I cannot boast
Of a king dethroned, or a murdered host;
But I can tell of hearts that were sad,
By my crystal drops made bright and glad;
Of thirsts I have quenched and brows I have laved,
Of hands I have cooled, and souls I have saved.
I have leaped through the valley, dashed down the mountain,
Slipped from the sunshine, and dripped from the fountain,
I have burst my cloud-fetters, and dropped from the sky,
And everywhere gladdened the prospect and eye;
I have eased the hot forehead of fever and pain,
I have made the parched meadows grow fertile with grain.
I can tell of the powerful wheel of the mill,
That ground out the flour, and turned at my will.
I can tell of manhood debased by you
That I have uplifted and crowned anew;
I cheer, I help, I strengthen and aid,
I gladden the heart of man and maid;

I set the wine-chained captive free,
And all are better for knowing me."

These are the tales they told each other,
The Glass of Wine, and its paler brother,
As they sat together, filled to the brim,
On a rich man's table, rim to rim.

Ella Wheeler Wilcox.

Abraham Lincoln

(*Written after Lincoln's death by Tom Taylor, famous cartoonist of the London "Punch."*)

You lay a wreath on murdered Lincoln's bier!
You, who with mocking pencil wont to trace,
Broad for the self-complacent British sneer,
His length of shambling limb, his furrowed face,

His gaunt, gnarled hands, his unkempt, bristling hair,
His garb uncouth, his bearing ill at ease,
His lack of all we prize as debonair,
Of power or will to shine, of art to please!

You, whose smart pen backed up the pencil's laugh,
Judging each step, as though the way were plain;
Reckless, so it could point its paragraph,
Of chief's perplexity, or people's pain!

Beside this corpse, that bears for winding-sheet
The Stars and Stripes he lived to rear anew,
Between the mourners at his head and feet—
Say, scurril jester, is there room for you?

Yes, he had lived to shame me from my sneer—
To lame my pencil and confute my pen—
To make me own this hind, of princes peer,
This rail-splitter, a true-born king of men.

My shallow judgment I had learned to rue,
Noting how to occasion's height he rose;
How his quaint wit made home-truth seem more true,
How, iron-like, his temper grew by blows;

How humble, yet how hopeful he could be;
How in good fortune and in ill the same;
Nor bitter in success, nor boastful he,
Thirsty for gold, nor feverish for fame.

He went about his work—such work as few
Ever had laid on head, and heart, and hand—
As one who knows where there's a task to do,
Man's honest will must Heaven's good grace command;

Who trusts the strength will with the burden grow,
That God makes instruments to work His will,
If but that will we can arrive to know,
Nor tamper with the weights of good and ill.

So he went forth to battle, on the side
That he felt clear was Liberty's and Right's,
As in his peasant boyhood he had plied
His warfare with rude nature's thwarting mights;—

The uncleared forest, the unbroken soil,
The iron bark that turns the lumberer's axe,
The rapid, that o'erbears the boatman's toil,
The prairie, hiding the mazed wanderer's tracks,

The ambushed Indian and the prowling bear—
Such were the needs that helped his youth to train:
Rough culture—but such trees large fruit may bear,
If but their stocks be of right girth and grain.

So he grew up, a destined work to do,
And lived to do it: four long, suffering years
Ill-fate, ill-feeling, ill-report, lived through,
And then he heard the hisses change to cheers,

The taunts to tribute, the abuse to praise,
And took both with the same unwavering mood;
Till, as he came on light, from darkling days,
And seemed to touch the goal from where he stood,

A felon hand, between the goal and him,
Reached from behind his back, a trigger prest—
And those perplexed and patient eyes were dim,
Those gaunt, long-laboring limbs were laid to rest!

The words of mercy were upon his lips,
Forgiveness in his heart and on his pen,
When this vile murderer brought swift eclipse
To thoughts of peace on earth, good-will to men.

The Old World and the New, from sea to sea,
Utter one voice of sympathy and shame!
Sore heart, so stopped when it at last beat high;
Sad life, cut short as its triumph came!

The Old Clock on the Stairs

Somewhat back from the village street
Stands the old-fashioned country-seat;
Across its antique portico
Tall poplar trees their shadows throw;
And, from its station in the hall,
An ancient timepiece says to all,
"Forever—never!
Never—forever!"

Half-way up the stairs it stands,
And points and beckons with its hands,
From its case of massive oak,
Like a monk who, under his cloak,
Crosses himself, and sighs, alas!
With sorrowful voice to all who pass,
"Forever—never!
Never—forever!"

By day its voice is low and light;
But in the silent dead of night,
Distinct as a passing footstep's fall,
It echoes along the vacant hall,
Along the ceiling, along the floor,
And seems to say at each chamber door,
"Forever—never!
Never—forever!"

Through days of sorrow and of mirth,
Through days of death and days of birth,
Through every swift vicissitude
Of changeful time, unchanged it has stood,
And as if, like God, it all things saw,
It calmly repeats those words of awe,
"Forever—never!
Never—forever!"

In that mansion used to be
Free-hearted Hospitality;
His great fires up the chimney roared;
The stranger feasted at his board;
But, like the skeleton at the feast,
That warning timepiece never ceased,—
"Forever—never!
Never—forever!"

There groups of merry children played;
There youths and maidens dreaming strayed;
Oh, precious hours! oh, golden prime
And affluence of love and time!
Even as a miser counts his gold,
Those hours the ancient timepiece told,—
"Forever—never!
Never—forever!"

From that chamber, clothed in white,
The bride came forth on her wedding night;
There, in that silent room below,
The dead lay, in his shroud of snow;
And, in the hush that followed the prayer,
Was heard the old clock on the stair,—
"Forever—never!
Never—forever!"

All are scattered, now, and fled,—
Some are married, some are dead;
And when I ask, with throbs of pain,
"Ah! when shall they all meet again?"
As in the days long since gone by,
The ancient timepiece makes reply,—
"Forever—never!
Never—forever!"

Never here, forever there,
Where all parting, pain, and care,
And death, and time, shall disappear,—
Forever there, but never here!
The horologe of Eternity
Sayeth this incessantly,—
"Forever—never!
Never—forever!"

H. W. Longfellow.

Christ in Flanders

We had forgotten You, or very nearly—
You did not seem to touch us very nearly—
Of course we thought about You now and then;
Especially in any time of trouble—
We knew that you were good in time of trouble—
But we were very ordinary men.

And there were always other things to think of—
There's lots of things a man has got to think of—
His work, his home, his pleasure, and his wife;
And so we only thought of You on Sunday—
Sometimes, perhaps, not even on a Sunday—
Because there's always lots to fill one's life.

And, all the while, in street or lane or byway—
In country lane, in city street, or byway—
You walked among us, and we did not see.

Your feet were bleeding as You walked our pavements—
How did we miss Your footprints on our pavements?—
Can there be other folk as blind as we?

Now we remember; over here in Flanders—
(It isn't strange to think of You in Flanders)—
This hideous warfare seems to make things clear.
We never thought about You much in England—
But now that we are far away from England—
We have no doubts, we know that You are here.

You helped us pass the jest along the trenches—
Where, in cold blood, we waited in the trenches—
You touched its ribaldry and made it fine.
You stood beside us in our pain and weakness—
We're glad to think You understand our weakness—
Somehow it seems to help us not to whine.

We think about You kneeling in the Garden—
Ah, God, the agony of that dread Garden—
We know You prayed for us upon the cross.
If anything could make us glad to bear it—
'Twould be the knowledge that You willed to bear it—
Pain—death—the uttermost of human loss.

Though we forgot You—You will not forget us—
We feel so sure that You will not forget us—
But stay with us until this dream is past.
And so we ask for courage, strength, and pardon—
Especially, I think, we ask for pardon—
And that You'll stand beside us to the last.

L. W. in London "Spectator."

We Are Seven

—A simple Child,
That lightly draws its breath,
And feels its life in every limb,
What should it know of death?

I met a little cottage Girl:
She was eight years old, she said;
Her hair was thick with many a curl
That clustered round her head.

She had a rustic, woodland air,
And she was wildly clad:
Her eyes were fair, and very fair;
—Her beauty made me glad.

"Sisters and brothers, little Maid,
How many may you be?"
"How many? Seven in all," she said,
And wondering looked at me.

"And where are they? I pray you tell."
She answered, "Seven are we;
And two of us at Conway dwell,
And two are gone to sea.

"Two of us in the church-yard lie,
My sister and my brother;
And, in the church-yard cottage, I
Dwell near them with my mother."

"You say that two at Conway dwell,
And two are gone to sea,

Yet ye are seven!—I pray you tell,
Sweet Maid, how this may be."

Then did the little Maid reply,
"Seven boys and girls are we;
Two of us in the church-yard lie,
Beneath the church-yard tree."

"You run about, my little Maid,
Your limbs they are alive;
If two are in the church-yard laid,
Then ye are only five."

"Their graves are green, they may be seen,"
The little Maid replied,
"Twelve steps or more from my mother's door,
And they are side by side.

"My stockings there I often knit,
My kerchief there I hem;
And there upon the ground I sit,
And sing a song to them.

"And often after sunset, Sir,
When it is light and fair,
I take my little porringer,
And eat my supper there.

"The first that died was sister Jane;
In bed she moaning lay,
Till God released her of her pain;
And then she went away.

"So in the church-yard she was laid;
And, when the grass was dry,
Together round her grave we played,
My brother John and I.

"And when the ground was white with snow,
And I could run and slide,
My brother John was forced to go,
And he lies by her side."

"How many are you, then," said I,
"If they two are in heaven?"
Quick was the little Maid's reply,
"O Master! we are seven."

"But they are dead; those two are dead!
Their spirits are in heaven!"
'T was throwing words away; for still
The little Maid would have her will,
And said, "Nay, we are seven!"

William Wordsworth.

Echo

"I asked of Echo, t'other day
(Whose words are often few and funny),
What to a novice she could say
Of courtship, love and matrimony.
Quoth Echo plainly,—'Matter-o'-money!'

"Whom should I marry? Should it be
A dashing damsel, gay and pert,
A pattern of inconstancy;
Or selfish, mercenary flirt?
Quoth Echo, sharply,—'Nary flirt!'

"What if, aweary of the strife
That long has lured the dear deceiver,
She promise to amend her life,
And sin no more; can I believe her?
Quoth Echo, very promptly,—'Leave her!'

"But if some maiden with a heart
On me should venture to bestow it,
Pray should I act the wiser part
To take the treasure or forego it?
Quoth Echo, with decision,—'Go it!'

"But what if, seemingly afraid
To bind her fate in Hymen's fetter,
She vow she means to die a maid,
In answer to my loving letter?
Quoth Echo, rather coolly,—'Let her!'

"What if, in spite of her disdain,
I find my heart entwined about
With Cupid's dear, delicious chain
So closely that I can't get out?
Quoth Echo, laughingly,—'Get out!'

"But if some maid with beauty blest,
As pure and fair as Heaven can make her,
Will share my labor and my rest
Till envious Death shall overtake her?
Quoth Echo (sotto voce),—'Take her!'"

John G. Saxe.

Engineers Making Love

It's noon when Thirty-five is due,
An' she comes on time like a flash of light,
An' you hear her whistle "Too-tee-too!"
Long 'fore the pilot swings in sight.
Bill Madden's drivin' her in to-day,
An' he's calling his sweetheart far away—
Gertrude Hurd lives down by the mill;
You might see her blushin'; she knows it's Bill.
"Tudie, tudie! Toot-ee! Tudie, tudie! Tu!"

Six-five, A. M. there's a local comes,
Makes up at Bristol, rúnnin' east;
An' the way her whistle sings and hums
Is a livin' caution to man and beast.
Every one knows who Jack White calls,—
Little Lou Woodbury, down by the falls;
Summer or Winter, always the same,
She hears her lover callin' her name—
"Lou-ie! Lou-ie! Lou-iee!"

But at one fifty-one, old Sixty-four—
Boston express, runs east, clear through—
Drowns her rattle and rumble and roar
With the softest whistle that ever blew.
An' away on the furthest edge of town
Sweet Sue Winthrop's eyes of brown
Shine like the starlight, bright and clear,
When she hears the whistle of Abel Gear,
"You-oo! Su-u-u-u-u-e!"

Along at midnight a freight comes in,
Leaves Berlin sometime—I don't know when;
But it rumbles along with a fearful din
Till it reaches the Y-switch there and then
The clearest notes of the softest bell
That out of a brazen goblet fell
Wake Nellie Minton out of her dreams;
To her like a wedding-bell it seems—
"Nell, Nell, Nell! Nell, Nell, Nell!"

Tom Willson rides on the right-hand side,
Givin' her steam at every stride;
An' he touches the whistle, low an' clear,
For Lulu Gray on the hill, to hear—
"Lu-Lu! Loo-Loo! Loo-oo!"

So it goes all day an' all night
Till the old folks have voted the thing a bore;
Old maids and bachelors say it ain't right
For folks to do courtin' with such a roar.
But the engineers their kisses will blow
From a whistle valve to the girls they know,
An' stokers the name of their sweethearts tell;
With the "Too-too-too" and the swinging bell.

R. J. Burdette.

Guilty or Not Guilty

She stood at the bar of justice,
  A creature wan and wild,
In form too small for a woman,
  In features too old for a child;
For a look so worn and pathetic
  Was stamped on her pale young face,
It seemed long years of suffering
  Must have left that silent trace.

"Your name?" said the judge, as he eyed her
  With kindly look yet keen,—
"Is Mary McGuire, if you please, sir."
  And your age?"—"I am turned fifteen."
"Well, Mary," and then from a paper
  He slowly and gravely read,
"You are charged here—I'm sorry to say it—
  With stealing three loaves of bread.

"You look not like an offender,
  And I hope that you can show
The charge to be false. Now, tell me,
  Are you guilty of this, or no?"
A passionate burst of weeping
  Was at first her sole reply,
But she dried her eyes in a moment,
  And looked in the judge's eye.

"I will tell you just how it was, sir:
  My father and mother are dead,
And my little brothers and sisters
  Were hungry and asked me for bread.
At first I earned it for them
  By working hard all day,
But somehow, times were bad, sir,
  And the work all fell away.

"I could get no more employment,
  The weather was bitter cold,
The young ones cried and shivered—
  (Little Johnny's but four years old)—
So what was I to do, sir?
  I am guilty, but do not condemn.
I *took*—oh, was it *stealing?*—
  The bread to give to them."

Every man in the court-room—
  Gray-beard and thoughtless youth—
Knew, as he looked upon her,
  That the prisoner spake the truth;
Out from their pockets came kerchiefs,
  Out from their eyes sprung tears,
And out from their old faded wallets
  Treasures hoarded for years.

The judge's face was a study,
  The strangest you ever saw,
As he cleared his throat and murmured
  Something about the *law;*
For one so learned in such matters,
  So wise in dealing with men,
He seemed, on a simple question,
  Sorely puzzled, just then.

But no one blamed him or wondered,
  When at last these words he heard,
"The sentence of this young prisoner
  Is, for the present, deferred."
And no one blamed him or wondered
  When he went to her and smiled
And tenderly led from the court-room,
  Himself, the "guilty" child.

The Baby

Where did you come from, baby dear?
Out of the everywhere into the here.

Where did you get your eyes so blue?
Out of the sky as I came through.

What makes the light in them sparkle and spin?
Some of the starry spikes left in.

Where did you get that little tear?
I found it waiting when I got here.

What makes your forehead so smooth and high?
A soft hand stroked it as I went by.

What makes your cheek like a warm white rose?
Something better than anyone knows.

Whence that three-cornered smile of bliss?
Three angels gave me at once a kiss.

Where did you get that pearly ear?
God spoke, and it came out to hear.

Where did you get those arms and hands?
Love made itself into hooks and bands.

Feet, whence did you come, you darling things?
From the same box as the cherubs' wings.

How did they all just come to be you?
God thought about me, and so I grew.

But how did you come to us, you dear?
God thought of you, and so I am here.

George Macdonald.

Song of the Sea

The sea! the sea! the open sea!
The blue, the fresh, the ever free!
Without a mark, without a bound,
It runneth the earth's wide regions round;
It plays with the clouds; it mocks the skies,
Or like a cradled creature lies.

I'm on the sea! I'm on the sea!
I am where I would ever be;
With the blue above and the blue below,
And silence wheresoe'er I go.
If a storm should come and awake the deep
What matter? *I* shall ride and sleep.

I love, oh, how I love to ride
On the fierce, foaming, bursting tide,
When every mad wave drowns the moon,
Or whistles aloud his tempest tune,
And tells how goeth the world below,
And why the southwest blasts do blow.

I never was on the dull, tame shore,
But I loved the great sea more and more,
And back I flew to her billowy breast,
Like a bird that seeketh its mother's nest;
And a mother she *was*, and *is*, to me,
For I was born on the open sea!

I've lived, since then, in calm and strife,
Full fifty summers a sailor's life,
With wealth to spend and a power to range,
But never have sought nor sighed for change;
And Death, whenever he comes to me,
Shall come on the wild, unbounded sea.

Barry Cornwall.

Diffidence

"I'm after axin', Biddy dear—"
And here he paused a while
To fringe his words the merest mite
With something of a smile—
A smile that found its image
In a face of beauteous mold,
Whose liquid eyes were peeping
From a broidery of gold.

"I've come to ax ye, Biddy dear,
If—" then he stopped again,
As if his heart had bubbled o'er
And overflowed his brain.
His lips were twitching nervously
O'er what they had to tell,
And timed the quavers with the eyes
That gently rose and fell.

"I've come—" and then he took her hands
And held them in his own,
"To ax—" and then he watched the buds
That on her cheeks had blown,—

"Me purty dear—" and then he heard
The throbbing of her heart,
That told how love had entered in
And claimed its every part.

"Och! don't be tazin' me," said she,
With just the faintest sigh,
"I've sinse enough to see you've come,
But what's the reason why?"
"To ax—" and once again the tongue
Forbore its sweets to tell,
"To ax—*if Mrs. Mulligan*
Has any pigs to sell."

Curfew Must Not Ring To-night

Slowly England's sun was setting o'er the hilltops far away,
Filling all the land with beauty at the close of one sad day,
And the last rays kissed the forehead of a man and maiden fair,—
He with footsteps slow and weary, she with sunny floating hair;
He with bowed head, sad and thoughtful, she with lips all cold and white,
Struggling to keep back the murmur, "Curfew must not ring to-night."

"Sexton," Bessie's white lips faltered, pointing to the prison old,
With its turrets tall and gloomy, with its walls dark, damp and cold,
"I've a lover in that prison, doomed this very night to die
At the ringing of the curfew, and no earthly help is nigh;
Cromwell will not come till sunset," and her lips grew strangely white
As she breathed the husky whisper: "Curfew must not ring to-night."

"Bessie," calmly spoke the sexton—every word pierced her young heart
Like the piercing of an arrow, like a deadly poisoned dart,—
"Long, long years I've rung the curfew from that gloomy shadowed tower;
Every evening, just at sunset, it has told the twilight hour;
I have done my duty ever, tried to do it just and right,
Now I'm old I will not falter,—curfew, it must ring to-night."

Wild her eyes and pale her features, stern and white her thoughtful brow.
As within her secret bosom Bessie made a solemn vow.
She had listened while the judges read without a tear or sigh:
"At the ringing of the curfew, Basil Underwood must die."
And her breath came fast and faster, and her eyes grew large and bright;
In an undertone she murmured, "Curfew must not ring to-night."

With quick step she bounded forward, sprung within the old church door,
Left the old man treading slowly paths so oft he'd trod before;
Not one moment paused the maiden, but with eye and cheek aglow
Mounted up the gloomy tower, where the bell swung to and fro,—
As she climbed the dusty ladder on which fell no ray of light,
Up and up,—her white lips saying: "Curfew must not ring to-night."

She has reached the topmost ladder; o'er her hangs the great, dark bell;
Awful is the gloom beneath her, like the pathway down to hell.
Lo, the ponderous tongue is swinging—'tis the hour of curfew now,
And the sight has chilled her bosom, stopped her breath and paled her brow.
Shall she let it ring? No, never! flash her eyes with sudden light,

As she springs and grasps it firmly—
"Curfew shall not ring to-night!"

Out she swung—far out; the city seemed a speck of light below,
There 'twixt heaven and earth suspended as the bell swung to and fro;
And the sexton at the bell-rope, old and deaf, heard not the bell,
Sadly thought, "That twilight curfew rang young Basil's funeral knell."
Still the maiden clung more firmly, and with trembling lips so white,
Said, to hush her heart's wild throbbing: "Curfew shall not ring to-night."

It was o'er; the bell ceased swaying, and the maiden stepped once more
Firmly on the dark old ladder where, for hundred years before
Human foot had not been planted. The brave deed that she had done
Should be told long ages after; as the rays of setting sun
Crimson all the sky with beauty, aged sires with heads of white,
Tell the eager, listening children, "Curfew did not ring that night."

O'er the distant hills came Cromwell; Bessie sees him, and her brow,
Lately white with fear and anguish, has no anxious traces now.
At his feet she tells her story, shows her hands all bruised and torn;
And her face so sweet and pleading, yet with sorrow pale and worn,
Touched his heart with sudden pity, lit his eyes with misty light:
"Go! your lover lives," said Cromwell, "Curfew shall not ring to-night."

Wide they flung the massive portal; led the prisoner forth to die,—
All his bright young life before him. 'Neath the darkening English sky
Bessie comes with flying footsteps, eyes aglow with love-light sweet;
Kneeling on the turf beside him, lays his pardon at his feet.
In his brave, strong arms he clasped her, kissed the face upturned and white,
Whispered, "Darling, you have saved me—curfew will not ring to-night."

Rose Hartwick Thorpe.

Kate Shelly

Have you heard how a girl saved the lightning express—
Of Kate Shelly, whose father was killed on the road?
Were he living to-day, he'd be proud to possess
Such a daughter as Kate. Ah! 'twas grit that she showed
On that terrible evening when Donahue's train
Jumped the bridge and went down, in the darkness and rain.

She was only eighteen, but a woman in size,
With a figure as graceful and lithe as a doe,
With peach-blossom cheeks, and with violet eyes,
And teeth and complexion like new-fallen snow;
With a nature unspoiled and unblemished by art—
With a generous soul, and a warm, noble heart!

'Tis evening—the darkness is dense and profound;
Men linger at home by their bright-blazing fires;
The wind wildly howls with a horrible sound,

And shrieks through the vibrating telegraph wires;
The fierce lightning flashes along the dark sky;
The rain falls in torrents; the river rolls by.

The scream of a whistle; the rush of a train!
The sound of a bell! a mysterious light
That flashes and flares through the fast falling rain!
A rumble! a roar! shrieks of human affright!
The falling of timbers! the space of a breath!
A splash in the river; then darkness and death!

Kate Shelly recoils at the terrible crash;
The sounds of destruction she happens to hear;
She springs to the window—she throws up the sash,
And listens and looks with a feeling of fear.
The tall tree-tops groan, and she hears the faint cry
Of a drowning man down in the river near by.

Her heart feebly flutters, her features grow wan,
And then through her soul in a moment there flies
A forethought that gives her the strength of a man—
She turns to her trembling old mother and cries:
"I must save the express—'twill be here in an hour!"
Then out through the door disappears in the shower.
She flies down the track through the pitiless rain;
She reaches the river—the water below
Whirls and seethes through the timbers. She shudders again;
"The bridge! To Moingona, God help me to go!"
Then closely about her she gathers her gown
And on the wet ties with a shiver sinks down.

Then carefully over the timbers she creeps
On her hands and knees, almost holding her breath.
The loud thunder peals and the wind wildly sweeps,
And struggles to hurry her downward to death;
But the thought of the train to destruction so near
Removes from her soul every feeling of fear.

With the blood dripping down from each torn, bleeding limb,
Slowly over the timbers her dark way she feels;
Her fingers grow numb and her head seems to swim;
Her strength is fast failing—she staggers! she reels!
She falls—Ah! the danger is over at last,
Her feet touch the earth, and the long bridge is passed!

In an instant new life seems to come to her form;
She springs to her feet and forgets her despair.
On, on to Moingona! she faces the storm,
She reaches the station—the keeper is there.
"Save the lightning express! No—hang out the red light!

There's death on the bridge at the river
to-night!"

Out flashes the signal-light, rosy and
red;
Then sounds the loud roar of the
swift-coming train,
The hissing of steam, and there, bright-
ly ahead,
The gleam of a headlight illumines
the rain.
"Down brakes!" shrieks the whistle,
defiant and shrill;
She heeds the red signal—she slackens,
she's still!

Ah! noble Kate Shelly, your mission is
done;
Your deed that dark night will not
fade from our gaze;
An endless renown you have worthily
won;
Let the nation be just, and accord you
its praise,
Let your name, let your fame, and
your courage declare
What a *woman* can do, and a *woman*
can dare!

Eugene J. Hall.

There's But One Pair of Stockings to Mend To-Night

An old wife sat by her bright fireside,
Swaying thoughtfully to and fro
In an easy chair, whose creaky craw
Told a tale of long ago;
While down by her side, on the kitchen
floor,
Stood a basket of worsted balls—a
score.

The good man dozed o'er the latest
news
Till the light in his pipe went out;
And, unheeded, the kitten with cunning
paws
Rolled and tangled the balls about;
Yet still sat the wife in the ancient
chair,
Swaying to and fro in the fire-light
glare.

But anon, a misty teardrop came
In her eyes of faded blue,
Then trickled down in a furrow deep
Like a single drop of dew;
So deep was the channel—so silent the
stream—
That the good man saw naught but the
dimmed eye-beam.

Yet marveled he much that the cheerful
light
Of her eye had heavy grown,
And marveled he more at the tangled
balls,
So he said in a gentle tone:
"I have shared thy joys since our mar-
riage vow,
Conceal not from me thy sorrows now."

Then she spoke of the time when the
basket there
Was filled to the very brim;
And now, there remained of the goodly
pile
But a single pair—for him;
"Then wonder not at the dimmed eye-
light,
There's but one pair of stockings to
mend to-night.

"I cannot but think of the busy feet
Whose wrappings were wont to lay
In the basket, awaiting the needle's
time—
Now wandering so far away;
How the sprightly steps to a mother
dear,
Unheeded fell on the careless ear.

"For each empty nook in the basket old
By the hearth there's a vacant seat;

And I miss the shadows from off the
wall,
And the patter of many feet;
'Tis for this that a tear gathered over
my sight,
At the one pair of stockings to mend
to-night.

" 'Twas said that far through the for-
est wild,
And over the mountains bold,
Was a land whose rivers and darkening
caves
Were gemmed with the rarest gold;
Then my first-born turned from the
oaken door—
And I knew the shadows were only
four.

"Another went forth on the foaming
wave,
And diminished the basket's store;
But his feet grew cold—so weary and
cold,
They'll never be warm any more.
And this nook, in its emptiness, seemeth
to me
To give forth no voice but the moan of
the sea.

"Two others have gone toward the set-
ting sun,
And made them a home in its light,
And fairy fingers have taken their
share,
To mend by the fireside bright;
Some other baskets their garments will
fill—
But mine, ah, mine is emptier still.

"Another—the dearest, the fairest, the
best—
Was taken by angels away,
And clad in a garment that waxeth not
old,
In a land of continual day;
Oh! wonder no more at the dimmed
eye-light,
When I mend the one pair of stockings
to-night."

The Young Man Waited

In the room below the young man sat,
With an anxious face and a white
cravat,
A throbbing heart and a silken hat,
And various other things like that
Which he had accumulated.
And the maid of his heart was up above
Surrounded by hat and gown and glove,
And a thousand things which women
love,
But no man knoweth the names there-
of—
And the young man sat and—waited.

You will scarce believe the things I tell,
But the truth thereof I know full well,
Though how may not be stated;
But I swear to you that the maiden took
A sort of half-breed, thin stove-hook,
And heated it well in the gaslight there,
And thrust it into her head, or hair.
Then she took something off the bed,
And hooked it onto her hair, or head,
And piled it high, and piled it higher,
And drove it home with staples of wire!
And the young man anxiously—
waited.

Then she took a thing she called a
"puff"
And some very peculiar whitish stuff,
And using about a half a peck,
She spread it over her face and neck,
(Deceit was a thing she hated!)
And she looked as fair as a lilied bower,
Or a pound of lard or a sack of flour;—
And the young man wearily—waited.

Then she took a garment of awful
shape
And it wasn't a waist, nor yet a cape,

But it looked like a piece of ancient mail,
Or an instrument from a Russian jail,
And then with a fearful groan and gasp,
She squeezed herself in its deathly clasp—
  So fair and yet so fated!
And then with a move like I don't know what,
She tied it on with a double knot;—
  And the young man wofully—waited.

Then she put on a dozen different things,
A mixture of buttons and hooks and strings,
Till she strongly resembled a notion store;
Then, taking some seventeen pins or more,
She thrust them into her ruby lips,
Then stuck them around from waist to hips,
  And never once hesitated.
And the maiden didn't know, perhaps,
That the man below had had seven naps,
  And that now he sleepily—waited.

And then she tried to put on her hat,
Ah me, a trying ordeal was that!
She tipped it high and she tried it low,
But every way that the thing would go
  Only made her more agitated.
It wouldn't go straight and it caught her hair,
And she wished she could hire a man to swear,
But alas, the only man lingering there
  Was the one who wildly—waited.

And then before she could take her leave,
She had to puff up her monstrous sleeve,
Then a little dab here and a wee pat there,
And a touch or two to her hindmost hair,
Then around the room with the utmost care
  She thoughtfully circulated.
Then she seized her gloves and a chamoiskin,
Some breath perfume and a long stick-pin,
A bonbon box and a cloak and some
Eau-de-cologne and chewing-gum,
Her opera glass and sealskin muff,
A fan and a heap of other stuff;
Then she hurried down, but ere she spoke,
Something about the maiden broke.
So she scurried back to the winding stair,
And the young man looked in wild despair,
  And then he—evaported.

Edmund Vance Cooke.

Invictus

Out of the night that covers me,
  Black as the Pit from pole to pole,
I thank whatever gods may be
  For my unconquerable soul.

In the fell clutch of circumstance
  I have not winced nor cried aloud.
Under the bludgeonings of chance
  My head is bloody, but unbowed.

Beyond this place of wrath and tears
  Looms but the Horror of the shade,
And yet the menace of the years
  Finds, and shall find, me unafraid.

It matters not how strait the gate,
  How charged with punishments the scroll,
I am the master of my fate;
  I am the captain of my soul.

William E. Henley.

Katie Lee and Willie Grey

Two brown heads with tossing curls,
Red lips shutting over pearls,
Bare feet, white and wet with dew,
Two eyes black, and two eyes blue;
Little girl and boy were they,
Katie Lee and Willie Grey.

They were standing where a brook,
Bending like a shepherd's crook,
Flashed its silver, and thick ranks
Of willow fringed its mossy banks;
Half in thought, and half in play,
Katie Lee and Willie Grey.

They had cheeks like cherries red;
He was taller—'most a head;
She, with arms like wreaths of snow,
Swung a basket to and fro
As she loitered, half in play,
Chattering to Willie Grey.

"Pretty Katie," Willie said—
And there came a dash of red
Through the brownness of his cheek—
"Boys are strong and girls are weak,
And I'll carry, so I will,
Katie's basket up the hill."

Katie answered with a laugh,
"You shall carry only half";
And then, tossing back her curls,
"Boys are weak as well as girls."
Do you think that Katie guessed
Half the wisdom she expressed?

Men are only boys grown tall;
Hearts don't change much, after all;
And when, long years from that day,
Katie Lee and Willie Grey
Stood again beside the brook,
Bending like a shepherd's crook,—

Is it strange that Willie said,
While again a dash of red
Crossed the brownness of his cheek,
"I am strong and you are weak;
Life is but a slippery steep,
Hung with shadows cold and deep.

"Will you trust me, Katie dear,—
Walk beside me without fear?
May I carry, if I will,
All your burdens up the hill?"
And she answered, with a laugh,
"No, but you may carry half."

Close beside the little brook,
Bending like a shepherd's crook,
Washing with its silver hands
Late and early at the sands,
Is a cottage, where to-day
Katie lives with Willie Grey.

In a porch she sits, and lo!
Swings a basket to and fro—
Vastly different from the one
That she swung in years agone,
This is long and deep and wide,
And has—*rockers at the side.*

Abou Ben Adhem

Abou Ben Adhem—may his tribe increase!—
Awoke one night from a deep dream of peace,
And saw, within the moonlight in his room,
Making it rich, and like a lily in bloom,
An angel, writing in a book of gold.
Exceeding peace had made Ben Adhem bold,
And to the Presence in the room he said,
"What writest thou?" The vision raised its head,
And, with a look made all of sweet accord,
Answered, "The names of those who love the Lord."
"And is mine one?" said Abou. "Nay, not so,"
Replied the angel.—Abou spoke more low,

But cheerily still; and said, "I pray
thee, then,
Write me as one that loves his fellow-
men."

The angel wrote, and vanished. The
next night
It came again, with a great wakening
light,
And showed the names whom love of
God had blessed:
And, lo! Ben Adhem's name led all the
rest. *Leigh Hunt.*

In School-Days

Still sits the school-house by the road,
A ragged beggar sunning;
Around it still the sumachs grow,
And blackberry vines are running.

Within, the master's desk is seen,
Deep scarred by raps official;
The warping floor, the battered seats,
The jack-knife's carved initial;

The charcoal frescoes on its wall;
Its door's worn sill, betraying
The feet that, creeping slow to school,
Went storming out to playing!

Long years ago a winter sun
Shone over it at setting;
Lit up its western window-panes,
And low eaves' icy fretting.

It touched the tangled golden curls,
And brown eyes full of grieving,
Of one who still her steps delayed
When all the school were leaving.

For near her stood the little boy
Her childish favor singled:
His cap pulled low upon a face
Where pride and shame were
mingled.

Pushing with restless feet the snow
To right and left, he lingered;—
As restlessly her tiny hands
The blue-checked apron fingered.

He saw her lift her eyes; he felt
The soft hand's light caressing,
And heard the tremble of her voice,
As if a fault confessing.

"I'm sorry that I spelt the word:
I hate to go above you,
Because,"—the brown eyes lower fell,—
"Because, you see, I love you!"

Still memory to a gray-haired man
That sweet child-face is showing.
Dear girl: the grasses on her grave
Have forty years been growing!

He lives to learn, in life's hard school,
How few who pass above him
Lament their triumph and his loss,
Like her,—because they love him.
John Greenleaf Whittier.

Mother's Fool

"Tis plain to see," said a farmer's wife,
"These boys will make their mark in
life;
They were never made to handle a hoe,
And at once to a college ought to go;
There's Fred, he's little better than a
fool,
But John and Henry must go to
school."

"Well, really, wife," quoth Farmer
Brown,
As he set his mug of cider down,
"Fred does more work in a day for me
Than both his brothers do in three.
Book larnin' will never plant one's corn,
Nor hoe potatoes, sure's you're born;
Nor mend a rod of broken fence—
For my part, give me common sense."

But his wife was bound the roost to
rule,

And John and Henry were sent to school,
While Fred, of course, was left behind,
Because his mother said he had no mind.

Five years at school the students spent;
Then into business each one went.
John learned to play the flute and fiddle,
And parted his hair, of course, in the middle;
While his brother looked rather higher than he,
And hung out a sign, "H. Brown, M. D."

Meanwhile, at home, their brother Fred
Had taken a notion into his head;
But he quietly trimmed his apple trees,
And weeded onions and planted peas,
While somehow or other, by hook or crook,
He managed to read full many a book;
Until at last his father said
He was getting "book larnin' " into his head;
"But for all that," added Farmer Brown,
"He's the smartest boy there is in town."

The war broke out, and Captain Fred
A hundred men to battle led,
And when the rebel flag came down,
Went marching home as General Brown.
But he went to work on the farm again,
And planted corn and sowed his grain;
He shingled the barn and mended the fence,
Till people declared he had common sense.

Now common sense was very rare,
And the State House needed a portion there;
So the "family dunce" moved into town—
The people called him Governor Brown;
And the brothers who went to the city school
Came home to live with "mother's fool."

Kentucky Philosophy

You Wi'yam, cum 'ere, suh, dis instunce.
 Wu' dat you got under dat box?
I do' want no foolin'—you hear me?
 Wut you say? Ain't nu'h'n but *rocks?*
'Peah ter me you's owdashus p'ticler.
 S'posin' dey's uv a new kine.
I'll des take a look at dem rocks. Hi yi! der you think dat I's bline?

I calls dat a plain water-million, you scamp, en I knows whah it growed;
It come fum de Jimmerson cawn fiel', dah on ter side er de road.
You stole it, you rascal—you stole it! I watched you fum down in de lot.
En time I gets th'ough wid you, nigger, you won't eb'n be a grease spot!

I'll fix you. Mirandy! Mi*ran*dy! go cut me a hick'ry—make 'ase!
En cut me de toughes' en keenes' you c'n fine anywhah on de place.
I'll larn you, Mr. Wi'yam Joe Vetters, ter steal en ter lie, you young sinner,
Disgracin' yo' ole Christian mammy, en makin' her leave cookin' dinner!

Now ain't you ashamed er yo'se'lf sur? I is. I's 'shamed you's my son!
En de holy accorjan angel he's 'shamed er wut you has done;
En he's tuk it down up yander in coal-black, blood-red letters—
"One water-million stoled by Wi'yam Josephus Vetters."

En wut you s'posen Brer Bascom, yo' teacher at Sunday school,
'Ud say ef he knowed how you's broke de good Lawd's Gol'n Rule?
Boy, whah's de raisin' I give you? Is you boun' fuh ter be a black villiun?
I's s'prised dat a chile er yo mammy 'ud steal any man's water-million.

En I's now gwinter cut it right open, en you shain't have nary bite,
Fuh a boy who'll steal water-millions—en dat in de day's broad light—
Ain't—*Lawdy!* it's *green!* Mirandy!
Mi-ran-dy! come on wi' dat switch!
Well, stealin' a g-r-e-e-n water-million! who ever yeered tell er des sich?

Cain't tell w'en dey's ripe? W'y you thump 'um, en w'en dey go pank dey is green;
But w'en dey go *punk,* now you mine me, dey's ripe—en dat's des wut I mean.
En nex' time you hook water-millions—*you* heered me, you ign'ant, you hunk,
Ef you do' want a lickin' all over, be sho dat dey allers go "punk"!

Harrison Robertson.

Give Us Men

God give us men; a time like this demands
Strong minds, great hearts, true faith and ready hands.
Men whom the lust of office cannot kill;
Men whom the spoils of office cannot buy;
Men who possess opinions and a will;
Men who have honor; men who will not lie;
Men who can stand before a demagogue,
And brave his treacherous flatteries without winking;
Tall men, sun-crowned, who live above the fog,
In public duty and in private thinking;
For while the rabble, with its thumb-worn creeds,
Its large professions, and its little deeds,
Mingle in selfish strife—lo! Freedom weeps,
Wrong rules the land, and waiting Justice sleeps.

J. G. Holland.

Never Trouble Trouble

My good man is a clever man, which no one will gainsay;
He lies awake to plot and plan 'gainst lions in the way,
While I, without a thought of ill, sleep sound enough for three,
For I never trouble trouble till trouble troubles me.

A holiday we never fix but he is sure 'twill rain;
And when the sky is clear at six he knows it won't remain.
He is always prophesying ill to which I won't agree,
For I never trouble trouble till trouble troubles me.

The wheat will never show a top—but soon how green the field!
We will not harvest half a crop—yet have a famous yield!
It will not sell, it never will! but I will wait and see,
For I never trouble trouble till trouble troubles me.

We have a good share of worldly gear, and fortune seems secure,
Yet my good man is full of fear—misfortune's coming sure!
He points me out the almshouse hill, but cannot make me see,

For I never trouble trouble till trouble
troubles me.

He has a sort of second sight, and when
the fit is strong,
He sees beyond the good and right the
evil and the wrong.
Heaven's cup of joy he'll surely spill
unless I with him be,
For I never trouble trouble till trouble
troubles me. *Fannie Windsor.*

What is Good

"What is the real good?" I asked in
musing mood.
Order, said the law court;
Knowledge, said the school;
Truth, said the wise man;
Pleasure, said the fool;
Love, said the maiden;
Beauty, said the page;
Freedom, said the dreamer;
Home, said the sage;
Fame, said the soldier;
Equity, the seer.
Spake my heart full sadly:
"The answer is not here."
Then within my bosom
Softly this I heard:
"Each heart holds the secret:
Kindness is the word."

John Boyle O'Reilly.

The Penny Ye Mean to Gie

There's a funny tale of a stingy man,
Who was none too good but might
have been worse,
Who went to his church on a Sunday
night
And carried along his well-filled
purse.

When the sexton came with the begging
plate,
The church was but dim with the
candle's light;
The stingy man fumbled all thro' his
purse,
And chose a coin by touch and not by
sight.

It's an odd thing now that guineas
should be
So like unto pennies in shape and
size.
"I'll gie a penny," the stingy man said:
"The poor must not gifts of pennies
despise."

The penny fell down with a clatter and
ring!
And back in his seat leaned the
stingy man.
"The world is full of the poor," he
thought,
"I can't help them all—I give wha
I can."

Ha! ha! how the sexton smiled, to b
sure,
To see the gold guinea fall in th
plate;
Ha! ha! how the stingy man's hear
was wrung,
Perceiving his blunder—but just to
late!

"No matter," he said; "in the Lord'
account
That guinea of gold is set down t
me—
They lend to him who give to the poor
It will not so bad an investment be.

"Na, na, mon," the chuckling sextc
cried out,
"The Lord is na cheated—he ken
thee well;
He knew it was only by accident
That out o' thy fingers the guin
fell!

"He keeps an account, na doubt, for the puir;
But in that account He'll set down to thee
Na mair o' that golden guinea, my mon,
Than the one bare penny ye mean to gie!"

There's comfort, too, in the little tale—
A serious side as well as a joke—
A comfort for all the generous poor
In the comical words the sexton spoke;

A comfort to think that the good Lord knows
How generous we really desire to be,
And will give us credit in his account,
For all the pennies we long "to gie."

Leedle Yawcob Strauss

I haf von funny leedle poy
Vot gomes shust to my knee,—
Der queerest schap, der createst rogue
As efer you dit see.
He runs, und schumps, und schmashes dings
In all barts off der house.
But vot off dot? He vas mine son,
Mine leedle Yawcob Strauss.

He gets der measels und der mumbs,
Und eferyding dot's oudt;
He sbills mine glass off lager bier,
Poots schnuff indo mine kraut;
He fills mine pipe mit Limburg cheese—
Dot vas der roughest chouse;
I'd dake dot vrom no oder poy
But leedle Yawcob Strauss.

He dakes der milkban for a dhrum,
Und cuts mine cane in dwo
To make der schticks to beat it mit—
Mine cracious, dot vas drue!
I dinks mine hed vas schplit abart
He kicks oup sooch a touse;
But nefer mind der poys vas few
Like dot young Yawcob Strauss.

He asks me questions sooch as dese:
Who baints mine nose so red?
Who vos it cuts dot schmoodth blace oudt
Vrom der hair ubon mine hed?
Und vhere der plaze goes vrom der lamp
Vene'er der glim I douse?
How gan I all dese dings eggsblain
To dot schmall Yawcob Strauss?

I somedimes dink I schall go vild
Mit sooch a grazy poy,
Und vish vonce more I gould haf rest
Und beaceful dimes enshoy.
But ven he vas asleep in ped,
So quiet as a mouse,
I prays der Lord, "Dake anydings,
But leaf dot Yawcob Strauss."

Charles F. Adams.

To-day

We shall do so much in the years to come,
But what have we done to-day?
We shall give out gold in princely sum,
But what did we give to-day?
We shall lift the heart and dry the tear,
We shall plant a hope in the place of fear,
We shall speak with words of love and cheer,
But what have we done to-day?
We shall be so kind in the after while,
But what have we been to-day?
We shall bring to each lonely life a smile,
But what have we brought to-day?
We shall give to truth a grander birth,
And to steadfast faith a deeper worth,
We shall feed the hungering souls of earth,
But whom have we fed to-day?

Nixon Waterman.

So Was I

My name is Tommy, an' I hates
That feller of my sister Kate's.
He's bigger'n I am an' you see
He's sorter lookin' down on me,
An' I resents it with a vim;
I think I am just as good as him.
He's older, an' he's mighty fly,
But's he's a kid, an' so am I.

One time he came,—down by the gate,
I guess it must have been awful late,—
An' Katie, she was there, an' they
Was feelin' very nice and gay,
An' he was talkin' all the while
About her sweet an' lovin' smile,
An' everythin' was as nice as pie,
An' they was there, an' so was I.

They didn't see me, 'cause I slid
Down underneath a bush, an' hid,
An' he was sayin' that his love
Was greater'n all the stars above
Up in the glorious heavens placed;
An' then his arms got 'round her waist,
An' clouds were floatin' in the sky,
And they was there, an' so was I.

I didn't hear just all they said,
But by an' by my sister's head
Was droopin' on his shoulder, an'
I seen him holdin' Katie's hand,
An' then he hugged her closer, some,
An' then I heerd a kiss—yum, yum;
An' Katie blushed an' drew a sigh,
An' sorter coughed,—an' so did I.

An' then that feller looked around
An' seed me there, down on the ground,
An'—was he mad? well, betcher boots
I gets right out of there an' scoots.
An' he just left my sister Kate
A-standin' right there by the gate;
An' I seen blood was in his eye,
An' he runned fast—an' so did I.

I runned the very best I could,
But he cotched up—I's 'fraid he would—
An' then he said he'd teach me how
To know my manners, he'd allow;
An' then he shaked me awful. Gee!
He jest—he frashed the ground with me.
An' then he stopped it by and by,
'Cause he was tired—an' so was I.

An' then he went back to the gate
An' couldn't find my sister Kate
'Cause she went in to bed, while he
Was runnin' 'round an' thumpin' me.
I got round in a shadder dim,
An' made a face, an' guffed at him;
An' then the moon larfed, in the sky,
'Cause he was there, an' so was I.

Joseph Bert Smiley.

Is It Worth While?

Is it worth while that we jostle a brother,
Bearing his load on the rough road of life?
Is it worth while that we jeer at each other
In blackness of heart that we war to the knife?
God pity us all in our pitiful strife.

God pity us all as we jostle each other;
God pardon us all for the triumph we feel
When a fellow goes down 'neath his load on the heather,
Pierced to the heart: Words are keener than steel,
And mightier far for woe than for weal.

Were it not well, in this brief little journey
On over the isthmus, down into the tide,

We give him a fish instead of a serpent,
Ere folding the hands to be and abide
Forever and aye in dust at his side?

Look at the roses saluting each other;
Look at the herds all at peace on the plain;
Man, and man only, makes war on his brother,
And laughs in his heart at his peril and pain,
Shamed by the beasts that go down on the plain.

Is it worth while that we battle to humble
Some poor fellow down into the dust?
God pity us all! Time too soon will tumble
All of us together, like leaves in a gust,
Humbled, indeed, down into the dust.

Joaquin Miller.

Life's Mirror

There are loyal hearts, there are spirits brave,
There are souls that are pure and true;
Then give to the world the best you have,
And the best will come back to you.

Give love, and love to your life will flow,
A strength in your utmost need;
Have faith, and a score of hearts will show
Their faith in your work and deed.

Give truth, and your gift will be paid in kind;
And honor will honor meet,
And the smile which is sweet will surely find
A smile that is just as sweet.

Give pity and sorrow to those who mourn;
You will gather in flowers again
The scattered seeds from your thought outborne,
Though the sowing seemed in vain.

For life is the mirror of king and slave;
'T is just what we are and do;
Then give to the world the best you have,
And the best will come back to you.

Madeline S. Bridges.

The Little Black-Eyed Rebel

A boy drove into the city, his wagon loaded down
With food to feed the people of the British-governed town;
And the little black-eyed rebel, so cunning and so sly,
Was watching for his coming from the corner of her eye.

His face was broad and honest, his hands were brown and tough,
The clothes he wore upon him were homespun, coarse, and rough;
But one there was who watched him, who long time lingered nigh,
And cast at him sweet glances from the corner of her eye.

He drove up to the market, he waited in the line—
His apples and potatoes were fresh and fair and fine.
But long and long he waited, and no one came to buy,
Save the black-eyed rebel, watching from the corner of her eye.

"Now, who will buy my apples?" he shouted, long and loud;
And, "Who wants my potatoes?" he repeated to the crowd.

But from all the people round him came no word of reply,
Save the black-eyed rebel, answering from the corner of her eye.

For she knew that 'neath the lining of the coat he wore that day
Were long letters from the husbands and the fathers far away,
Who were fighting for the freedom that they meant to gain, or die;
And a tear like silver glistened in the corner of her eye.

But the treasures—how to get them? crept the question through her mind,
Since keen enemies were watching for what prizes they might find;
And she paused a while and pondered, with a pretty little sigh,
Then resolve crept through her features, and a shrewdness fired her eye.

So she resolutely walked up to the wagon old and red—
"May I have a dozen apples for a kiss?" she sweetly said;
And the brown face flushed to scarlet, for the boy was somewhat shy,
And he saw her laughing at him from the corner of her eye.

"You may have them all for nothing, and more, if you want," quoth he.
"I will have them, my good fellow, but can pay for them," said she.
And she clambered on the wagon, minding not who all were by,
With a laugh of reckless romping in the corner of her eye.

Clinging round his brawny neck, she clasped her fingers white and small,
And then whispered, "Quick! the letters! thrust them underneath my shawl!
Carry back again *this* package, and be sure that you are spry!"
And she sweetly smiled upon him from the corner of her eye.

Loud the motley crowd was laughing at the strange, ungirlish freak;
And the boy was scared and panting, and so dashed he could not speak.
And "Miss, I have good apples," a bolder lad did cry;
But she answered, "No, I thank you," from the corner of her eye.

With the news from loved ones absent to the dear friends they would greet,
Searching them who hungered for them, swift she glided through the street.
"There is nothing worth the doing that it does not pay to try,"
Thought the little black-eyed rebel with a twinkle in her eye.

Will Carleton.

A Day Well Spent

If you sit down at set of sun
And count the deeds that you have done,
And, counting, find
One self-denying act, one word that eased the heart of him that heard;
One glance most kind, which felt like sunshine where it went,
Then you may count that day well spent.

But if through all the livelong day
You've eased no heart by yea or nay,
If through it all you've nothing done that you can trace
That brought the sunshine to one face
No act most small that helped some soul and nothing cost,
Then count that day as worse than lost

Say Not the Struggle Nought Availeth

ay not the struggle nought availeth,
 The labor and the wounds are vain,
he enemy faints not, nor faileth,
 And as things have been they remain.

f hopes were dupes, fears may be
 liars;
 It may be, in yon smoke concealed,
our comrades chase e'en now the
 fliers,
 And, but for you, possess the field.

or while the tired waves, vainly
 breaking,
 Seem here no painful inch to gain,
ar back, through creeks and inlets
 making,
 Comes silent, flooding in, the main,

nd not by eastern windows only,
 When daylight comes, comes in the
 light,
n front, the sun climbs slow, how
 slowly,
 But westward, look, the land is
 bright.

A. H. Clough.

The Miller of the Dee

here dwelt a miller, hale and bold,
 Beside the river Dee;
e worked and sang from morn till
 night—
 No lark more blithe than he;
nd this the burden of his song
 Forever used to be:
I envy nobody—no, not I—
 And nobody envies me!"

Thou 'rt wrong, my friend," said good
 King Hal,
 "As wrong as wrong can be;
or could my heart be light as thine,
 I'd gladly change with thee.
And tell me now, what makes thee sing,
 With voice so loud and free,
While I am sad, though I'm a king,
 Beside the river Dee?"

The miller smiled and doffed his cap,
 "I earn my bread," quoth he;
"I love my wife, I love my friend,
 I love my children three;
I owe no penny I cannot pay,
 I thank the river Dee
That turns the mill that grinds the
 corn
 That feeds my babes and me."

"Good friend," said Hal, and sighed
 the while,
 "Farewell, and happy be;
But say no more, if thou'dst be true
 That no one envies thee;
Thy mealy cap is worth my crown,
 Thy mill my kingdom's fee;
Such men as thou art England's boast,
 O miller of the Dee!"

Charles Mackay.

The Old Red Cradle

Take me back to the days when the
 old red cradle rocked,
 In the sunshine of the years that are
 gone;
To the good old trusty days, when the
 door was never locked,
 And we slumbered unmolested till
 the dawn.

I remember of my years I had num-
 bered almost seven,
 And the old cradle stood against the
 wall—
I was youngest of the five, and two
 were gone to heaven,
 But the old red cradle rocked us all.

And if ever came a day when my
 cheeks were flushed and hot,

When I did not mind my porridge or my play,
I would clamber up its side and the pain would be forgot,
When the old red cradle rocked away.

It has been a hallowed spot where I've turned through all the years,
Which have brought me the evil with the good,
And I turn again to-night, aye, and see it through my tears,
The place where the dear old cradle stood.

By its side my father paused with a little time to spare,
And the care-lines would soften on his brow,
Ah! 't was but a little while that I knew a father's care,
But I fancy in my dreams I see him now.

By my mother it was rocked when the evening meal was laid,
And again I seem to see her as she smiled;
When the rest were all in bed, 't was there she knelt and prayed,
By the old red cradle and her child.

Aye, it cradled one and all, brothers, sisters in it lay,
And it gave me the sweetest rest I've known;
But to-night the tears will flow, and I let them have their way,
For the passing years are leaving me alone.

And it seems of those to come, I would gladly give them all
For a slumber as free from care as then,
Just to wake to-morrow morn where the rising sun would fall
Round the old red cradle once again.

But the cradle long has gone and the burdens that it bore,
One by one, have been gathered to the fold;
Still the flock is incomplete, for it numbers only four,
With one left out straying in the cold.

Heaven grant again we may in each other's arms be locked,
Where no sad tears of parting ever fall;
God forbid that one be lost that the old red cradle rocked;
And the dear old cradle rocked us all.

Annie J. Granniss.

The Moo Cow Moo

My papa held me up to the Moo Cow Moo
So close I could almost touch,
And I fed him a couple of times or so,
And I wasn't a fraid-cat, much.

But if my papa goes in the house,
And my mamma she goes in too,
I keep still like a little mouse
For the Moo Cow Moo might Moo.

The Moo Cow's tail is a piece of rope
All raveled out where it grows;
And it's just like feeling a piece of soap
All over the Moo Cow's nose.

And the Moo Cow Moo has lots of fun
Just switching his tail about,
But if he opens his mouth, why then I run,
For that's where the Moo comes out.

The Moo Cow Moo has deers on his head,
And his eyes stick out of their place,
And the nose of the Moo Cow Moo is spread
All over the Moo Cow's face.

And his feet are nothing but finger-
nails,
And his mamma don't keep them cut,
And he gives folks milk in water pails,
When he don't keep his handles shut.

But if you or I pull his handles, why
The Moo Cow Moo says it hurts,
But the hired man sits down close by
And squirts, and squirts, and squirts.
Edmund Vance Cooke.

All Things Bright and Beautiful

All things bright and beautiful,
All creatures great and small,
All things wise and wonderful,—
The Lord God made them all.

Each little flower that opens,
Each little bird that sings,—
He made their glowing colors,
He made their tiny wings.

The rich man in his castle,
The poor man at his gate,
God made them, high or lowly,
And ordered their estate.

The purple-headed mountain,
The river running by,
The morning, and the sunset
That lighteth up the sky,

The cold wind in the winter,
The pleasant summer sun,
The ripe fruits in the garden,—
He made them, every one.

The tall trees in the greenwood,
The meadows where we play,
The rushes by the water
We gather every day,—

He gave us eyes to see them,
And lips that we might tell
How great is God Almighty,
Who hath made all things well.
Cecil Frances Alexander.

An Order for a Picture

Oh, good painter, tell me true,
Has your hand the cunning to draw
Shapes of things that you never saw?
Aye? Well, here is an order for you.

Woods and cornfields, a little brown,—
The picture must not be over-
bright,—
Yet all in the golden and gracious
light
Of a cloud, when the summer sun is
down.
Alway and alway, night and morn,
Woods upon woods, with fields of
corn
Lying between them, not quite sere,
And not in the full, thick, leafy bloom,
When the wind can hardly find breath-
ing-room
Under their tassels,—cattle near,
Biting shorter the short green grass,
And a hedge of sumach and sassafras,
With bluebirds twittering all around,—
(Ah, good painter, you can't paint
sound!)—
These, and the little house where I
was born,
Low and little, and black and old,
With children, many as it can hold,
All at the windows, open wide,—
Heads and shoulders clear outside,
And fair young faces all ablush:
Perhaps you have seen, some day,
Roses crowding the self-same way,
Out of a wilding, wayside bush.

Listen closer. When you have done
With woods and cornfields and graz-
ing herds,
A lady, the loveliest ever the sun
Looked down upon you must paint for
me:
Oh, if I could only make you see
The clear blue eyes, the tender smile,
The sovereign sweetness, the gentle
grace,

The woman's soul, and the angel's face
That are beaming on me all the while,
I need not speak these foolish words:
Yet one word tells you all I would say,—
She is my mother: you will agree
That all the rest may be thrown away.

Two little urchins at her knee
You must paint, sir: one like me,—
The other with a clearer brow,
And the light of his adventurous eyes
Flashing with boldest enterprise:
At ten years old he went to sea,—
God knoweth if he be living now;
He sailed in the good ship "Commodore,"—
Nobody ever crossed her track
To bring us news, and she never came back.
Ah, it is twenty long years and more
Since that old ship went out of the bay
With my great-hearted brother on her deck:
I watched him till he shrank to a speck,
And his face was toward me all the way.
Bright his hair was, a golden brown,
The time we stood at our mother's knee:
That beauteous head, if it did go down,
Carried sunshine into the sea!

Out in the fields one summer night
We were together, half afraid
Of the corn-leaves' rustling, and of the shade
Of the high hills, stretching so still and far,—
Loitering till after the low little light
Of the candle shone through the open door,
And over the hay-stack's pointed top,
All of a tremble and ready to drop,
The first half-hour, the great yellow star,
That we, with staring, ignorant eyes,
Had often and often watched to see
Propped and held in its place in the skies
By the fork of a tall red mulberry-tree,
Which close in the edge of our flax-field grew,—
Dead at the top, just one branch full
Of leaves, notched round, and lined with wool,
From which it tenderly shook the dew
Over our heads, when we came to play
In its hand-breadth of shadow, day after day.
Afraid to go home, sir; for one of us bore
A nest full of speckled and thin-shelled eggs,—
The other, a bird, held fast by the legs,
Not so big as a straw of wheat:
The berries we gave her she wouldn't eat,
But cried and cried, till we held her bill,
So slim and shining, to keep her still.

At last we stood at our mother's knee.
Do you think, sir, if you try,
You can paint the look of a lie?
If you can, pray have the grace
To put it solely in the face
Of the urchin that is likest me:
I think 'twas solely mine, indeed:
But that's no matter,—paint it so;
The eyes of our mother—(take good heed)—
Looking not on the nestful of eggs,
Nor the fluttering bird, held so fast by the legs,
But straight through our faces down to our lies,

And, oh, with such injured, reproachful surprise!
I felt my heart bleed where that glance went, as though
A sharp blade struck through it.

You, sir, know
That you on the canvas are to repeat
Things that are fairest, things most sweet,—
Woods and cornfields and mulberry-tree,—
The mother,—the lads, with their bird at her knee:
But, oh, that look of reproachful woe!
High as the heavens your name I'll shout,
If you paint me the picture, and leave that out.

Alice Cary.

Who Won the War?

Who won the war?
'T was little Belgium stemmed the tide
Of ruthless hordes who thought to ride
Her borders through and prostrate France
Ere yet she'd time to raise her lance.
'T was plucky Belgium.

Who won the war?
Italia broke the galling chain
Which bound her to the guilty twain;
Then fought 'gainst odds till one of these
Lay prone and shattered at her knees.
'T was gallant Italy.

Who won the war?
Old England's watch dogs of the main
Their vigil kept, and not in vain;
For not a ship their wrath dared brave
Save those which skulked beneath the wave.
'T was mighty England.

Who won the war?
'T was France who wrote in noble rage
The grandest words on history's page,
"They shall not pass"—the devilish Hun;
And he could never pass Verdun.
'T was sturdy France.

Who won the war?
In darkest hour there rose a cry,
"Liberty, sweet Liberty, thou shalt not die!"
Thank God! they came across the sea,
Two million men and victory!
'T was glorious America.

Who won the war?
No one of these; not one, but all
Who answered Freedom's clarion call.
Each humble man who did his bit
In God's own book of fame is writ.
These won the war.

Woodbury Pulsifer.

Mothers of Men

The bravest battle that ever was fought!
Shall I tell you where and when?
On the map of the world you will find it not,
"Twas fought by the mothers of men.

Nay, not with cannon or battle shot,
With sword or nobler pen,
Nay, not with eloquent words or thought
From mouths of wonderful men;

But deep in the walled-up woman's heart—
Of woman that would not yield,
But bravely, silently, bore her part—
Lo, there is the battle field!

No marshaling troup, no bivouac song,
No banner to gleam or wave,

But oh, these battles, they last so long—
From babyhood to the grave.

Yet, faithful as a bridge of stars,
She fights in her walled-up town—
Fights on and on in the endless wars,
Then, silent, unseen, goes down.

Oh, ye with banner and battle shot,
And soldiers to shout and praise,
I tell you the kingliest victories fought
Were fought in those silent ways.

Oh, spotless in a world of shame,
With splendid and silent scorn,
Go back to God as white as you came—
The kingliest warrior born!

Joaquin Miller.

Plain Bob and a Job

Bob went lookin' for a job—
Didn't want a situation; didn't ask a lofty station:
Didn't have a special mission for a topnotcher's position;
Didn't have such fine credentials—but he had the real essentials—
Had a head that kept on workin' and two hands that were not shirkin';
Wasn't either shirk or snob;
Wasn't Mister—just plain Bob,
Who was lookin' for a job.

Bob went lookin' for a job;
And he wasn't scared or daunted when he saw a sign—"Men Wanted."
Walked right in with manner fittin' up to where the Boss was sittin',
And he said: "My name is Bob, and I'm lookin' for a job;
And if you're the Boss that hires 'em, starts 'em workin', and that fires 'em,
Put my name right down here, Neighbor, as a candidate for labor;
For my name is just plain Bob,
And my pulses sort o' throb
For that thing they call a job."
Bob kept askin' for a job,
And the Boss, he says: "What kind?"
And Bob answered: "Never mind;
For I am not a bit partic'ler and I never was a stickler
For proprieties in workin'—if you got some labor lurkin'
Anywhere around about kindly go and trot it out.
It's a job I want, you see—
Any kind that there may be
Will be good enough for me."

Well, sir, Bob he got a job.
But the Boss went 'round all day in a dreamy sort of way;
And he says to me: "By thunder, we have got the world's Eighth Wonder!
Got a feller name of Bob who just asked me for a job—
Never asks when he engages about overtime in wages;
Never asked if he'd get pay by the hour or by the day;
Never asked me if it's airy work and light and sanitary;
Never asked me for my notion of the chances of promotion;
Never asked for the duration of his annual vacation;
Never asked for Saturday half-a-holiday with pay;
Never took me on probation till he tried the situation;
Never asked me if it's sittin' work or standin', or befittin'
Of his birth and inclination—he just filed his application,
Hung his coat up on a knob,
Said his name was just plain Bob—
And went workin' at a job!"

James W. Foley.

Aunt Tabitha

Whatever I do and whatever I say,
Aunt Tabitha tells me it isn't the way
When *she* was a girl (forty summers ago);
Aunt Tabitha tells me they never did so.

Dear aunt! If I only would take her advice!
But I like my own way, and I find it *so* nice!
And besides, I forget half the things I am told;
But they all will come back to me—when I am old.

If a youth passes by, it may happen, no doubt,
He may chance to look in as I chance to look out;
She would never endure an impertinent stare—
It is *horrid*, she says, and I mustn't sit there.

A walk in the moonlight has pleasures, I own,
But it isn't quite safe to be walking alone;
So I take a lad's arm—just for safety you know—
But Aunt Tabitha tells me *they* didn't do so.

How wicked we are, and how good they were then!
They kept at arm's length those detestable men;
What an era of virtue she lived in!—But stay—
Were the *men* all such rogues in Aunt Tabitha's day?

If the men *were* so wicked, I'll ask my papa
How he dared to propose to my darling mamma;
Was he like the rest of them? Goodness! Who knows?
And what shall *I* say, if a wretch should propose?

I am thinking if aunt knew so little of sin,
What a wonder Aunt Tabitha's aunt must have been!
And her grand-aunt—it scares me—how shockingly sad
That we girls of to-day are so frightfully bad!

A martyr will save us, and nothing else can,
Let *me perish*—to rescue some wretched young man!
Though when to the altar a victim I go,
Aunt Tabitha 'll tell me *she* never did so!

The Flag Goes By

Hats off!
Along the street there comes
A blare of bugles, a ruffle of drums,
A flash of color beneath the sky:
Hats off!
The flag is passing by!

Blue and crimson and white it shines,
Over the steel-tipped, ordered lines.
Hats off!
The colors before us fly;
But more than the flag is passing by.

Sea-fights and land-fights, grim and great,
Fought to make and to save the State;
Weary marches and sinking ships;
Cheers of victory on dying lips;

Days of plenty and years of peace,
March of a strong land's swift increase:

Equal justice, right and law,
Stately honor and reverent awe;

Sign of a nation, great and strong,
To ward her people from foreign wrong;
Pride and glory and honor, all
Live in the colors to stand or fall.

Hats off!
Along the street there comes
A blare of bugles, a ruffle of drums,
And loyal hearts are beating high:
Hats off!
The flag is passing by!

H. H. Bennett.

The Rivers of France

The rivers of France are ten score and twain,
But five are the names that we know:
The Marne, the Vesle, the Ourcq and the Aisne,
And the Somme of the swampy flow.

The rivers of France, from source to sea,
Are nourished by many a rill,
But these five, if ever a drouth there be
The fountains of sorrow would fill.

The rivers of France shine silver white,
But the waters of five are red
With the richest blood, in the fiercest fight
For freedom that ever was shed.

The rivers of France sing soft as they run,
But five have a song of their own,
That hymns the fall of the arrogant one
And the proud cast down from his throne.

The rivers of France all quietly tak
To sleep in the house of their birtl
But the carnadined wave of five sha break
On the uttermost strands of earth.

Five rivers of France—see! thei names are writ
On a banner of crimson and gold,
And the glory of those who fashione it
Shall nevermore cease to be told.

H. J. M., in London "Times."

Seven Times One

There's no dew left on the daisies an clover,
There's no rain left in heaven;
I've said my "seven times" over an over:
Seven times one are seven.

I am old, so old I can write a letter;
My birthday lessons are done;
The lambs play always, they know r better,
They are only one times one.

O Moon! in the night I have seen y sailing
And shining so round and low;
You were bright! but your light failing,
You are nothing now but a bow.

You Moon, have you done somethi wrong in heaven,
That God has hidden your face?
I hope if you have, you'll soon be fc given,
And shine again in your place.

O velvet Bee, you're a dusty fellow;
You've powdered your legs with go
O brave Marshmary buds, rich and y low,
Give me your money to hold!

O Columbine, open your folded wrapper,
Where two twin turtle-doves dwell!
O Cuckoo-pint, toll me the purple clapper
That hangs in your clear green bell!

And show me your nest, with the young ones in it,
I will not steal them away;
I am old! you may trust me, linnet, linnet,
I am seven times one to-day.

Jean Ingelow.

Seven Times Two

You bells in the steeple, ring, ring out your changes,
How many soever they be,
And let the brown meadow-lark's note as he ranges,
Come over, come over to me.

Yet birds' clearest carol by fall or by swelling
No magical sense conveys,
And bells have forgotten their old art of telling
The fortune of future days.

"Turn again, turn again," once they rang cheerily,
While a boy listened alone;
Made his heart yearn again, musing so wearily
All by himself on a stone.

Poor bells! I forgive you; your good days are over,
And mine, they are yet to be;
No listening, no longing shall aught, aught discover:
You leave the story to me.

The foxglove shoots out of the green matted heather,
Preparing her hoods of snow;
She was idle, and slept till the sunshiny weather:
Oh, children take long to grow.

I wish and I wish that the spring would go faster,
Nor long summer bide so late;
And I could grow on like the foxglove and aster,
For some things are ill to wait.

I wait for the day when dear hearts shall discover,
While dear hands are laid on my head:
"The child is a woman, the book may close over,
For all the lessons are said."

I wait for my story—the birds cannot sing it,
Not one, as he sits on the tree;
The bells cannot ring it, but long years, oh bring it!
Such as I wish it to be.

Jean Ingelow.

Seven Times Three

LOVE

I leaned out of window, I smelt the white clover,
Dark, dark was the garden, I saw not the gate;
"Now, if there be footsteps, he comes, my one lover—
Hush, nightingale, hush! O sweet nightingale, wait
Till I listen and hear
If a step draweth near,
For my love he is late!

"The skies in the darkness stoop nearer and nearer,
A cluster of stars hangs like fruit in the tree,
The fall of the water comes sweeter, comes clearer:

To what art thou listening, and what dost thou see?
Let the star-clusters grow,
Let the sweet waters flow,
And cross quickly to me.

"You night-moths that hover where honey brims over
From sycamore blossoms, or settle or sleep;
You glowworms, shine out, and the pathway discover
To him that comes darkling along the rough steep.
Ah, my sailor, make haste,
For the time runs to waste,
And my love lieth deep,

"Too deep for swift telling; and yet, my one lover,
I've conned thee an answer, it waits thee to-night."
By the sycamore passed he, and through the white clover;
Then all the sweet speech I had fashioned took flight;
But I'll love him more, more
Than e'er wife loved before,
Be the days dark or bright.

Jean Ingelow.

Seven Times Four

MATERNITY

Heigh-ho! daisies and buttercups,
Fair yellow daffodils, stately and tall!
When the wind wakes, how they rock in the grasses,
And dance with the cuckoo-buds slender and small!
Here's two bonny boys, and here's mother's own lasses
Eager to gather them all.

Heigh-ho! daisies and buttercups!
Mother shall thread them a daisy chain;
Sing them a song of the pretty hedge-sparrow,
That loved her brown little ones, loved them full fain;
Sing, "Heart, thou art wide, though the house be but narrow,"—
Sing once, and sing it again.

Heigh-ho! daisies and buttercups,
Sweet wagging cowslips, they bend and they bow;
A ship sails afar over warm ocean waters,
And haply one musing doth stand at her prow.
O bonny brown sons, and O sweet little daughters,
Maybe he thinks on you now!

Heigh-ho! daisies and buttercups,
Fair yellow daffodils, stately and tall!
A sunshiny world full of laughter and leisure,
And fresh hearts unconscious of sorrow and thrall!
Send down on their pleasure smiles passing its measure,
God that is over us all!

Jean Ingelow.

Autumn Woods

Ere, in the northern gale,
The summer tresses of the trees are gone,
The woods of Autumn, all around our vale,
Have put their glory on.

The mountains that infold,
In their wide sweep, the colored landscape round,
Seem groups of giant kings, in purple and gold,
That guard the enchanted ground.

I roam the woods that crown
The upland, where the mingled splendors glow,
Where the gay company of trees look down
On the green fields below.

My steps are not alone
In these bright walks; the sweet southwest, at play,
Flies, rustling, where the painted leaves are strown
Along the winding way.

And far in heaven, the while,
The sun, that sends that gale to wander here,
Pours out on the fair earth his quiet smile,—
The sweetest of the year.

Where now the solemn shade,
Verdure and gloom where many branches meet;
So grateful, when the noon of summer made
The valleys sick with heat?

Let in through all the trees
Come the strange rays; the forest depths are bright;
Their sunny-colored foliage, in the breeze,
Twinkles, like beams of light.

The rivulet, late unseen,
Where bickering through the shrubs its waters run,
Shines with the image of its golden screen
And glimmerings of the sun.

But 'neath yon crimson tree,
Lover to listening maid might breathe his flame,
Nor mark, within its roseate canopy,
Her blush of maiden shame.

Oh, Autumn! why so soon
Depart the hues that make thy forests glad;
Thy gentle wind and thy fair sunny noon,
And leave thee wild and sad?

Ah! 'twere a lot too blessed
Forever in thy colored shades to stray;
Amid the kisses of the soft southwest
To rove and dream for aye;

And leave the vain low strife
That makes men mad—the tug for wealth and power,
The passions and the cares that wither life,
And waste its little hour.

William Cullen Bryant.

The Drummer Boy of Mission Ridge

Did you ever hear of the Drummer Boy of Mission Ridge, who lay
With his face to the foe, 'neath the enemy's guns, in the charge of that terrible day?
They were firing above him and firing below, and the tempest of shot and shell
Was raging like death, as he moaned in his pain, by the breastworks where he fell.

"Go back with your corps," our colonel had said, but he waited the moment when
He might follow the ranks and shoulder a gun with the best of us bearded men:
And so when the signals from old Fort Wood set an army of veterans wild,
He flung down his drum, which spun down the hill like the ball of a wayward child.

And then he fell in with the foremost ranks of brave old company G,
As we charged by the flank, with our colors ahead, and our columns closed up like a V,
In the long, swinging lines of that splendid advance, when the flags of our corps floated out,
Like the ribbons that dance in the jubilant lines of the march of a gala day rout.

He charged with the ranks, though he carried no gun, for the colonel had said him nay,
And he breasted the blast of the bristling guns, and the shock of the sickening fray;
And when by his side they were falling like hail he sprang to a comrade slain,
And shouldered his musket and bore it as true as the hand that was dead in pain.

'Twas dearly we loved him, our Drummer Boy, with a fire in his bright, black eye,
That flashed forth a spirit too great for his form—he only was just so high,
As tall, perhaps, as your little lad who scarcely reaches your shoulder—
Though his heart was the heart of a veteran then, a trifle, it may be, bolder.

He pressed to the front, our lad so leal, and the works were almost won,
A moment more and our flags had swung o'er the muzzle of murderous gun;
But a raking fire swept the van, and he fell 'mid the wounded and slain,
With his wee wan face turned up to Him who feeleth His children's pain.

Again and again our lines fell back, and again with shivering shocks
They flung themselves on the rebels' works as ships are tossed on rocks;
To be crushed and broken and scattered amain, as the wrecks of the surging storm,
Where none may rue and none may reck of aught that has human form.

So under the ridge we were lying for the order to charge again,
And we counted our comrades missing, and we counted our comrades slain;
And one said, "Johnny, our Drummer Boy, is grievously shot and lies
Just under the enemy's breastwork; if left on the field he dies."

Then all the blood that was in me surged up to my aching brow,
And my heart leaped up like a ball in my throat—I can feel it even now,
And I said I would bring that boy from the field, if God would spare my breath,
If all the guns in Mission Ridge should thunder the threat of death.

I crept and crept up the ghastly ridge, by the wounded and the dead,
With the moans of my comrades right and left, behind me and yet ahead,
Till I came to the form of our Drummer Boy, in his blouse of dusty blue,
With his face to the foe, 'neath the enemy's guns, where the blast of the battle blew.

And his gaze as he met my own just there would have melted a heart of stone,
As he tried like a wounded bird to rise and placed his hand in my own;

And he said in a voice half smothered, though its whispering thrills me yet,
"I think in a moment more that I would have stood on that parapet.

"But now I nevermore will climb, and, Sergeant, when you see
The men go up those breastworks there, just stop and waken me;
For though I cannot make the charge and join the cheers that rise,
I may forget my pain to see the old flag kiss the skies."

Well, it was hard to treat him so, his poor limb shattered sore,
But I raised him on my shoulder and to the surgeon bore;
And the boys who saw us coming each gave a shout of joy,
And uttered fervent prayers for him, our valiant Drummer Boy.

When sped the news that "Fighting Joe" had saved the Union right,
With his legions fresh from Lookout; and that Thomas massed his might
And forced the rebel center; and our cheering ran like wild;
And Sherman's heart was happy as the heart of a little child;

When Grant from his lofty outlook saw our flags by the hundred fly
Along the slopes of Mission Ridge, where'er he cast his eye;
And when we heard the thrilling news of the mighty battle done,
The fearful contest ended, and the glorious victory won;

Then his bright black eyes so yearning grew strangely rapt and wide,
And in that hour of conquest our little hero died.
But ever in our hearts he dwells, with a grace that ne'er is old,
For him the heart to duty wed can nevermore grow cold!

And when they tell of heroes, and the laurels they have won,
Of the scars they are doomed to carry, of the deeds that they have done;
Of the horror to be biding among the ghastly dead,
The gory sod beneath them, the bursting shell o'erhead,

My heart goes back to Mission Ridge and the Drummer Boy who lay
With his face to the foe, 'neath the enemy's guns, in the charge of that terrible day;
And I say that the land that bears such sons is crowned and dowered with all
The dear God giveth nations to stay them lest they fall.

Oh, glory of Mission Ridge, stream on, like the roseate light of morn,
On the sons that now are living, on the sons that are yet unborn!
And cheers for our comrades living, and tears as they pass away!
And three times three for the Drummer Boy who fought at the front that day!

If——

If you can keep your head when all about you
  Are losing theirs and blaming it on you;
If you can trust yourself when all men doubt you,
  But make allowance for their doubting too;
If you can wait and not be tired by waiting,
  Or being lied about don't deal in lies,
Or being hated don't give way to hating,

And yet don't look too good, nor talk too wise;

If you can dream and not make dreams your master;
If you can think and not make thoughts your aim;
If you can meet with Triumph and Disaster
And treat those two impostors just the same;
If you can bear to hear the truth you've spoken
Twisted by knaves to make a trap for fools,
Or watch the things you gave your life to broken,
And stoop and build 'em up with worn-out tools;

If you can make one heap of all your winnings
And risk it on one turn of pitch and toss,
And lose, and start again at your beginnings
And never breathe a word about your loss;
If you can force your heart and nerve and sinew
To serve your turn long after they are gone,
And so hold on when there is nothing in you
Except the Will which says to them: "Hold on!"

If you can talk with crowds and keep your virtue,
Or walk with Kings nor lose the common touch;
If neither foes nor loving friends can hurt you;
If all men count with you, but none too much;
If you can fill the unforgiving minute
With sixty seconds' worth of distance run,
Yours is the Earth and everything that's in it,
And—which is more—you'll be a Man, my son!

Rudyard Kipling.

Second Table

Some boys are mad when comp'ny comes to stay for meals. They hate
To have the other people eat while boys must wait and wait,
But I've about made up my mind I'm different from the rest,
For as for me, I b'lieve I like the second table best.

To eat along with comp'ny is so trying, for it's tough
To sit and watch the victuals when you dassent touch the stuff.
You see your father serving out the dark meat and the light
Until a boy is sure he'll starve before he gets a bite.

And when he asks you what you'll have,—you've heard it all before,—
You know you'll get just what you get and won't get nothing more;
For, when you want another piece, your mother winks her eye,
And so you say, "I've plenty, thanks!" and tell a whopping lie.

When comp'ny is a-watching you, you've got to be polite,
And eat your victuals with a fork and take a little bite.
You can't have nothing till you're asked and, 'cause a boy is small,
Folks think he isn't hungry, and he's never asked at all.

Since I can first remember I've been told that when the cake

Is passed around, the proper thing is for a boy to take
The piece that's nearest to him, and so all I ever got,
When comp'ny's been to our house, was the smallest in the lot.

It worries boys like everything to have the comp'ny stay
A-setting round the table, like they couldn't get away.
But when they've gone and left the whole big shooting match to me,
Say! ain't it fun to just wade in and help myself? Oh, gee!

With no one round to notice what you're doing—bet your life!—
Boys don't use forks to eat with when they'd rather use a knife,
Nor take such little bites as when they're eating with the rest
And so, for lots of things, I like the second table best.

Nixon Waterman.

The Children

When the lessons and tasks are all ended,
And the school for the day is dismissed,
And the little ones gather around me,
To bid me good night and be kissed;
Oh, the little white arms that encircle
My neck in their tender embrace!
Oh, the smiles that are halos of heaven,
Shedding sunshine of love on my face!

And when they are gone, I sit dreaming
Of my childhood, too lovely to last;
Of love that my heart will remember
When it wakes to the pulse of the past,
Ere the world and its wickedness made me
A partner of sorrow and sin,—
When the glory of God was about me,
And the glory of gladness within.

All my heart grows weak as a woman's
And the fountains of feeling will flow,
When I think of the paths steep and stony,
Where the feet of the dear ones must go;
Of the mountains of sin hanging o'er them,
Of the tempest of Fate blowing wild;
Oh, there's nothing on earth half so holy
As the innocent heart of a child!

They are idols of hearts and of households;
They are angels of God in disguise;
His sunlight still sleeps in their tresses,
His glory still gleams in their eyes;
Oh, these truants from home and from heaven,—
They have made me more manly and mild;
And I know now how Jesus could liken
The kingdom of God to a child!

I ask not a life for the dear ones
All radiant, as others have done,
But that life may have just enough shadow
To temper the glare of the sun;
I would pray God to guard them from evil,
But my prayer would bound back to myself;
Ah! a seraph may pray for a sinner,
But a sinner must pray for himself.

The twig is so easily bended,
I have banished the rule and the rod;
I have taught them the goodness of knowledge,
They have taught me the goodness of God.

My heart is the dungeon of darkness,
Where I shut them for breaking a rule;
My frown is sufficient correction;
My love is the law of the school.

I shall leave the old house in the autumn,
To traverse its threshold no more;
Ah! how shall I sigh for the dear ones
That meet me each morn at the door!
I shall miss the "good nights" and the kisses,
And the gush of their innocent glee,
The group on its green, and the flowers
That are brought every morning to me.

I shall miss them at morn and at even,
Their song in the school and the street;
I shall miss the low hum of their voices,
And the tread of their delicate feet.
When the lessons of life are all ended,
And death says, "The school is dismissed!"
May the little ones gather around me
To bid me good night and be kissed!

Charles M. Dickinson.

A Visit from St. Nicholas

'Twas the night before Christmas, when all through the house
Not a creature was stirring, not even a mouse;
The stockings were hung by the chimney with care,
In hopes that St. Nicholas soon would be there;
The children were nestled all snug in their beds,
While visions of sugar-plums danced in their heads;
And mamma in her kerchief, and I in my cap,
Had just settled our brains for a long winter's nap,—
When out on the lawn there arose such a clatter,
I sprang from my bed to see what was the matter.
Away to the window I flew like a flash,
Tore open the shutters and threw up the sash.
The moon, on the breast of the new-fallen snow,
Gave a luster of midday to objects below:
When what to my wondering eyes should appear,
But a miniature sleigh and eight tiny reindeer,
With a little old driver, so lively and quick,
I knew in a moment it must be St. Nick.
More rapid than eagles his coursers they came,
And he whistled and shouted, and called them by name:
"Now, Dasher! now Dancer! now, Prancer! now Vixen!
On, Comet, on, Cupid! on, Donder and Blitzen!—
To the top of the porch, to the top of the wall!
Now, dash away, dash away, dash away all!"
As dry leaves that before the wild hurricane fly,
When they meet with an obstacle, mount to the sky,
So, up to the house-top the coursers they flew,
With the sleigh full of toys,—and St. Nicholas too,
And then in a twinkling I heard on the roof
The prancing and pawing of each little hoof.
As I drew in my head, and was turning around,
Down the chimney St. Nicholas came with a bound,

He was dressed all in fur from his head to his foot,
And his clothes were all tarnished with ashes and soot;
A bundle of toys he had flung on his back,
And he looked like a peddler just opening his pack.
His eyes how they twinkled; his dimples how merry!
His cheeks were like roses, his nose like a cherry;
His droll little mouth was drawn up like a bow,
And the beard on his chin was as white as the snow.
The stump of a pipe he held tight in his teeth,
And the smoke, it encircled his head like a wreath.
He had a broad face and a little round belly
That shook, when he laughed, like a bowl full of jelly.
He was chubby and plump—a right jolly old elf—
And I laughed when I saw him, in spite of myself.
A wink of his eye, and a twist of his head,
Soon gave me to know I had nothing to dread.
He spake not a word, but went straight to his work,
And filled all the stockings; then turned with a jerk,
And laying his finger aside of his nose
And giving a nod, up the chimney he rose.
He sprang to his sleigh, to his team gave a whistle,
And away they all flew like the down of a thistle;
But I heard him exclaim, ere they drove out of sight,
"Happy Christmas to all, and to all a good-night!" *Clement C. Moore.*

Your Mission

If you cannot on the ocean
  Sail among the swiftest fleet,
Rocking on the highest billows,
  Laughing at the storms you meet,
You can stand among the sailors,
  Anchored yet within the bay,
You can lend a hand to help them,
  As they launch their boats away.

If you are too weak to journey
  Up the mountain steep and high,
You can stand within the valley,
  While the multitudes go by;
You can chant in happy measure,
  As they slowly pass along;
Though they may forget the singer,
  They will not forget the song.

If you have not gold and silver
  Ever ready to command,
If you cannot towards the needy
  Reach an ever-open hand,
You can visit the afflicted,
  O'er the erring you can weep,
You can be a true disciple,
  Sitting at the Savior's feet.

If you cannot in the conflict,
  Prove yourself a soldier true,
If where fire and smoke are thickest,
  There's no work for you to do,
When the battle-field is silent,
  You can go with careful tread,
You can bear away the wounded,
  You can cover up the dead.

Do not then stand idly waiting
  For some greater work to do,
Fortune is a lazy goddess,
  She will never come to you.
Go and toil in any vineyard,
  Do not fear to do or dare,
If you want a field of labor,
  You can find it anywhere.

Ellen H. Gates.

The House by the Side of the Road

There are hermit souls that live withdrawn
In the peace of their self-content;
There are souls, like stars, that dwell apart,
In a fellowless firmament;
There are pioneer souls that blaze their paths
Where highways never ran;
But let me live by the side of the road
And be a friend to man.

Let me live in a house by the side of the road,
Where the race of men go by,
The men who are good and the men who are bad,
As good and as bad as I.
I would not sit in the scorner's seat,
Or hurl the cynic's ban;
Let me live in a house by the side of the road
And be a friend to man.

I see from my house by the side of the road,
By the side of the highway of life,
The men who press with the ardor of hope,
The men who are faint with the strife.
But I turn not away from their smiles nor their tears,
Both parts of an infinite plan;
Let me live in my house by the side of the road
And be a friend to man.

I know there are brook-gladdened meadows ahead
And mountains of wearisome height;
That the road passes on through the long afternoon
And stretches away to the night.
But still I rejoice when the travelers rejoice,
And weep with the strangers that moan,
Nor live in my house by the side of the road
Like a man who dwells alone.

Let me live in my house by the side of the road
Where the race of men go by;
They are good, they are bad, they are weak, they are strong,
Wise, foolish—so am I.
Then why should I sit in the scorner's seat,
Or hurl the cynic's ban?
Let me live in my house by the side of the road
And be a friend to man.

Sam Walter Foss.

Asleep at the Switch

The first thing that I remember was Carlo tugging away,
With the sleeve of my coat fast in his teeth, pulling, as much as to say:
"Come, master, awake, attend to the switch, lives now depend upon you.
Think of the souls in the coming train, and the graves you are sending them to.
Think of the mother and the babe at her breast, think of the father and son,
Think of the lover and the loved one too, think of them doomed every one
To fall (as it were by your very hand) into yon fathomless ditch,
Murdered by one who should guard them from harm, who now lies asleep at the switch."

I sprang up amazed—scarce knew where I stood, sleep had o'ermastered me so;

I could hear the wind hollowly howling, and the deep river dashing below,
I could hear the forest leaves rustling, as the trees by the tempest were fanned,
But what was that noise in the distance? That, I could not understand.
I heard it at first indistinctly, like the rolling of some muffled drum,
Then nearer and nearer it came to me, till it made my very ears hum;
What is this light that surrounds me and seems to set fire to my brain?
What whistle's that, yelling so shrill? Ah! I know now; it's the train.

We often stand facing some danger, and seem to take root to the place;
So I stood—with this demon before me, its heated breath scorching my face;
Its headlight made day of the darkness, and glared like the eyes of some witch,—
The train was almost upon me before I remembered the switch.
I sprang to it, seizing it wildly, the train dashing fast down the track;
The switch resisted my efforts, some devil seemed holding it back;
On, on came the fiery-eyed monster, and shot by my face like a flash;
I swooned to the earth the next moment, and knew nothing after the crash.

How long I lay there unconscious 'twas impossible for me to tell;
My stupor was almost a heaven, my waking almost a hell,—
For then I heard the piteous moaning and shrieking of husbands and wives,
And I thought of the day we all shrink from, when I must account for their lives;
Mothers rushed by me like maniacs, their eyes glaring madly and wild;
Fathers, losing their courage, gave way to their grief like a child;
Children searching for parents, I noticed, as by me they sped,
And lips, that could form naught but "Mamma," were calling for one perhaps dead.

My mind was made up in a moment, the river should hide me away,
When, under the still burning rafters I suddenly noticed there lay
A little white hand; she who owned it was doubtless an object of love
To one whom her loss would drive frantic, though she guarded him now from above;
I tenderly lifted the rafters and quietly laid them one side;
How little she thought of her journey when she left for this dark, fatal ride!
I lifted the last log from off her, and while searching for some spark of life,
Turned her little face up in the starlight, and recognized—Maggie, my wife!

O Lord! my scourge is a hard one, at a blow thou hast shattered my pride;
My life will be one endless nightmare, with Maggie away from my side.
How often I'd sat down and pictured the scenes in our long, happy life;
How I'd strive through all my lifetime, to build up a home for my wife;
How people would envy us always in our cozy and neat little nest;
How I should do all the labor, and Maggie should all the day rest;
How one of God's blessings might cheer

us, how some day I perhaps should be rich:—
But all of my dreams had been shattered, while I lay there asleep at the switch!

I fancied I stood on my trial, the jury and judge I could see;
And every eye in the court room was steadily fixed upon me;
And fingers were pointed in scorn, till I felt my face blushing blood-red,
And the next thing I heard were the words, "Hanged by the neck until dead."
Then I felt myself pulled once again, and my hand caught tight hold of a dress,
And I heard, "What's the matter, dear Jim? You've had a bad nightmare, I guess!"
And there stood Maggie, my wife, with never a scar from the ditch,
I'd been taking a nap in my bed, and had not been "asleep at the switch."

George Hoey.

Each in His Own Tongue

A fire-mist and a planet,
A crystal and a cell,
A jellyfish and a saurian,
And caves where the cavemen dwell;
Then a sense of law and beauty,
And a face turned from the clod,—
Some call it Evolution,
And others call it God.

A haze in the far horizon,
The infinite, tender sky;
The ripe, rich tints of the cornfields,
And the wild geese sailing high;
And all over upland and lowland
The charm of the goldenrod,—
Some of us call it Nature,
And others call it God.

Like tides on a crescent sea-beach,
When the moon is new and thin,
Into our hearts high yearnings
Come welling and surging in,—
Come from the mystic ocean
Whose rim no foot has trod,—
Some of us call it Longing,
And others call it God.

A picket frozen on duty,
A mother starved for her brood,
Socrates drinking the hemlock,
And Jesus on the rood;
The millions who, humble and nameless,
The straight, hard pathway trod,—
Some call it Consecration,
And others call it God.

William Herbert Carruth.

How Cyrus Laid the Cable

Come, listen all unto my song;
It is no silly fable;
'Tis all about the mighty cord
They call the Atlantic Cable.

Bold Cyrus Field he said, says he,
I have a pretty notion
That I can run the telegraph
Across the Atlantic Ocean.

Then all the people laughed, and said
They'd like to see him do it;
He might get half-seas over, but
He never could go through it;

To carry out his foolish plan
He never would be able;
He might as well go hang himself
With his Atlantic Cable.

But Cyrus was a valiant man,
A fellow of decision;
And heeded not their mocking words,
Their laughter and derision.

Twice did his bravest efforts fail,
And yet his mind was stable;

He wa'n't the man to break his heart
  Because he broke his cable.

"Once more, my gallant boys!" he cried;
  "*Three times!*—you know the fable,—
(*I'll make it thirty,*" muttered he,
  "But I will lay this cable!")

Once more they tried—hurrah! hurrah!
  What means this great commotion?
The Lord be praised! the cable's laid
  Across the Atlantic Ocean.

Loud ring the bells,—for, flashing through
  Six hundred leagues of water,
Old Mother England's benison
  Salutes her eldest daughter.

O'er all the land the tidings speed,
  And soon, in every nation,
They'll hear about the cable with
  Profoundest admiration!

* * * *

And may we honor evermore
  The manly, bold, and stable;
And tell our sons, to make them brave,
  How Cyrus laid the cable.

John G. Saxe.

Jane Jones

Jane Jones keeps talkin' to me all the time,
  An' says you must make it a rule
To study your lessons 'nd work hard 'nd learn,
  An' never be absent from school.
Remember the story of Elihu Burritt,
  An' how he clum up to the top,
Got all the knowledge 'at he ever had
  Down in a blacksmithing shop?
Jane Jones she honestly said it was so!
    Mebbe he did—
    I dunno!
O' course what's a-keepin' me 'way from the top,
Is not never havin' no blacksmithing shop.

She said 'at Ben Franklin was awfully poor,
  But full of ambition an' brains;
An' studied philosophy all his hull life,
  An' see what he got for his pains!
He brought electricity out of the sky,
  With a kite an' a bottle an' key,
An' we're owing him more'n any one else
  For all the bright lights 'at we see.
Jane Jones she honestly said it was so!
    Mebbe he did—
    I dunno!
O' course what's allers been hinderin' me
Is not havin' any kite, lightning er key.

Jane Jones said Abe Lincoln had no books at all,
  An' used to split rails when a boy;
An' General Grant was a tanner by trade
  An' lived 'way out in Ill'nois.
So when the great war in the South first broke out
  He stood on the side o' the right,
An' when Lincoln called him to take charge o' things,
  He won nearly every blamed fight.
Jane Jones she honestly said it was so!
    Mebbe he did—
    I dunno!
Still I ain't to blame, not by a big sight,
For I ain't never had any battles to fight.

She said 'at Columbus was out at the knees
  When he first thought up his big scheme,

An' told all the Spaniards 'nd Italians, too,
An' all of 'em said 'twas a dream.
But Queen Isabella jest listened to him,
'Nd pawned all her jewels o' worth,
'Nd bought him the Santa Maria 'nd said,
"Go hunt up the rest o' the earth!"
Mebbe he did—
I dunno!
O' course that may be, but then you must allow
They ain't no land to discover jest now!

Ben King.

The Leap of Roushan Beg

Mounted on Kyrat strong and fleet,
His chestnut steed with four white feet,
Roushan Beg, called Kurroglou,
Son of the road and bandit chief,
Seeking refuge and relief,
Up the mountain pathway flew.

Such was Kyrat's wondrous speed,
Never yet could any steed
Reach the dust-cloud in his course.
More than maiden, more than wife,
More than gold and next to life
Roushan the Robber loved his horse.

In the land that lies beyond
Erzeroum and Trebizond,
Garden-girt his fortress stood;
Plundered khan, or caravan
Journeying north from Koordistan,
Gave him wealth and wine and food.

Seven hundred and fourscore
Men at arms his livery wore,
Did his bidding night and day.
Now, through regions all unknown,
He was wandering, lost, alone,
Seeking without guide his way.

Suddenly the pathway ends,
Sheer the precipice descends,
Loud the torrent roars unseen;
Thirty feet from side to side
Yawns the chasm; on air must ride
He who crosses this ravine.

Following close in his pursuit,
At the precipice's foot
Reyhan the Arab of Orfah
Halted with his hundred men,
Shouting upward from the glen,
"La Illah illa Allah!"

Gently Roushan Beg caressed
Kyrat's forehead, neck, and breast,
Kissed him upon both his eyes;
Sang to him in his wild way,
As upon the topmost spray
Sings a bird before it flies.

"O my Kyrat, O my steed,
Round and slender as a reed,
Carry me this peril through!
Satin housings shall be thine,
Shoes of gold, O Kyrat mine,
O thou soul of Kurroglou!

"Soft thy skin as silken skein,
Soft as woman's hair thy mane,
Tender are thine eyes and true;
All thy hoofs like ivory shine,
Polished bright; O life of mine,
Leap, and rescue Kurroglou!"

Kyrat, then, the strong and fleet,
Drew together his four white feet,
Paused a moment on the verge,
Measured with his eye the space,
And into the air's embrace
Leaped, as leaps the ocean surge.

As the ocean surge o'er sand
Bears a swimmer safe to land,
Kyrat safe his rider bore;
Rattling down the deep abyss,
Fragments of the precipice
Rolled like pebbles on a shore.

Roushan's tasseled cap of red
Trembled not upon his head,
  Careless sat he and upright;
Neither hand nor bridle shook,
Nor his head he turned to look,
  As he galloped out of sight.

Flash of harness in the air,
Seen a moment like the glare
  Of a sword drawn from its sheath;
Thus the phantom horseman passed,
And the shadow that he cast
  Leaped the cataract underneath.

Reyhan the Arab held his breath
While this vision of life and death
  Passed above him. "Allahu!"
Cried he. "In all Koordistan
Lives there not so brave a man
  As this Robber Kurroglou!"

Henry W. Longfellow.

Old Ironsides

Ay, tear her tattered ensign down!
  Long has it waved on high,
And many an eye has danced to see
  That banner in the sky;
Beneath it rung the battle shout,
  And burst the cannon's roar;—
The meteor of the ocean air
  Shall sweep the clouds no more!

Her deck, once red with heroes' blood,
  Where knelt the vanquished foe,
When winds were hurrying o'er the flood,
  And waves were white below,
No more shall feel the victor's tread,
  Or know the conquered knee;—
The harpies of the shore shall pluck
  The eagle of the sea!

Oh, better that her shattered hulk
  Should sink beneath the wave!
Her thunders shook the mighty deep,
  And there should be her grave;
Nail to the mast her holy flag,
  Set every threadbare sail,
And give her to the god of storms,
  The lightning and the gale!

Oliver Wendell Holmes.

A Psalm of Life

Tell me not, in mournful numbers,
  "Life is but an empty dream!"
For the soul is dead that slumbers,
  And things are not what they seem.

Life is real! Life is earnest!
  And the grave is not its goal;
"Dust thou art, to dust returnest,"
  Was not spoken of the soul.

Not enjoyment, and not sorrow,
  Is our destined end or way;
But to act that each to-morrow
  Finds us farther than to-day.

Art is long, and Time is fleeting,
  And our hearts, though stout and brave,
Still, like muffled drums, are beating
  Funeral marches to the grave.

In the world's broad field of battle,
  In the bivouac of Life,
Be not like dumb, driven cattle!
  Be a hero in the strife!

Trust no Future, howe'er pleasant!
  Let the dead Past bury its dead!
Act, act in the living Present!
  Heart within, and God o'erhead!

Lives of great men all remind us
  We can make our lives sublime,
And, departing, leave behind us
  Footprints on the sands of time;

Footprints, that perhaps another,
  Sailing o'er life's solemn main,

A forlorn and shipwrecked brother,
Seeing, shall take heart again.

Let us, then, be up and doing,
With a heart for any fate;
Still achieving, still pursuing,
Learn to labor and to wait.

Henry W. Longfellow.

Johnny's Hist'ry Lesson

I think, of all the things at school
A boy has got to do,
That studyin' hist'ry, as a rule,
Is worst of all, don't you?
Of dates there are an awful sight,
An' though I study day an' night,
There's only one I've got just right—
That's fourteen ninety-two.

Columbus crossed the Delaware
In fourteen ninety-two;
We whipped the British, fair an' square,
In fourteen ninety-two.
At Concord an' at Lexington
We kept the redcoats on the run,
While the band played Johnny Get Your Gun,
In fourteen ninety-two.

Pat Henry, with his dyin' breath—
In fourteen ninety-two—
Said, "Gimme liberty or death!"
In fourteen ninety-two.
An' Barbara Frietchie, so 'tis said,
Cried, "Shoot if you must this old, gray head,
But I'd rather 'twould be your own instead!"
In fourteen ninety-two.

The Pilgrims came to Plymouth Rock
In fourteen ninety-two,
An' the Indians standin' on the dock
Asked, "What are you goin' to do?"
An' they said, "We seek your harbor drear
That our children's children's children dear
May boast that their forefathers landed here
In fourteen ninety-two."

Miss Pocahontas saved the life—
In fourteen ninety-two—
Of John Smith, an' became his wife
In fourteen ninety-two.
An' the Smith tribe started then an' there,
An' now there are John Smiths ev'rywhere,
But they didn't have any Smiths to spare
In fourteen ninety-two.

Kentucky was settled by Daniel Boone
In fourteen ninety-two,
An' I think the cow jumped over the moon
In fourteen ninety-two.
Ben Franklin flew his kite so high
He drew the lightnin' from the sky,
An' Washington couldn't tell a lie,
In fourteen ninety-two.

Nixon Waterman.

Riding on the Rail

Singing through the forests, rattling over ridges,
Shooting under arches, rumbling over bridges,
Whizzing through the mountains, buzzing o'er the vale,—
Bless me! this is pleasant, riding on the rail!

Men of different stations in the eye of Fame,
Here are very quickly coming to the same;
High and lowly people, birds of every feather,
On a common level, traveling together!

Gentlemen in shorts, blooming very tall;
Gentlemen at large, talking very small;
Gentlemen in tights, with a loosish mien;
Gentlemen in gray, looking very green!

Gentlemen quite old, asking for the news;
Gentlemen in black, with a fit of blues;
Gentlemen in claret, sober as a vicar;
Gentlemen in tweed, dreadfully in liquor!

Stranger on the right looking very sunny,
Obviously reading something very funny.
Now the smiles are thicker—wonder what they mean?
Faith, he's got the Knickerbocker Magazine!

Stranger on the left, closing up his peepers;
Now he snores again, like the Seven Sleepers;
At his feet a volume gives the explanation,
How the man grew stupid from "association"!

Ancient maiden lady anxiously remarks
That there must be peril 'mong so many sparks;
Roguish-looking fellow, turning to the stranger,
Says 'tis his opinion *she* is out of danger!

Woman with her baby, sitting *vis a vis;*
Baby keeps a-squalling, woman looks at me;
Asks about the distance—says 'tis tiresome talking,
Noises of the cars are so very shocking!

Market woman, careful of the precious casket,
Knowing eggs are eggs, tightly holds her basket;
Feeling that a smash, if it came, would surely
Send her eggs to pot rather prematurely.

Singing through the forests, rattling over ridges,
Shooting under arches, rumbling over bridges,
Whizzing through the mountains, buzzing o'er the vale,—
Bless me! this is pleasant, riding on the rail!

J. G. Saxe.

The Building of the Ship

EXTRACT

Thou, too, sail on, O Ship of State!
Sail on, O Union, strong and great!
Humanity with all its fears,
With all the hopes of future years,
Is hanging breathless on thy fate!
We know what Master laid thy keel,
What Workmen wrought thy ribs of steel,
Who made each mast, and sail, and rope,
What anvils rang, what hammers beat,
In what a forge and what a heat
Were shaped the anchors of thy hope!
Fear not each sudden sound and shock,
'Tis of the wave and not the rock;
'Tis but the flapping of the sail,
And not a rent made by the gale!
In spite of rock and tempest's roar,
In spite of false lights on the shore,
Sail on, nor fear to breast the sea!
Our hearts, our hopes, are all with thee,
Our hearts, our hopes, our prayers, our tears,
Our faith triumphant o'er our fears,
Are all with thee,—are all with thee!

H. W. Longfellow.

The Dead Pussy Cat

You's as stiff an' as cold as a stone,
Little cat!
Dey's done frowed you out an' left you alone,
Little cat!
I 's a-strokin' you's fur,
But you don't never purr
Nor hump up anywhere,
Little cat.
W'y is dat?
Is you's purrin' an' humpin'-up done?

An' w'y fer is you's little foot tied,
Little cat?
Did dey pisen you's tummick inside,
Little cat?
Did dey pound you wif bricks,
Or wif big nasty sticks,
Or abuse you wif kicks,
Little cat?
Tell me dat,
Did dey holler at all when you cwied?

Did it hurt werry bad w'en you died,
Little cat?
Oh, w'y didn't yo wun off and hide,
Little cat?
I is wet in my eyes,
'Cause I most always cwies
W'en a pussy cat dies,
Little cat,
Tink of dat,
An' I's awfully solly besides!

Dest lay still dere in de sof' gwown',
Little cat,
W'ile I tucks de gween gwass all awoun',
Little cat.
Dey can't hurt you no more
W'en you's tired an' so sore,
Dest sleep twiet, you pore
Little cat,
Wif a pat,
An' fordet all de kicks of de town.

Marion Short.

The Owl Critic

"Who stuffed that white owl?" No one spoke in the shop;
The barber was busy, and he couldn't stop;
The customers, waiting their turns, were all reading
The *Daily*, the *Herald*, the *Post*, little heeding
The young man who blurted out such a blunt question;
Not one raised a head, or even made a suggestion;
And the barber kept on shaving.

"Don't you see, Mister Brown,"
Cried the youth, with a frown,
"How wrong the whole thing is,
How preposterous each wing is,
How flattened the head is, how jammed down the neck is—
In short, the whole owl, what an ignorant wreck 'tis!
I make no apology; I've learned owl-eology.
I've passed days and nights in a hundred collections,
And cannot be blinded to any deflections
Arising from unskilful fingers that fail
To stuff a bird right, from his beak to his tail.
Mister Brown! Mister Brown! Do take that bird down,
Or you'll soon be the laughing-stock all over town!"
And the barber kept on shaving.

"I've *studied* owls,
And other night fowls,
And I tell you
What I know to be true:
An owl cannot roost
With his limbs so unloosed;
No owl in this world
Ever had his claws curled,

Ever had his legs slanted,
Ever had his bill canted,
Ever had his neck screwed
Into that attitude.
He can't *do* it, because
'Tis against all bird laws.
Anatomy teaches,
Ornithology preaches,
An owl has a toe
That *can't* turn out so!
I've made the white owl my study for years,
And to see such a job almost moves me to tears!
Mister Brown, I'm amazed
You should be so gone crazed
As to put up a bird
In that posture absurd!
To *look* at that owl really brings on a dizziness;
The man who stuffed him don't half know his business!"
And the barber kept on shaving.

"Examine those eyes.
I'm filled with surprise
Taxidermists should pass
Off on you such poor glass;
So unnatural they seem
They'd make Audubon scream,
And John Burroughs laugh
To encounter such chaff.
Do take that bird down;
Have him stuffed again, Brown!"
And the barber kept on shaving.

"With some sawdust and bark
I could stuff in the dark
An owl better than that.
I could make an old hat
Look more like an owl
Than that horrid fowl,
Stuck up here so stiff like a side of coarse leather.
In fact, about *him* there's not one natural feather."

Just then, with a wink and a sly normal lurch,
The owl, very gravely, got down from his perch,
Walked round, and regarded his fault-finding critic
(Who thought he was stuffed) with a glance analytic,
And then fairly hooted, as if he should say:
"Your learning's at fault this time, anyway;
Don't waste it again on a live bird, I pray.
I'm an owl; you're another. Sir Critic, good-day!"
And the barber kept on shaving.

James T. Fields.

At School-Close

The end has come, as come it must
To all things; in these sweet June days
The teacher and the scholar trust
Their parting feet to separate ways.

They part: but in the years to be
Shall pleasant memories cling to each,
As shells bear inland from the sea
The murmur of the rhythmic beach.

One knew the joys the sculptor knows
When, plastic to his lightest touch,
His clay-wrought model slowly grows
To that fine grace desired so much.

So daily grew before her eyes
The living shapes whereon she wrought,
Strong, tender, innocently wise,
The child's heart with the woman's thought.

And one shall never quite forget
The voice that called from dream and play,

The firm but kindly hand that set
Her feet in learning's pleasant way,—

The joy of Undine soul-possessed,
The wakening sense, the strange delight
That swelled the fabled statue's breast
And filled its clouded eyes with sight!

O Youth and Beauty, loved of all!
Ye pass from girlhood's gate of dreams;
In broader ways your footsteps fall,
Ye test the truth of all that seems

Her little realm the teacher leaves,
She breaks her wand of power apart,
While, for your love and trust, she gives
The warm thanks of a grateful heart.

Hers is the sober summer noon
Contrasted with your morn of spring;
The waning with the waxing moon,
The folded with the outspread wing.

Across the distance of the years
She sends her God-speed back to you;
She has no thought of doubts or fears;
Be but yourselves, be pure, be true,

And prompt in duty; heed the deep,
Low voice of conscience; through the ill
And discord round about you, keep
Your faith in human nature still.

Be gentle: unto griefs and needs
Be pitiful as woman should,
And, spite of all the lies of creeds,
Hold fast the truth that God is good.

Give and receive; go forth and bless
The world that needs the hand and heart
Of Martha's helpful carefulness
No less than Mary's better part.

So shall the stream of time flow by
And leave each year a richer good,
And matron loveliness outvie
The nameless charm of maidenhood.

And, when the world shall link your names
With gracious lives and manners fine,
The teacher shall assert her claims,
And proudly whisper, "These were mine!"

John G. Whittier.

The Wild White Rose

Oh, that I might have my request, and that God would grant me the thing that I long for.—*Job 6:8.*

It was peeping through the brambles, that little wild white rose,
Where the hawthorn hedge was planted, my garden to enclose.
All beyond was fern and heather, on the breezy, open moor;
All within was sun and shelter, and the wealth of beauty's store.
But I did not heed the fragrance of flow'ret or of tree,
For my eyes were on that rosebud, and it grew too high for me.
In vain I strove to reach it through the tangled mass of green,
It only smiled and nodded behind its thorny screen.
Yet through that summer morning I lingered near the spot:
Oh, why do things seem sweeter if we possess them not?
My garden buds were blooming, but all that I could see
Was that little mocking wild rose, hanging just too high for me.

So in life's wider garden there are buds of promise, too,

Beyond our reach to gather, but not beyond our view;
And like the little charmer that tempted me astray,
They steal out half the brightness of many a summer's day.
Oh, hearts that fail with longing for some forbidden tree,
Look up and learn a lesson from my white rose and me.
'Tis wiser far to number the blessings at my feet,
Than ever to be sighing for just one bud more sweet.
My sunbeams and my shadows fall from a pierced Hand,
I can surely trust His wisdom since His heart I understand;
And maybe in the morning, when His blessed face I see,
He will tell me why my white rose grew just too high for me.

Ellen H. Willis.

L'Envoi

When Earth's last picture is painted, and the tubes are twisted and dried,
When the oldest colors have faded, and the youngest critic has died,
We shall rest, and, faith, we shall need it—lie down for an æon or two,
Till the Master of All Good Workmen shall set us to work anew!

And those who were good shall be happy: they shall sit in a golden chair;
They shall splash at a ten-league canvas with brushes of comet's hair;
They shall find real saints to draw from —Magdalene, Peter and Paul;
They shall work for an age at a sitting and never be tired at all.

And only the Master shall praise us, and only the Master shall blame;
And no one shall work for money, and no one shall work for fame;
But each for the joy of the working, and each, in his separate star,
Shall draw the Thing as he sees It for the God of Things as They Are!

Rudyard Kipling.

Whistling in Heaven

You're surprised that I ever should say so?
Just wait till the reason I've given
Why I say I sha'n't care for the music,
Unless there is whistling in heaven.
Then you'll think it no very great wonder,
Nor so strange, nor so bold a conceit,
That unless there's a boy there a-whistling,
Its music will not be complete.

It was late in the autumn of '40;
We had come from our far Eastern home
Just in season to build us a cabin,
Ere the cold of the winter should come;
And we lived all the while in our wagon
That husband was clearing the place
Where the house was to stand; and the clearing
And building it took many days.

So that our heads were scarce sheltered
In under its roof when our store
Of provisions was almost exhausted,
And husband must journey for more;
And the nearest place where he could get them
Was yet such a distance away,
That it forced him from home to be absent
At least a whole night and a day.

You see, we'd but two or three neighbors,

And the nearest was more than a mile;
And we hadn't found time yet to know them,
For we had been busy the while.
And the man who had helped at the raising
Just staid till the job was well done;
And as soon as his money was paid him
Had shouldered his axe and had gone.

Well, husband just kissed me and started—
I could scarcely suppress a deep groan
At the thought of remaining with baby
So long in the house alone;
For, my dear, I was childish and timid,
And braver ones might well have feared,
For the wild wolf was often heard howling,
And savages sometimes appeared.

But I smothered my grief and my terror
Till husband was off on his ride,
And then in my arms I took Josey,
And all the day long sat and cried,
As I thought of the long, dreary hours
When the darkness of night should fall,
And I was so utterly helpless,
With no one in reach of my call.

And when the night came with its terrors,
To hide ev'ry ray of light,
I hung up a quilt by the window,
And, almost dead with affright,
I kneeled by the side of the cradle,
Scarce daring to draw a full breath,
Lest the baby should wake, and its crying
Should bring us a horrible death.

There I knelt until late in the evening
And scarcely an inch had I stirred,
When suddenly, far in the distance,
A sound as of whistling I heard.
I started up dreadfully frightened,
For fear 'twas an Indian's call;
And then very soon I remembered
The red man ne'er whistles at all.

And when I was sure 'twas a white man,
I thought, were he coming for ill,
He'd surely approach with more caution—
Would come without warning, and still.
Then the sound, coming nearer and nearer,
Took the form of a tune light and gay,
And I knew I needn't fear evil
From one who could whistle that way.

Very soon I heard footsteps approaching,
Then came a peculiar dull thump,
As if some one was heavily striking
An ax in the top of a stump;
And then, in another brief moment,
There came a light tap on the door,
When quickly I undid the fast'ning,
And in stepped a boy, and before

There was either a question or answer
Or either had time to speak,
I just threw my glad arms around him,
And gave him a kiss on the cheek.
Then I started back, scared at my boldness,
But he only smiled at my fright,
As he said, "I'm your neighbor's boy, Elick,
Come to tarry with you through the night.

"We saw your husband go eastward,
And made up our minds where he'd gone,
And I said to the rest of our people,
'That woman is there all alone,
And I venture she's awfully lonesome,
And though she may have no great fear,
I think she would feel a bit safer
If only a boy were but near.'

"So, taking my axe on my shoulder,
For fear that a savage might stray
Across my path and need scalping,
I started right down this way;
And coming in sight of the cabin,
And thinking to save you alarm,
I whistled a tune, just to show you
I didn't intend any harm.

"And so here I am, at your service;
But if you don't want me to stay,
Why, all you need do is to say so,
And should'ring my axe, I'll away."
I dropped in a chair and near fainted,
Just at thought of his leaving me then,
And his eye gave a knowing bright twinkle
As he said, "I guess I'll remain."

And then I just sat there and told him
How terribly frightened I'd been,
How his face was to me the most welcome
Of any I ever had seen;
And then I lay down with the baby,
And slept all the blessed night through,
For I felt I was safe from all danger
Near so brave a young fellow, and true.

So now, my dear friend, do you wonder,
Since such a good reason I've given,
Why I say I sha'n't care for the music,
Unless there is whistling in heaven?
Yes, often I've said so in earnest,
And now what I've said I repeat,
That unless there's a boy there a-whistling,
Its music will not be complete.

Sleep, Baby, Sleep

Sleep, baby, sleep!
Thy father's watching the sheep,
Thy mother's shaking the dreamland tree,
And down drops a little dream for thee.
Sleep, baby, sleep!

Sleep, baby, sleep!
The large stars are the sheep,
The little stars are the lambs, I guess,
The bright moon is the shepherdess.
Sleep, baby, sleep!

Sleep, baby, sleep!
Thy Savior loves His sheep;
He is the Lamb of God on high
Who for our sakes came down to die.
Sleep, baby, sleep!

Elizabeth Prentiss.

The Lost Chord

Seated one day at the organ,
I was weary and ill at ease,
And my fingers wandered idly
Over the noisy keys.

I do not know what I was playing,
Or what I was dreaming then;
But I struck one chord of music,
Like the sound of a great Amen.

It flooded the crimson twilight,
Like the close of an angel's psalm;
And it lay on my fevered spirit
With a touch of infinite calm.

It quieted pain and sorrow,
Like love overcoming strife;
It seemed the harmonious echo
From our discordant life.

It linked all perplexing meanings
  Into one perfect peace,
And trembled away into silence
  As if it were loth to cease.

I have sought, but I seek it vainly,
  That one lost chord divine,
That came from the soul of the organ,
  And entered into mine.

It may be that Death's bright angel
  Will speak in that chord again;
It may be that only in Heaven
  I shall hear that grand Amen.

Adelaide A. Procter.

The Children's Hour

Between the dark and the daylight,
  When the night is beginning to lower,
Comes a pause in the day's occupations,
  That is known as the Children's Hour.

I hear in the chamber above me
  The patter of little feet,
The sound of a door that is opened,
  And voices soft and sweet.

From my study I see in the lamplight,
  Descending the broad hall stair,
Grave Alice, and laughing Allegra,
  And Edith with golden hair.

A whisper, and then a silence:
  Yet I know by their merry eyes
They are plotting and planning together
  To take me by surprise.

A sudden rush from the stairway,
  A sudden raid from the hall!
By three doors left unguarded
  They enter my castle wall!

They climb up into my turret
  O'er the arms and back of my chair;
If I try to escape, they surround me;
  They seem to be everywhere.

They almost devour me with kisses,
  Their arms about me entwine,
Till I think of the Bishop of Bingen
  In his Mouse-tower on the Rhine!

Do you think, O blue-eyed banditti,
  Because you have scaled the wall,
Such an old mustache as I am
  Is not a match for you all!

I have you fast in my fortress,
  And will not let you depart,
But put you down into the dungeon
  In the round-tower of my heart.

And there will I keep you forever,
  Yes, forever and a day,
Till the walls shall crumble to ruin,
  And moulder in dust away!

Henry W. Longfellow.

Woodman, Spare That Tree!

Woodman, spare that tree!
  Touch not a single bough!
In youth it sheltered me,
  And I'll protect it now.
'T was my forefather's hand
  That placed it near his cot;
There, woodman, let it stand,
  Thy ax shall harm it not!

That old familiar tree,
  Whose glory and renown
Are spread o'er land and sea—
  And wouldst thou hew it down?
Woodman, forbear thy stroke!
  Cut not its earth-bound ties;
Oh, spare that aged oak,
  Now towering to the skies!

When but an idle boy,
  I sought its grateful shade;
In all their gushing joy
  Here, too, my sisters played.
My mother kissed me here;
  My father pressed my hand—
Forgive this foolish tear,
  But let that old oak stand!

My heart-strings round thee cling,
Close as thy bark, old friend!
Here shall the wild-bird sing,
And still thy branches bend.
Old tree! the storm still brave!
And, woodman, leave the spot;
While I've a hand to save,
Thy ax shall harm it not!

George Pope Morris.

Little Brown Hands

They drive home the cows from the pasture,
Up through the long shady lane,
Where the quail whistles loud in the wheat-fields,
That are yellow with ripening grain.
They find, in the thick waving grasses,
Where the scarlet-lipped strawberry grows.
They gather the earliest snowdrops,
And the first crimson buds of the rose.

They toss the new hay in the meadow,
They gather the elder-bloom white,
They find where the dusky grapes purple
In the soft-tinted October light.
They know where the apples hang ripest,
And are sweeter than Italy's wines;
They know where the fruit hangs the thickest
On the long, thorny blackberry vines.

They gather the delicate sea-weeds,
And build tiny castles of sand;
They pick up the beautiful sea shells—
Fairy barks that have drifted to land.
They wave from the tall, rocking tree-tops,
Where the oriole's hammock-nest swings,
And at night time are folded in slumber
By a song that a fond mother sings.

Those who toil bravely are strongest;
The humble and poor become great;
And so from these brown-handed children
Shall grow mighty rulers of state.
The pen of the author and statesman,—
The noble and wise of the land,—
The sword, and the chisel, and palette,
Shall be held in the little brown hand.

Mary H. Krout.

Barbara Frietchie

Up from the meadows rich with corn
Clear in the cool September morn,

The clustered spires of Frederick stand
Green-walled by the hills of Maryland.

Round about them orchards sweep,
Apple and peach tree fruited deep,

Fair as the garden of the Lord
To the eyes of the famished rebel horde,

On that pleasant morn of the early fall
When Lee marched over the mountain-wall,—

Over the mountains winding down,
Horse and foot, into Frederick town.

Forty flags with their silver stars,
Forty flags with their crimson bars,

Flapped in the morning wind; the sun
Of noon looked down, and saw not one.

Up rose old Barbara Frietchie then,
Bowed with her fourscore years and ten;

Bravest of all in Frederick town,
She took up the flag the men hauled down;

In her attic window the staff she set,
To show that one heart was loyal yet.

Up the street came the rebel tread,
Stonewall Jackson riding ahead.

Under his slouched hat left and right
He glanced; the old flag met his sight.

"Halt!"—the dust-brown ranks stood fast.
"Fire!"—out blazed the rifle-blast.

It shivered the window, pain and sash;
It rent the banner with seam and gash.

Quick, as it fell, from the broken staff
Dame Barbara snatched the silken scarf;

She leaned far out on the window-sill,
And shook it forth with a royal will.

"Shoot, if you must, this old gray head,
But spare your country's flag," she said.

A shade of sadness, a blush of shame,
Over the face of the leader came;

The nobler nature within him stirred
To life at that woman's deed and word:

"Who touches a hair of yon gray head
Dies like a dog; march on!" he said.

All day long through Frederick street
Sounded the tread of marching feet;

All day long that free flag tost
Over the heads of the rebel host.

Ever its torn folds rose and fell
On the loyal winds that loved it well;

And through the hill-gaps sunset light
Shone over it a warm good night.

Barbara Frietchie's work is o'er,
And the Rebel rides on his raids no more.

Honor to her! and let a tear
Fall, for her sake, on Stonewall's bier.

Over Barbara Frietchie's grave,
Flag of freedom and Union wave!

Peace and order and beauty draw
Round thy symbol of light and law;

And ever the stars above look down
On thy stars below in Frederick town.

John G. Whittier.

I Want to Go to Morrow

I started on a journey just about a week ago,
For the little town of Morrow, in the State of Ohio.
I never was a traveler, and really didn't know
That Morrow had been ridiculed a century or so.
I went down to the depot for my ticket and applied
For the tips regarding Morrow, not expecting to be guyed.
Said I, "My friend, I want to go to Morrow and return
Not later than to-morrow, for I haven't time to burn."

Said he to me, "Now let me see if I have heard you right,
You want to go to Morrow and come back to-morrow night.
You should have gone to Morrow yesterday and back to-day,
For if you started yesterday to Morrow, don't you see,
You could have got to Morrow and returned to-day at three.
The train that started yesterday—now understand me right—
To-day it gets to Morrow, and returns to-morrow night."

Said I, "My boy, it seems to me you're talking through your hat,
Is there a town named Morrow on your line? Now tell me that."
"There is," said he, "and take from me a quiet little tip—
To go from here to Morrow is a fourteen-hour trip.
The train that goes to Morrow leaves to-day eight-thirty-five;
Half after ten to-morrow is the time it should arrive.
Now if from here to Morrow is a fourteen-hour jump,

Can you go to-day to Morrow and come back to-day, you chump?"

Said I, "I want to go to Morrow; can I go to-day
And get to Morrow by to-night, if there is no delay?"
"Well, well," said he, "explain to me and I've no more to say;
Can you go anywhere to-morrow and come back from there to-day?"
For if to-day you'd get to Morrow, surely you'll agree
You should have started not to-day, but yesterday, you see.
So if you start to Morrow, leaving here to-day, you're flat,
You won't get to Morrow till the day that follows that.

"Now if you start to-day to Morrow, it's a cinch you'll land
To-morrow into Morrow, not to-day, you understand.
For the train to-day to Morrow, if the schedule is right,
Will get you into Morrow by about to-morrow night."
Said I, "I guess you know it all, but kindly let me say,
How can I go to Morrow, if I leave the town to-day?"
Said he, "You cannot go to Morrow any more to-day,
For the train that goes to Morrow is a mile upon its way."

FINALE

I was so disappointed I was mad enough to swear;
The train had gone to Morrow and had left me standing there.
The man was right in telling me I was a howling jay;
I didn't go to Morrow, so I guess I'll go to-day.

Out in the Fields

The little cares that fretted me,
I lost them yesterday
Among the fields above the seas,
Among the winds at play;
Among the lowing of the herds,
The rustling of the trees,
Among the singing of the birds,
The humming of the bees.

The foolish fears of what might happen,—
I cast them all away
Among the clover-scented grass,
Among the new-mown hay;
Among the husking of the corn,
Where drowsy poppies nod,
Where ill thoughts die and good are born,
Out in the fields with God.

Elizabeth Barrett Browning.

The Bluebird's Song

I know the song that the bluebird is singing,
Out in the apple tree where he is swinging.
Brave little fellow! the skies may be dreary—
Nothing cares he while his heart is so cheery.

Hark! how the music leaps out from his throat!
Hark! was there ever so merry a note?
Listen a while, and you'll hear what he's saying,
Up in the apple tree swinging and swaying.

"Dear little blossoms down under the snow,
You must be weary of winter I know.
Listen, I'll sing you a message of cheer!
Summer is coming! and springtime is here!

"Little white snowdrop! I pray you arise;
Bright yellow crocus! please open your eyes;
Sweet little violets, hid from the cold,
Put on your mantles of purple and gold;
Daffodils! Daffodils! say, do you hear?—
Summer is coming, and springtime is here!"

Emily Huntington Miller.

The Main Truck, or a Leap for Life

Old Ironsides at anchor lay,
In the harbor of Mahon;
A dead calm rested on the bay,—
The waves to sleep had gone;
When little Hal, the Captain's son,
A lad both brave and good,
In sport, up shroud and rigging ran,
And on the main truck stood!

A shudder shot through every vein,—
All eyes were turned on high!
There stood the boy, with dizzy brain,
Between the sea and sky;
No hold had he above, below;
Alone he stood in air:
To that far height none dared to go,—
No aid could reach him there.

We gazed, but not a man could speak,—
With horror all aghast,—
In groups, with pallid brow and cheek,—
We watched the quivering mast.
The atmosphere grew thick and hot,
And of a lurid hue;—
As riveted unto the spot,
Stood officers and crew.

The father came on deck:—he gasped,
"Oh, God; thy will be done!"
Then suddenly a rifle grasped,
And aimed it at his son.
"Jump, far out, boy, into the wave!
Jump, or I fire," he said;
"That only chance your life can save;
Jump, jump, boy!" He obeyed.

He sunk,—he rose,—he lived,—he moved,—
And for the ship struck out.
On board we hailed the lad beloved,
With many a manly shout.
His father drew, in silent joy,
Those wet arms round his neck,
And folded to his heart his boy,—
Then fainted on the deck.

Morris.

The Arrow and the Song

I shot an arrow into the air,
It fell to earth, I knew not where;
For, so swiftly it flew, the sight
Could not follow it in its flight.

I breathed a song into the air,
It fell to earth, I knew not where;
For who has sight so keen and strong,
That it can follow the flight of song?

Long, long afterward, in an oak
I found the arrow, still unbroke;
And the song, from beginning to end,
I found again in the heart of a friend.

H. W. Longfellow.

The Green Mountain Justice

"The snow is deep," the Justice said;
"There's mighty mischief overhead."
"High talk, indeed!" his wife exclaimed;
"What, sir! shall Providence be blamed?"
The Justice, laughing, said, "Oh no!
I only meant the loads of snow
Upon the roofs. The barn is weak;
I greatly fear the roof will break,

So hand me up the spade, my dear,
I'll mount the barn, the roof to clear."
"No!" said the wife; "the barn is high,
And if you slip, and fall, and die,
How will my living be secured?—
Stephen, your life is not insured.
But tie a rope your waist around,
And it will hold you safe and sound."
"I will," said he. "Now for the roof—
All snugly tied, and danger-proof!
Excelsior! Excel—But no!
The rope is not secured below!"
Said Rachel, "Climb, the end to throw
Across the top, and I will go
And tie that end around my waist."
"Well, every woman to her taste;
You always would be tightly laced.
Rachel, when you became my bride,
I thought the knot securely tied;
But lest the bond should break in twain,
I'll have it fastened once again."
Below the arm-pits tied around,
She takes her station on the ground,
While on the roof, beyond the ridge,
He shovels clear the lower edge.
But, sad mischance! the loosened snow
Comes sliding down, to plunge below.
And as he tumbles with the slide,
Up Rachel goes on t'other side.
Just half-way down the Justice hung;
Just half-way up the woman swung.
"Good land o' Goshen!" shouted she;
"Why, do you see it?" answered he.

The couple, dangling in the breeze,
Like turkeys hung outside to freeze,
At their rope's end and wits' end, too,
Shout back and forth what best to do.
Cried Stephen, "Take it coolly, wife;
All have their ups and downs in life."
Quoth Rachel, "What a pity 'tis
To joke at such a thing as this!
A man whose wife is being hung
Should know enough to hold his tongue."
"Now, Rachel, as I look below,
I see a tempting heap of snow.
Suppose, my dear, I take my knife,
And cut the rope to save my life?"
She shouted, "Don't! 'twould be my death—
I see some pointed stones beneath.
A better way would be to call,
With all our might, for Phebe Hall."
"Agreed!" he roared. First he, then she
Gave tongue; "O Phebe! Phebe! *Phe-e-be* Hall!" in tones both fine and coarse.
Enough to make a drover hoarse.

Now Phebe, over at the farm,
Was sitting, sewing, snug and warm;
But hearing, as she thought, her name,
Sprang up, and to the rescue came;
Beheld the scene, and thus she thought:
"If now a kitchen chair were brought,
And I could reach the lady's foot,
I'd draw her downward by the boot,
Then cut the rope, and let him go;
He cannot miss the pile of snow."
He sees her moving toward his wife.
Armed with a chair and carving-knife,
And, ere he is aware, perceives
His head ascending to the eaves;
And, guessing what the two are at,
Screams from beneath the roof, "Stop that!
You make me fall too far, by half!"
But Phebe answers, with a laugh,
"Please tell a body by what right
You've brought your wife to such a plight!"
And then, with well-directed blows,
She cuts the rope and down he goes.
The wife untied, they walk around
When lo! no Stephen can be found.
They call in vain, run to and fro;
They look around, above, below;
No trace or token can they see,
And deeper grows the mystery.
Then Rachel's heart within her sank;
But, glancing at the snowy bank,
She caught a little gleam of hope,—

A gentle movement of the rope.
They scrape away a little snow;
What's this? A hat! Ah! he's below;
Then upward heaves the snowy pile,
And forth he stalks in tragic style,
Unhurt, and with a roguish smile;
And Rachel sees, with glad surprise,
The missing found, the fallen rise.

Rev. Henry Reeves.

Jane Conquest

About the time of Christmas
(Not many months ago),
When the sky was black
With wrath and rack,
And the earth was white with snow,
When loudly rang the tumult
Of winds and waves of strife,
In her home by the sea,
With her babe on her knee,
Sat Harry Conquest's wife.

And he was on the ocean,
Although she knew not where,
For never a lip
Could tell of the ship,
To lighten her heart's despair.
And her babe was fading and dying;
The pulse in the tiny wrist
Was all but still,
And the brow was chill,
And pale as the white sea mist.

Jane Conquest's heart was hopeless;
She could only weep and pray
That the Shepherd mild
Would take her child
Without a pain away.
The night was dark and darker,
And the storm grew stronger still,
And buried in deep
And dreamless sleep
Lay the hamlet under the hill.

The fire was dead on the hearthstone
Within Jane Conquest's room,
And still sat she,
With her babe on her knee,
At prayer amid the gloom.
When, borne above the tempest,
A sound fell on her ear,
Thrilling her through,
For well she knew
'Twas the voice of mortal fear.

And a light leaped in at the lattice,
Sudden and swift and red;
Crimsoning all,
The whited wall,
And the floor, and the roof o'erhead.
For one brief moment, heedless
Of the babe upon her knee,
With the frenzied start
Of a frightened heart,
Upon her feet rose she.

And through the quaint old casement
She looks upon the sea;
Thank God that the sight
She saw that night
So rare a sight should be!
Hemmed in by many a billow
With mad and foaming lip,
A mile from shore,
Or hardly more,
She saw a gallant ship.

And to her horror she beheld it
Aflame from stem to stern;
For there seemed no speck
On all that wreck
Where the fierce fire did not burn;
Till the night was like a sunset,
And the sea like a sea of blood,
And the rocks and shore
Were bathed all o'er
And drenched with the gory flood.

She looked and looked, till the terror
Went creeping through every limb;
And her breath came quick,
And her heart grew sick,
And her sight grew dizzy and dim;

And her lips had lost their utterance,
For she tried but could not speak;
And her feelings found
No channel of sound
In prayer, or sob, or shriek.

Once more that cry of anguish
Thrilled through the tempest's strife,
And it stirred again
In heart and brain
The active thinking life;
And the light of an inspiration
Leaped to her brightened eye,
And on lip and brow
Was written now
A purpose pure and high.

Swiftly she turns, and softly
She crosses the chamber floor,
And faltering not,
In his tiny cot
She laid the babe she bore.
And then with a holy impulse,
She sank to her knees, and made
A lowly prayer,
In the silence there,
And this was the prayer she prayed:

"O Christ, who didst bear the scourging,
And who now dost wear the crown,
I at Thy feet,
O True and Sweet,
Would lay my burden down.
Thou bad'st me love and cherish
The babe Thou gavest me,
And I have kept
Thy word, nor stept
Aside from following Thee.

"And lo! my boy is dying!
And vain is all my care;
And my burden's weight
Is very great,
Yea, greater than I can bear!
O Lord, Thou know'st what peril
Doth threat these poor men's lives,
And I, a woman,
Most weak and human,
Do plead for their waiting wives.

"Thou canst not let them perish;
Up, Lord, in Thy strength, and save
From the scorching breath
Of this terrible death
On this cruel winter wave.
Take Thou my babe and watch it,
No care is like to Thine;
And let Thy power
In this perilous hour
Supply what lack is mine."

And so her prayer she ended,
And rising to her feet,
Gave one long look
At the cradle nook
Where the child's faint pulses beat;
And then with softest footsteps
Retrod the chamber floor,
And noiselessly groped
For the latch, and oped,
And crossed the cottage door.

And through the tempest bravely
Jane Conquest fought her way,
By snowy deep
And slippery steep
To where her duty lay.
And she journeyed onward, breathless,
And weary and sore and faint,
Yet forward pressed
With the strength, and the zest,
And the ardor of a saint.

Solemn, and weird, and lonely
Amid its countless graves,
Stood the old gray church
On its tall rock perch,
Secure from the sea and its waves;
And beneath its sacred shadow
Lay the hamlet safe and still;
For however the sea
And the wind might be,
There was quiet under the hill.

Jane Conquest reached the churchyard,
  And stood by the old church door,
    But the oak was tough
    And had bolts enough,
  And her strength was frail and poor;
So she crept through a narrow window,
  And climbed the belfry stair,
    And grasped the rope,
    Sole cord of hope,
  For the mariners in despair.

And the wild wind helped her bravely,
  And she wrought with an earnest will,
    And the clamorous bell
    Spoke out right well
  To the hamlet under the hill.
And it roused the slumbering fishers,
  Nor its warning task gave o'er
    Till a hundred fleet
    And eager feet
  Were hurrying to the shore.

And then it ceased its ringing,
  For the woman's work was done,
    And many a boat
    That was now afloat
  Showed man's work had begun.
But the ringer in the belfry
  Lay motionless and cold,
    With the cord of hope,
    The church-bell rope,
  Still in her frozen hold.

How long she lay it boots not,
  But she woke from her swoon at last
    In her own bright room,
    To find the gloom,
  And the grief, and the peril past,
With the sense of joy within her,
  And the Christ's sweet presence near;
    And friends around,
    And the cooing sound
  Of her babe's voice in her ear.

And they told her all the story,
  How a brave and gallant few
    O'ercame each check,
    And reached the wreck,
  And saved the hopeless crew.
And how the curious sexton
  Had climbed the belfry stair,
    And of his fright
    When, cold and white,
  He found her lying there;

And how, when they had borne her
  Back to her home again,
    The child she left
    With a heart bereft
  Of hope, and weary with pain,
Was found within his cradle
  In a quiet slumber laid;
    With a peaceful smile
    On his lips the while,
  And the wasting sickness stayed.

And she said "'Twas the Christ who watched it,
  And brought it safely through";
    And she praised His truth
    And His tender ruth
  Who had saved her darling too.

Nathan Hale

To drum beat and heart beat,
  A soldier marches by,
There is color in his cheek,
  There is courage in his eye;
Yet to drum beat and heart beat,
  In a moment he must die.

By starlight and moonlight,
  He seeks the Britons' camp;
He hears the rustling flag,
  And the armed sentry's tramp;
And the starlight and moonlight
  His silent wanderings lamp.

With a slow tread and still tread,
  He scans the tented line,

And he counts the battery guns
  By the gaunt and shadowy pine,
And his slow tread and still tread
  Gives no warning sign.

The dark wave, the plumed wave,
  It meets his eager glance;
And it sparkles 'neath the stars,
  Like the glimmer of a lance—
A dark wave, a plumed wave,
  On an emerald expanse.

A sharp clang, a steel clang,
  And terror in the sound!
For the sentry, falcon-eyed,
  In the camp a spy has found;
With a sharp clang, a steel clang,
  The patriot is bound.

With calm brow, steady brow,
  He listens to his doom.
In his look there is no fear,
  Nor a shadow trace of gloom,
But with calm brow, steady brow,
  He robes him for the tomb.

In the long night, the still night,
  He kneels upon the sod;
And the brutal guards withhold
  E'en the solemn word of God!
In the long night, the still night,
  He walks where Christ hath trod.

'Neath the blue morn, the sunny morn,
  He dies upon the tree;
And he mourns that he can give
  But one life for liberty;
And in the blue morn, the sunny morn
  His spent wings are free.

But his last words, his message words,
  They burn, lest friendly eye
Should read how proud and calm
  A patriot could die.
With his last words, his dying words,
  A soldier's battle cry.

From Fame-leaf and Angel-leaf,
  From monument and urn,
The sad of earth, the glad of Heaven,
  His tragic fate shall learn;
And on Fame-leaf and Angel-leaf,
  The name of Hale shall burn.

Francis M. Finch.

The Lips That Touch Liquor Must Never Touch Mine

You are coming to woo me, but not as of yore,
When I hastened to welcome your ring at the door;
For I trusted that he who stood waiting me then,
Was the brightest, the truest, the noblest of men.
Your lips on my own when they printed "Farewell,"
Had never been soiled by "the beverage of hell";
But they come to me now with the bacchanal sign,
And the lips that touch liquor must never touch mine.

I think of that night in the garden alone,
When in whispers you told me your heart was my own,
That your love in the future should faithfully be
Unshared by another, kept only for me.
Oh, sweet to my soul is the memory still
Of the lips which met mine, when they murmured "I will";
But now to their pressure no more they incline,
For the lips that touch liquor must never touch mine!

O John! how it crushed me, when first in your face

The pen of the "Rum Fiend" had written "disgrace";
And turned me in silence and tears from that breath
All poisoned and foul from the chalice of death.
It scattered the hopes I had treasured to last;
It darkened the future and clouded the past;
It shattered my idol, and ruined the shrine,
For the lips that touch liquor must never touch mine.

I loved you—Oh, dearer than language can tell,
And you saw it, you proved it, you knew it too well!
But the man of my love was far other than he
Who now from the "Tap-room" comes reeling to me;
In manhood and honor so noble and right—
His heart was so true, and his genius so bright—
And his soul was unstained, unpolluted by wine;
But the lips that touch liquor must never touch mine.

You promised reform, but I trusted in vain;
Your pledge was but made to be broken again:
And the lover so false to his promises now,
Will not, as a husband, be true to his vow.
The word must be spoken that bids you depart—
Though the effort to speak it should shatter my heart—
Though in silence, with blighted affection, I pine,
Yet the lips that touch liquor must never touch mine!

If one spark in your bosom of virtue remain,
Go fan it with prayer till it kindle again;
Resolved, with "God helping," in future to be
From wine and its follies unshackled and free!
And when you have conquered this foe of your soul,—
In manhood and honor beyond his control—
This heart will again beat responsive to thine,
And the lips free from liquor be welcome to mine.

George W. Young.

A Perfect Day

When you come to the end of a perfect day
And you sit alone with your thought
While the chimes ring out with a carol gay
For the joy that the day has brought,
Do you think what the end of a perfect day
Can mean to a tired heart?
When the sun goes down with a flaming ray
And the dear friends have to part?

Well, this is the end of a perfect day,
Near the end of a journey, too;
But it leaves a thought that is big and strong,
With a wish that is kind and true;
For mem'ry has painted this perfect day
With colors that never fade,
And we find, at the end of a perfect day,
The soul of a friend we've made.

Carrie Jacobs Bond.

Kate Ketchem

Kate Ketchem on a winter's night
Went to a party dressed in white.
Her chignon in a net of gold,
Was about as large as they ever sold.
Gayly she went, because her "pap"
Was supposed to be a rich old chap.

But when by chance her glances fell
On a friend who had lately married well,
Her spirits sunk, and a vague unrest
And a nameless longing filled her breast——
A wish she wouldn't have had made known,
To have an establishment of her own.

Tom Fudge came slowly through the throng,
With chestnut hair, worn pretty long
He saw Kate Ketchem in the crowd,
And knowing her slightly, stopped and bowed;
Then asked her to give him a single flower,
Saying he'd think it a priceless dower.

Out from those with which she was decked,
She took the poorest she could select.
And blushed as she gave it, looking down
To call attention to her gown.
"Thanks," said Fudge, and he thought how dear
Flowers must be at that time of year.

Then several charming remarks he made,
Asked if she sang, or danced, or played;
And being exhausted, inquired whether
She thought it was going to be pleasant weather.
And Kate displayed her "jewelry,"
And dropped her lashes becomingly;
And listened, with no attempt to disguise
The admiration in her eyes.
At last, like one who has nothing to say,
He turned around and walked away.

Kate Ketchem smiled, and said, "You bet
I'll catch that Fudge and his money yet.
He's rich enough to keep me in clothes,
And I think I could manage him as I chose.
He could aid my father as well as not,
And buy my brother a splendid yacht.
My mother for money should never fret,
And all it cried for the baby should get;
And after that, with what he could spare,
I'd make a show at a charity fair."

Tom Fudge looked back as he crossed the sill,
And saw Kate Ketchem standing still.
"A girl more suited to my mind
It isn't an easy thing to find;
And every thing that she has to wear
Proves her as rich as she is fair.
Would she were mine, and I to-day
Had the old man's cash my debts to pay!
No creditors with a long account,
No tradesmen wanting 'that little amount';
But all my scores paid up when due
By a father-in-law as rich as a Jew!"

But he thought of her brother, not worth a straw,
And her mother, that would be his, in law;
So, undecided, he walked along,
And Kate was left alone in the throng.

But a lawyer smiled, whom he sought by stealth,
To ascertain old Ketchem's wealth;
And as for Kate, she schemed and planned
Till one of the dancers claimed her hand.

He married her for her father's cash;
She married him to cut a dash.
But as to paying his debts, do you know,
The father couldn't see it so;
And at hints for help, Kate's hazel eyes
Looked out in their innocent surprise.
And when Tom thought of the way he had wed
He longed for a single life instead,
And closed his eyes in a sulky mood,
Regretting the days of his bachelorhood;
And said, in a sort of reckless vein,
"I'd like to see her catch me again,
If I were free, as on that night
When I saw Kate Ketchem dressed in white!"

She wedded him to be rich and gay;
But husband and children didn't pay.
He wasn't the prize she hoped to draw,
And wouldn't live with his mother-in-law.
And oft when she had to coax and pout
In order to get him to take her out,
She thought how very attentive and bright
He seemed at the party that winter's night;
Of his laugh, as soft as a breeze of the south,
('Twas now on the other side of his mouth);
How he praised her dress and gems in his talk,
As he took a careful account of stock.

Sometimes she hated the very walls—
Hated her friends, her dinners, and calls;
Till her weak affection, to hatred turned,
Like a dying tallow-candle burned.
And for him who sat there, her peace to mar,
Smoking his everlasting cigar—
He wasn't the man she thought she saw,
And grief was duty, and hate was law.
So she took up her burden with a groan,
Saying only, "I might have known!"

Alas for Kate! and alas for Fudge!
Though I do not owe them any grudge;
And alas for any who find to their shame
That two can play at their little game!
For of all hard things to bear and grin,
The hardest is knowing you're taken in.
Ah, well! as a general thing, we fret
About the one we didn't get;
But I think we needn't make a fuss,
If the one we don't want didn't get us.

Phoebe Cary.

Mandalay

By the old Moulmein Pagoda, lookin' eastward to the sea,
There's a Burma girl a-settin', an' I know she thinks o' me;
For the wind is in the palm-trees, an' the temple-bells they say:
"Come you back, you British soldier: come you back to Mandalay!"
Come you back to Mandalay,
Where the old flotilla lay:
Can't you 'ear their paddles chunkin' from Rangoon to Mandalay?
On the road to Mandalay,
Where the flyin'-fishes play,
An' the dawn comes up like

thunder outer China 'crost the Bay!

'Er petticut was yaller an' 'er little cap was green,
An' 'er name was Supi-yaw-lat—jes' the same as Theebaw's Queen,
An' I seed her fust a-smokin' of a whackin' white cheroot,
An' a-wastin' Christian kisses on an 'eathen idol's foot;
Bloomin' idol made o' mud—
Wot they called the Great Gawd Budd—
Plucky lot she cared for idols when I kissed 'er where she stud!
On the road to Mandalay—

When the mist was on the rice-fields an' the sun was droppin' low,
She'd git 'er little banjo an' she'd sing *"Kul-la-lo-lo!"*
With 'er arm upon my shoulder an' her cheek agin my cheek
We useter watch the steamers and the *hathis* pilin' teak.
Elephints a-pilin' teak
In the sludgy, squdgy creek,
Where the silence 'ung that 'eavy you was arf afraid to speak!
On the road to Mandalay—

But that's all shove be'ind me—long ago an' fur away,
An' there ain't no 'buses runnin' from the Benk to Mandalay;
An' I'm learnin' 'ere in London what the ten-year sodger tells:
"If you've 'eard the East a-callin', why, you won't 'eed nothin' else."
No! you won't 'eed nothin' else
But them spicy garlic smells
An' the sunshine an' the palm-trees an' the tinkly temple-bells!
On the road to Mandalay—

I am sick o' wastin' leather on these gutty pavin'-stones,
An' the blasted Henglish drizzle wakes the fever in my bones;
Tho' I walks with fifty 'ousemaids outer Chelsea to the Strand,
An' they talk a lot o' lovin', but wot do they understand?
Beefy face an' grubby 'and—
Law! wot *do* they understand?
I've a neater, sweeter maiden in a cleaner, greener land!
On the road to Mandalay—

Ship me somewheres east of Suez where the best is like the worst,
Where there aren't no Ten Commandments, an' a man can raise a thirst;
For the temple-bells are callin', an' it's there that I would be—
By the old Moulmein Pagoda, lookin' lazy at the sea—
On the road to Mandalay,
Where the old Flotilla lay,
With our sick beneath the awnings when we went to Mandalay!
On the road to Mandalay!
Where the flyin'- fishes play,
An' the dawn comes up like thunder outer China 'crost the Bay!

Rudyard Kipling.

Columbus

Behind him lay the gray Azores,
Behind the Gates of Hercules;
Before him not the ghost of shores,
Before him only shoreless seas.
The good mate said: "Now must we pray,
For lo! the very stars are gone.
Brave Adm'r'l, speak; what shall I say?"
"Why, say: 'Sail on! sail on! and on!' "

"My men grow mutinous day by day;
My men grow ghastly wan and weak."
The stout mate thought of home; a spray
Of salt wave washed his swarthy cheek.
"What shall I say, brave Adm'r'l, say,
If we sight naught but seas at dawn?"
"Why, you shall say at break of day:
'Sail on! sail on! sail on! and on!' "

They sailed and sailed, as winds might blow,
Until at last the blanched mate said:
"Why, now not even God would know
Should I and all my men fall dead.
These very winds forget their way,
For God from these dread seas is gone.
Now speak, brave Adm'r'l, speak and say—"
He said: "Sail on! Sail on! and on!"

They sailed. They sailed. Then spake the mate:
"This mad sea shows his teeth to-night.
He curls his lips, he lies in wait
With lifted teeth, as if to bite!
Brave Adm'r'l, say but one good word:
What shall we do when hope is gone?
The words leapt like a leaping sword;
"Sail on! sail on! sail on! and on!"

Then, pale and worn, he kept his deck,
And peered through darkness. Ah, that night
Of all dark nights! And then a speck—
A light! a light! a light! a light!
It grew, a starlit flag unfurled!
It grew to be Time's burst of dawn.
He gained a world; he gave that world
Its grandest lesson: "On! sail on!"

Joaquin Miller.

"Sister's Best Feller"

My sister's best feller is 'most six-foot-three,
And handsome and strong as a feller can be;
And Sis, she's so little, and slender, and small,
You never would think she could boss him at all;
But, my jing!
She don't do a thing
But make him jump 'round, like he worked with a string!
It jest made me 'shamed of him sometimes, you know,
To think that he'll let a girl bully him so.

He goes to walk with her and carries her muff
And coat and umbrella, and that kind of stuff;
She loads him with things that must weigh 'most a ton;
And, honest, he *likes* it,—as if it was fun!
And, oh, say!
When they go to a play,
He'll sit in the parlor and fidget away,
And she won't come down till it's quarter past eight,
And then she'll scold *him* 'cause they get there so late.

He spends heaps of money a-buyin' her things,
Like candy, and flowers, and presents, and rings;
And all he's got for 'em's a handkerchief case—
A fussed-up concern, made of ribbons and lace;
But, my land! He thinks it's just grand,
" 'Cause she made it," he says, "with her own little hand";

He calls her "an angel"—I heard him
—and "saint,"
And "beautif'lest bein' on earth"—but
she ain't.

'Fore I go on an errand for her any
time,
I just make her coax me, and give me
a dime;
But that great big silly—why, honest
and true—
He'd run forty miles if she wanted him
to.
Oh, gee whiz!
I tell you what 'tis!
I jest think it's *awful*—those actions of
his.
I won't fall in love, when I'm grown—
no sir-ee!
My sister's best feller's a warnin' to
me! *Joseph C. Lincoln.*

Where the West Begins

Out where the handclasp's a little
stronger,
Out where a smile dwells a little longer,
That's where the West begins.
Out where the sun's a little brighter,
Where the snow that falls is a trifle
whiter,
Where the bonds of home are a wee bit
tighter,
That's where the West begins.

Out where the skies are a trifle bluer,
Out where friendship's a little truer,
That's where the West begins.
Out where a fresher breeze is blowing,
Where there is laughter in every
streamlet flowing,
Where there's more of reaping and less
of sowing,
That's where the West begins.

Out where the world is in the making,
Where fewer hearts with despair are
aching;
That's where the West begins.
Where there is more of singing and less
of sighing,
Where there is more of giving and less
of buying,
And a man makes friends without half
trying—
That's where the West begins.
Arthur Chapman.

The Tapestry Weavers

Let us take to our hearts a lesson—no
lesson can braver be—
From the ways of the tapestry weav-
ers on the other side of the sea.
Above their heads the pattern hangs,
they study it with care,
The while their fingers deftly move,
their eyes are fastened there.

They tell this curious thing, besides, of
the patient, plodding weaver:
He works on the wrong side evermore,
but works for the right side ever.
It is only when the weaving stops, and
the web is loosed and turned,
That he sees his real handiwork—that
his marvelous skill is learned.

Ah, the sight of its delicate beauty,
how it pays him for all his cost!
No rarer, daintier work than his was
ever done by the frost.
Then the master bringeth him golden
hire, and giveth him praise as well,
And how happy the heart of the weav-
er is, no tongue but his can tell.

The years of man are the looms of God,
let down from the place of the sun,
Wherein we are weaving ever, till the
mystic web is done.
Weaving blindly but weaving surely
each for himself his fate—
We may not see how the right side
looks, we can only weave and wait.

But, looking above for the pattern, no weaver hath to fear;
Only let him look clear into heaven, the Perfect Pattern is there.
If he keeps the face of the Savior forever and always in sight
His toil shall be sweeter than honey, his weaving sure to be right.

And when the work is ended, and the web is turned and shown,
He shall hear the voice of the Master, it shall say unto him, "Well done!"
And the white-winged Angels of Heaven, to bear him shall come down;
And God shall give him gold for his hire—not coin—but a glowing crown.

When the Teacher Gets Cross

When the teacher gets cross, and her blue eyes gets black,
And the pencil comes down on the desk with a whack,
We chillen all sit up straight in a line,
As if we had rulers instead of a spine,
And it's scary to cough, and it a'n't safe to grin,
When the teacher gets cross, and the dimples goes in.

When the teacher gets cross, the tables get mixed,
The ones and the twos begins to play tricks,
The pluses and minuses is just little smears,
When the cry babies cry their slates full of tears,
And the figgers won't add, but just act up like sin,
When the teacher gets cross, and the dimples goes in.

When the teacher gets cross, the reading gets bad,
The lines jingle round till the chillen is sad.
And Billy boy puffs and gets red in the face,
As if he and the lesson were running a race,
Until she hollers out, "Next!" as sharp as a pin,
When the teacher gets cross, and the dimples goes in.

When the teacher gets good, her smile is so bright,
That the tables gets straight, and the reading gets right.
The pluses and minuses comes trooping along,
And the figgers add up and stop being wrong,
And we chillen would like, but we dassent, to shout,
When the teacher gets good, and the dimples comes out.

Recessional

God of our fathers, known of old,
Lord of our far-flung battle line,
Beneath whose awful Hand we hold
Dominion over palm and pine—
Lord God of Hosts, be with us yet,
Lest we forget—lest we forget!

The tumult and the shouting dies;
The captains and the kings depart:
Still stands Thine ancient sacrifice,
An humble and a contrite heart.
Lord God of Hosts, be with us yet,
Lest we forget—lest we forget!

Far-called, our navies melt away;
On dune and headland sinks the fire:
Lo, all our pomp of yesterday
Is one with Nineveh and Tyre!
Judge of the Nations, spare us yet,
Lest we forget—lest we forget!

If, drunk with sight of power, we loose
Wild tongues that have not Thee in awe—
Such boasting as the Gentiles use,
Or lesser breeds without the Law—
Lord God of Hosts, be with us yet,
Lest we forget—lest we forget!

For heathen heart that puts her trust
In reeking tube and iron shard,
All valiant dust that builds on dust,
And guarding, calls not Thee to guard,
For frantic boast and foolish word,
Thy Mercy on Thy People, Lord!
Amen.

Rudyard Kipling.

The Eternal Goodness

O Friends! with whom my feet have trod
The quiet aisles of prayer,
Glad witness to your zeal for God
And love of man I bear.

I trace your lines of argument;
Your logic linked and strong
I weigh as one who dreads dissent,
And fears a doubt as wrong.

But still my human hands are weak
To hold your iron creeds:
Against the words ye bid me speak
My heart within me pleads.

Who fathoms the Eternal Thought?
Who talks of scheme and plan?
The Lord is God! He needeth not
The poor device of man.

I walk with bare, hushed feet the ground
Ye tread with boldness shod;
I dare not fix with mete and bound
The love and power of God.

Ye praise His justice; even such
His pitying love I deem;
Ye seek a king; I fain would touch
The robe that hath no seam.

Ye see the curse which overbroods
A world of pain and loss;
I hear our Lord's beatitudes
And prayer upon the cross.

More than your schoolmen teach, within
Myself, alas! I know;
Too dark ye cannot paint the sin,
Too small the merit show.

I bow my forehead to the dust,
I veil mine eyes for shame,
And urge, in trembling self-distrust,
A prayer without a claim.

I see the wrong that round me lies,
I feel the guilt within;
I hear, with groan and travail-cries,
The world confess its sin.

Yet, in the maddening maze of things,
And tossed by storm and flood,
To one fixed stake my spirit clings;
I know that God is good!

Not mine to look where cherubim
And seraphs may not see,
But nothing can be good in Him
Which evil is in me.

The wrong that pains my soul below
I dare not throne above;
I know not of His hate,—I know
His goodness and His love.

I dimly guess from blessings known
Of greater out of sight,
And, with the chastened Psalmist, own
His judgments too are right.

I long for household voices gone,
For vanished smiles I long,
But God hath led my dear ones on,
And he can do no wrong.

I know not what the future hath
Of marvel or surprise,
Assured alone that life and death
His mercy underlies.

And if my heart and flesh are weak
To bear an untried pain,
The bruised reed He will not break,
But strengthen and sustain.

No offering of my own I have,
Nor works my faith to prove;
I can but give the gifts He gave,
And plead His love for love.

And so beside the Silent Sea,
I wait the muffled oar;
No harm from Him can come to me
On ocean or on shore.

I know not where His islands lift
Their fronded palms in air;
I only know I cannot drift
Beyond His love and care.

O brothers! if my faith is vain,
If hopes like these betray,
Pray for me that my feet may gain
The sure and safer way.

And Thou, O Lord! by whom are seen
Thy creatures as they be,
Forgive me if too close I lean
My human heart on Thee!

John G. Whittier.

Driving Home the Cows

Out of the clover and blue-eyed grass
He turned them into the river-lane;
One after another he let them pass,
Then fastened the meadow-bars again.

Under the willows and over the hill,
He patiently followed their sober pace;
The merry whistle for once was still,
And something shadowed the sunny face.

Only a boy! and his father had said
He never could let his youngest go;
Two already were lying dead
Under the feet of the trampling foe.

But after the evening work was done,
And the frogs were loud in the meadow swamp,
Over his shoulder he slung his gun,
And stealthily followed the foot-path damp,—

Across the clover and through the wheat,
With resolute heart and purpose grim,
Though cold was the dew on his hurrying feet,
And the blind bat's flitting startled him.

Thrice since then had the lanes been white,
And the orchards sweet with apple bloom;
And now, when the cows came back at night,
The feeble father drove them home.

For news had come to the lonely farm
That three were lying where two had lain;
And the old man's tremulous, palsied arm
Could never lean on a son's again.

The summer day grew cool and late;
He went for the cows when the work was done;
But down the lane, as he opened the gate,
He saw them coming, one by one,—

Brindle, Ebony, Speckle, and Bess,
Shaking their horns in the evening wind,
Cropping the buttercups out of the grass—
But who was it following close behind?

Loosely swung in the idle air
The empty sleeve of army blue;
And worn and pale, from the crisping hair,
Looked out a face that the father knew.

For southern prisons will sometimes yawn,
And yield their dead unto life again;
And the day that comes with a cloudy dawn
In golden glory at last may wane.

The great tears sprang to their meeting eyes;
For the heart must speak when the lips are dumb,
And under the silent evening skies
Together they followed the cattle home.
Kate P. Osgood.

A Song of Our Flag

Your Flag and my Flag!
And, oh, how much it holds—
Your land and my land—
Secure within its folds!
Your heart and my heart
Beat quicker at the sight;
Sun-kissed and wind-tossed,
Red and blue and white.
The one Flag—the great Flag—the Flag for me and you—
Glorified all else beside—the red and white and blue!

Your Flag and my Flag!
To every star and stripe
The drums beat as hearts beat
And fifers shrilly pipe!
Your Flag and my Flag—
A blessing in the sky;
Your hope and my hope—
It never hid a lie!
Home land and far land and half the world around,
Old Glory hears our glad salute and ripples to the sound!
Wilbur D. Nesbit.

When the Minister Comes to Tea

Oh! they've swept the parlor carpet, and they've dusted every chair,
And they've got the tidies hangin' jest exactly on the square;
And the what-not's fixed up lovely, and the mats have all been beat,
And the pantry's brimmin' over with the bully things ter eat;
Sis has got her Sunday dress on, and she's frizzin' up her bangs;
Ma's got on her best alpacky, and she's askin' how it hangs;
Pa has shaved as slick as can be, and I'm rigged way up in G,—
And it's all because we're goin' ter have the minister ter tea.
Oh! the table's fixed up gaudy, with the gilt-edged chiny set,
And we'll use the silver tea-pot and the comp'ny spoons, you bet;
And we're goin' ter have some fruit-cake and some thimbleberry jam,
And "riz biscuits," and some doughnuts, and some chicken, and some ham.
Ma, she'll 'polergize like fury and say everything is bad,
And "Sich awful luck with cookin'," she is sure she never had;
But, er course, she's only bluffin,' for it's as prime as it can be,
And she's only talkin' that way 'cause the minister's ter tea.

Everybody'll be a-smilin' and as good as ever was,
Pa won't growl about the vittles, like he generally does,
And he'll ask me would I like another piece er pie; but, sho!
That, er course, is only manners, and I'm s'posed ter answer "No."
Sis'll talk about the church-work and about the Sunday-school,
Ma'll tell how she liked that sermon that was on the Golden Rule,
And if I upset my tumbler they won't say a word ter me:—
Yes, a boy can eat in comfort with the minister ter tea!
Say! a minister, you'd reckon, never'd say what wasn't true;
But that isn't so with ours, and I jest can prove it, too;
'Cause when Sis plays on the organ so it makes yer want ter die,
Why, he sets and says it's lovely; and that, seems ter me, 's a lie:
But I like him all the samey, and I only wish he'd stay
At our house fer good and always, and eat with us every day;
Only think of havin' goodies *every* evenin'! Jimmin*ee!*
And I'd *never* git a scoldin' with the minister ter tea!

Joseph C. Lincoln.

When the Cows Come Home

When klingle, klangle, klingle,
Far down the dusty dingle,
The cows are coming home;

Now sweet and clear, now faint and low,
The airy tinklings come and go,
Like chimings from the far-off tower,
Or patterings of an April shower
That makes the daisies grow;
Ko-ling, Ko-lang, kolinglelingle
Far down the darkening dingle,
The cows come slowly home.

And old-time friends, and twilight plays,
And starry nights and sunny days,
Come trooping up the misty ways
When the cows come home.
With jingle, jangle, jingle,
Soft tones that sweetly mingle—
The cows are coming home;

Malvine, and Pearl, and Florimel,
DeKamp, Red Rose, and Gretchen Schell.
Queen Bess and Sylph, and Spangled Sue,
Across the fields I hear her "loo-oo"
And clang her silver bell;
Go-ling, go-lang, golingledingle,
With faint, far sounds that mingle,
The cows come slowly home.

And mother-songs of long-gone years,
And baby-joys and childish fears,
And youthful hopes and youthful tears,
When the cows come home.
With ringle, rangle, ringle,
By twos and threes and single,
The cows are coming home.

Through violet air we see the town,
And the summer sun a-sliding down,
And the maple in the hazel glade
Throws down the path a longer shade,
And the hills are growing brown;
To-ring, to-rang, toringleringle,
By threes and fours and single,
The cows come slowly home.

The same sweet sound of wordless psalm,

The same sweet June-day rest and calm,
The same sweet smell of buds and balm,
When the cows come home.
With tinkle, tankle, tinkle,
Through fern and periwinkle,
The cows are coming home.

A-loitering in the checkered stream,
Where the sun-rays glance and gleam,
Clarine, Peach-bloom and Phebe Phillis
Stand knee-deep in the creamy lilies,
In a drowsy dream;
To-link, to-lank, tolinklelinkle,
O'er banks with buttercups a-twinkle,
The cows come slowly home.

And up through memory's deep ravine
Come the brook's old song and its old-time sheen,
And the crescent of the silver queen,
When the cows come home.
With klingle, klangle, klingle,
With loo-oo, and moo-oo and jingle,
The cows are coming home.

And over there on Merlin Hill
Sounds the plaintive cry of the whip-poor-will,
And the dew-drops lie on the tangled vines,
And over the poplars Venus shines,
And over the silent mill.
Ko-ling, ko-lang, kolinglelin-gle,
With ting-a-ling and jingle,
The cows come slowly home.

Let down the bars; let in the train
Of long-gone songs, and flowers, and rain;
For dear old times come back again,
When the cows come home.

Agnes E. Mitchell.

Custer's Last Charge

Dead! Is it possible? He, the bold rider,
Custer, our hero, the first in the fight,
Charming the bullets of yore to fly wider,
Shunning our battle-king's ringlets of light!
Dead! our young chieftain, and dead all forsaken!
No one to tell us the way of his fall!
Slain in the desert, and never to waken,
Never, not even to victory's call!

Comrades, he's gone! but ye need not be grieving;
No, may my death be like his when I die!
No regrets wasted on words I am leaving,
Falling with brave men, and face to the sky.
Death's but a journey, the greatest must take it:
Fame is eternal, and better than all;
Gold though the bowl be, 'tis fate that must break it,
Glory can hallow the fragments that fall.

Proud for his fame that last day that he met them!
All the night long he had been on their track,
Scorning their traps and the men that had set them,
Wild for a charge that should never give back.
There, on the hilltop he halted and saw them—
Lodges all loosened and ready to fly;
Hurrying scouts with the tidings to awe them,
Told of his coming before he was nigh.

All the wide valley was full of their forces,
  Gathered to cover the lodges' retreat,—
Warriors running in haste to their horses,
  Thousands of enemies close to his feet!
Down in the valleys the ages had hollowed,
  There lay the Sitting Bull's camp for a prey!
Numbers! What recked he? What recked those who followed?
  Men who had fought ten to one ere that day?

Out swept the squadrons, the fated three hundred,
  Into the battle-line steady and full;
Then down the hillside exultingly thundered
  Into the hordes of the Old Sitting Bull!
Wild Ogalallah, Arapahoe, Cheyenne,
  Wild Horse's braves, and the rest of their crew,
Shrank from that charge like a herd from a lion,
  Then closed around the great hell of wild Sioux.

Right to their center he charged, and then, facing—
  Hark to those yells and around them, Oh, see!
Over the hilltops the devils come racing,
  Coming as fast as the waves of the sea!
Red was the circle of fire about them,
  No hope of victory, no ray of light,
Shot through that terrible black cloud about them,
  Brooding in death over Custer's last fight.

THEN DID HE BLENCH? Did he die like a craven,
  Begging those torturing fiends for his life?
Was there a soldier who carried the Seven
  Flinched like a coward or fled from the strife?
No, by the blood of our Custer, no quailing!
  There in the midst of the devils they close,
Hemmed in by thousands, but ever assailing,
  Fighting like tigers, all bayed amid foes!

Thicker and thicker the bullets came singing;
  Down go the horses and riders and all;
Swiftly the warriors round them were ringing,
  Circling like buzzards awaiting their fall.
See the wild steeds of the mountain and prairie,
  Savage eyes gleaming from forests of mane;
Quivering lances with pennons so airy;
  War-painted warriors charging amain.

Backward again and again they were driven,
  Shrinking to close with the lost little band;
Never a cap that had worn the bright Seven
  Bowed till its wearer was dead on the strand.
Closer and closer the death-circle growing,
  Even the leader's voice, clarion clear,
Rang out his words of encouragement glowing,

"We can but die once, boys. but SELL YOUR LIVES DEAR!"

Dearly they sold them, like Berserkers raging,
Facing the death that encircled them round;
Death's bitter pangs by their vengeance assuaging,
Marking their tracks by their dead on the ground.
Comrades, our children shall yet tell their story,—
Custer's last charge on the Old Sitting Bull;
And ages shall swear that the cup of his glory
Needed but that death to render it full.
Frederick Whittaker.

A Boy and His Stomach

What's the matter, stummick? Ain't I always been your friend?
Ain't I always been a pardner to you? All my pennies don't I spend
In getting nice things for you? Don't I give you lots of cake?
Say, stummick, what's the matter,
You had to go an' ache?

Why, I loaded you with good things yesterday;
I gave you more corn an' chicken than you'd ever had before;
I gave you fruit an' candy, apple pie an' chocolate cake,
An' last night when I got to bed you had to go an' ache.

Say, what's the matter with you? Ain't you satisfied at all?
I gave you all you wanted; you was hard jes' like a ball,
An' you couldn't hold another bit of puddin'; yet last night
You ached most awful, stummick!
That ain't treatin' me jest right.

I've been a friend to you, I have!
Why ain't you a friend o' mine?
They gave me castor oil becoz you made me whine.
I'm feelin' fine this mornin'; yes it's true;
But I tell you, stummick, you better appreciate things I do for you.

On the Shores of Tennessee

"'Move my arm-chair, faithful Pompey,
In the sunshine bright and strong,
For this world is fading, Pompey—
Massa won't be with you long;
And I fain would hear the south wind
Bring once more the sound to me,
Of the wavelets softly breaking
On the shores of Tennessee.

"Mournful though the ripples murmur
As they still the story tell,
How no vessels float the banner
That I've loved so long and well,
I shall listen to their music,
Dreaming that again I see
Stars and Stripes on sloop and shallop
Sailing up the Tennessee;

"And Pompey, while old Massa's waiting
For Death's last dispatch to come,
If that exiled starry banner
Should come proudly sailing home,
You shall greet it, slave no longer—
Voice and hand shall both be free
That shout and point to Union colors
On the waves of Tennessee."

"Massa's berry kind to Pompey;
But old darkey's happy here,
Where he's tended corn and cotton
For dese many a long-gone year.
Ober yonder, Missis' sleeping—
No one tends her grave like me;
Mebbe she would miss the flowers
She used to love in Tennessee.

"'Pears like, she was watching Massa—
If Pompey should beside him stay,
Mebbe she'd remember better
How for him she used to pray;
Telling him that way up yonder
White as snow his soul would be,
If he served the Lord of Heaven
While he lived in Tennessee."

Silently the tears were rolling
Down the poor old dusky face,
As he stepped behind his master,
In his long-accustomed place.
Then a silence fell around them,
As they gazed on rock and tree
Pictured in the placid waters
Of the rolling Tennessee;—

Master, dreaming of the battle
Where he fought by Marion's side,
Where he bid the haughty Tarleton
Stoop his lordly crest of pride:—
Man, remembering how yon sleeper
Once he held upon his knee,
Ere she loved the gallant soldier,
Ralph Vervair of Tennessee.

Still the south wind fondly lingers
'Mid the veteran's silver hair;
Still the bondman, close beside him
Stands behind the old arm-chair,
With his dark-hued hand uplifted,
Shading eyes, he bends to see
Where the woodland, boldly jutting,
Turns aside the Tennessee.

Thus he watches cloud-born shadows
Glide from tree to mountain-crest,
Softly creeping, aye and ever
To the river's yielding breast.
Ha! above the foliage yonder
Something flutters wild and free!
"Massa! Massa! Hallelujah!
The flag's come back to Tennessee!"

"Pompey, hold me on your shoulder,
Help me stand on foot once more,
That I may salute the colors
As they pass my cabin door.
Here's the paper signed that frees you,
Give a freeman's shout with me—
'God and Union!' be our watchword
Evermore in Tennessee!"

Then the trembling voice grew fainter,
And the limbs refused to stand;
One prayer to Jesus—and the soldier
Glided to the better land.
When the flag went down the river
Man and master both were free;
While the ring-dove's note was mingled
With the rippling Tennessee.

Ethel Lynn Beers.

The White-Footed Deer

It was a hundred years ago,
When, by the woodland ways,
The traveler saw the wild deer drink,
Or crop the birchen sprays.

Beneath a hill, whose rocky side
O'er-browed a grassy mead,
And fenced a cotttage from the wind,
A deer was wont to feed.

She only came when on the cliffs
The evening moonlight lay,
And no man knew the secret haunts
In which she walked by day.

White were her feet, her forehead showed
A spot of silvery white,
That seemed to glimmer like a star
In autumn's hazy night.

And here, when sang the whippoorwill,
She cropped the sprouting leaves,
And here her rustling steps were heard
On still October eves.

But when the broad midsummer moon
Rose o'er the grassy lawn,

Beside the silver-footed deer
  There grazed a spotted fawn.

The cottage dame forbade her son
  To aim the rifle here;
"It were a sin," she said, "to harm
  Or fright that friendly deer.

"This spot has been my pleasant home
  Ten peaceful years and more;
And ever, when the moonlight shines,
  She feeds before our door.

"The red men say that here she walked
  A thousand moons ago;
They never raise the war-whoop here,
  And never twang the bow.

"I love to watch her as she feeds,
  And think that all is well
While such a gentle creature haunts
  The place in which we dwell."

The youth obeyed, and sought for game
  In forests far away,
Where, deep in silence and in moss,
  The ancient woodland lay.

But once, in autumn's golden time,
  He ranged the wild in vain,
Nor roused the pheasant nor the deer,
  And wandered home again.

The crescent moon and crimson eve
  Shone with a mingling light;
The deer, upon the grassy mead,
  Was feeding full in sight.

He raised the rifle to his eye,
  And from the cliffs around
A sudden echo, shrill and sharp,
  Gave back its deadly sound.

Away, into the neighboring wood,
  The startled creature flew,
And crimson drops at morning lay
  Amid the glimmering dew.

Next evening shone the waxing moon
  As sweetly as before;
The deer upon the grassy mead
  Was seen again no more.

But ere that crescent moon was old,
  By night the red men came,
And burnt the cottage to the ground,
  And slew the youth and dame.

Now woods have overgrown the mead,
  And hid the cliffs from sight;
There shrieks the hovering hawk at noon,
  And prowls the fox at night.

W. C. Bryant.

Mount Vernon's Bells

Where Potomac's stream is flowing
  Virginia's border through,
Where the white-sailed ships are going
  Sailing to the ocean blue;

Hushed the sound of mirth and singing,
  Silent every one!
While the solemn bells are ringing
  By the tomb of Washington.

Tolling and knelling,
  With a sad, sweet sound,
O'er the waves the tones are swelling
  By Mount Vernon's sacred ground.

Long ago the warrior slumbered—
  Our country's father slept;
Long among the angels numbered
  They the hero soul have kept.

But the children's children love him,
  And his name revere,
So where willows wave above him,
  Sweetly still his knell you hear.

Sail, oh ships, across the billows,
  And bear the story far;

How he sleeps beneath the willows,—
"First in peace and first in war."

Tell while sweet adieus are swelling,
Till you come again,
He within the hearts is dwelling,
Of his loving countrymen.

M. B. C. Slade.

Gradatim

Heaven is not reached at a single bound;
But we build the ladder by which we rise
From the lowly earth to the vaulted skies,
And we mount to the summit round by round.

I count this thing to be grandly true:
That a noble deed is a step toward God,
Lifting a soul from the common sod
To a purer air and a broader view.

We rise by things that are under our feet;
By what we have mastered of good and gain,
By the pride deposed and the passion slain,
And the vanquished ills that we hourly meet.

We hope, we aspire, we resolve, we trust,
When the morning calls us to life and light;
But our hearts grow weary, and ere the night
Our lives are trailing the sordid dust.

We hope, we resolve, we aspire, we pray,
And we think that we mount the air on wings,
Beyond the recall of sensual things,
While our feet still cling to the heavy clay.

Only in dreams is a ladder thrown
From the weary earth to the sapphire walls;
But the dreams depart, and the vision falls,
And the sleeper awakes on his pillow of stone.

Heaven is not reached at a single bound;
But we build the ladder by which we rise
From the lowly earth to the vaulted skies,
And we mount to the summit round by round.

J. G. Holland.

Mr. Finney's Turnip

Mr. Finney had a turnip
And it grew behind the barn;
It grew there, and it grew there,
And the turnip did no harm.

It grew and it grew,
Till it could get no taller;
Mr. Finney pulled it up
And put it in his cellar.

It lay there and it lay there,
Till it began to rot;
His daughter Sallie took it up,
And put it in the pot.

She boiled it, and she boiled it,
As long as she was able;
His daughter Peggy fished it out,
And put it on the table.

Mr. Finney and his wife,
They sat down to sup,
And they ate, and they ate,
Until they ate the turnip up.

The Village Blacksmith

Under a spreading chestnut tree
The village smithy stands;
The smith, a mighty man is he,
With large and sinewy hands;
And the muscles of his brawny arms
Are strong as iron bands.

His hair is crisp, and black and long,
His face is like the tan;
His brow is wet with honest sweat,
He earns whate'er he can,
And looks the whole world in the face,
For he owes not any man.

Week in, week out, from morn till night,
You can hear his bellows blow;
You can hear him swing his heavy sledge,
With measured beat and slow,
Like a sexton ringing the village bell,
When the evening sun is low.

And children coming home from school
Look in at the open door;
They love to see the flaming forge,
And hear the bellows roar,
And catch the burning sparks that fly
Like chaff from a threshing floor.

He goes on Sunday to the church,
And sits among his boys;
He hears the parson pray and preach,
He hears his daughter's voice,
Singing in the village choir,
And it makes his heart rejoice.

It sounds to him like her mother's voice,
Singing in Paradise!
He needs must think of her once more,
How in the grave she lies;
And with his hard, rough hand he wipes
A tear out cf his eyes.

Toiling,—rejoicing,—sorrowing,
Onward through life he goes;
Each morning sees some task begun,
Each evening sees it close;
Something attempted, something done,
Has earned a night's repose.

Thanks, thanks to thee, my worthy friend,
For the lesson thou hast taught!
Thus at the flaming forge of life
Our fortunes must be wrought;
Thus on its sounding anvil shaped
Each burning deed and thought.

H. W. Longfellow.

You and You

To the American Private in the Great War

Every one of you won the war—
You and you and you—
Each one knowing what it was for,
And what was his job to do.

Every one of you won the war,
Obedient, unwearied, unknown,
Dung in the trenches, drift on the shore,
Dust to the world's end blown;
Every one of you, steady and true,
You and you and you—
Down in the pit or up in the blue,
Whether you crawled or sailed or flew,
Whether your closest comrade knew
Or you bore the brunt alone—

All of you, all of you, name after name,
Jones and Robinson, Smith and Brown,
You from the piping prairie town,
You from the Fundy fogs that came,
You from the city's roaring blocks,
You from the bleak New England rocks
With the shingled roof in the apple boughs,
You from the brown adobe house——

You from the Rockies, you from the Coast,
You from the burning frontier-post
And you from the Klondyke's frozen flanks,
You from the cedar-swamps, you from the pine,
You from the cotton and you from the vine,
You from the rice and the sugar-brakes,
You from the Rivers and you from the Lakes,
You from the Creeks and you from the Licks
And you from the brown bayou—
You and you and you—
You from the pulpit, you from the mine,
You from the factories, you from the banks,
Closer and closer, ranks on ranks,
Airplanes and cannon, and rifles and tanks,
Smith and Robinson, Brown and Jones,
Ruddy faces or bleaching bones,
After the turmoil and blood and pain
Swinging home to the folks again
Or sleeping alone in the fine French rain—
Every one of you won the war.

Every one of you won the war—
You and you and you—
Pressing and pouring forth, more and more,
Toiling and straining from shore to shore
To reach the flaming edge of the dark
Where man in his millions went up like a spark,
You, in your thousands and millions coming,
All the sea ploughed with you, all the air humming,
All the land loud with you,
All our hearts proud with you,
All our souls bowed with the awe of your coming!

Where's the Arch high enough,
Lads, to receive you,
Where's the eye dry enough,
Dears, to perceive you,
When at last and at last in your glory you come,
Tramping home?

Every one of you won the war,
You and you and you—
You that carry an unscathed head,
You that halt with a broken tread,
And oh, most of all, you Dead, you Dead!
Lift up the Gates for these that are last,
That are last in the great Procession.
Let the living pour in, take possession,
Flood back to the city, the ranch, the farm,
The church and the college and mill,
Back to the office, the store, the exchange,
Back to the wife with the babe on her arm,
Back to the mother that waits on the sill,
And the supper that's hot on the range.

And now, when the last of them all are by,
Be the Gates lifted up on high
To let those Others in,
Those Others, their brothers, that softly tread,
That come so thick, yet take no ground,
That are so many, yet make no sound,
Our Dead, our Dead, our Dead!

O silent and secretly-moving throng,
In your fifty thousand strong,
Coming at dusk when the wreaths have dropt

And streets are empty, and music
 stopt,
Silently coming to hearts that wait
Dumb in the door and dumb at the gate,
And hear your step and fly to your
 call—
Every one of you won the war,
But you, you Dead, most of all!

Edith Wharton (Copyright 1919 by Charles Scribner's Sons).

The First Snow-fall

The snow had begun in the gloaming,
 And busily all the night
Had been heaping field and highway
 With a silence deep and white.

Every pine and fir and hemlock
 Wore ermine too dear for an earl,
And the poorest twig on the elm tree
 Was ridged inch-deep with pearl.

From sheds new-roofed with Carrara
 Came Chanticleer's muffled crow,
The stiff rails were softened to swan's-
 down,
 And still fluttered down the snow.

I stood and watched by the window
 The noiseless work of the sky,
And the sudden flurries of snow-birds,
 Like brown leaves whirling by.

I thought of a mound in sweet Auburn
 Where a little headstone stood;
How the flakes were folding it gently,
 As did robins the babes in the wood.

Up spoke our own little Mabel,
 Saying, "Father, who makes it
 snow?"
And I told of the good All-father
 Who cares for us here below.

Again I looked at the snow-fall,
 And thought of the leaden sky
That arched o'er our first great sorrow,
 When that mound was heaped so
 high.

I remembered the gradual patience
 That fell from that cloud like snow,
Flake by flake, healing and hiding
 The scar of our deep-plunged woe.

And again to the child I whispered,
 "The snow that husheth all,
Darling, the merciful Father
 Alone can make it fall!"

Then, with eyes that saw not, I kissed
 her;
 And she, kissing back, could not
 know
That *my* kiss was given to her sister,
 Folded close under deepening snow.

James Russell Lowell.

The Concord Hymn

Sung at the completion of the Concord Monument, April 19, 1836.

By the rude bridge that arched the
 flood,
 Their flag to April's breeze unfurled,
Here once the embattled farmers stood,
 And fired the shot heard round the
 world.

The foe long since in silence slept;
 Alike the conqueror silent sleeps;
And Time the ruined bridge has swept
 Down the dark stream which sea-
 ward creeps.

On this green bank, by this soft stream,
 We set to-day a votive stone,
That memory may their deed redeem,
 When, like our sires, our sons are
 gone.

Spirit, that made these heroes dare
 To die, to leave their children free,
Bid Time and Nature gently spare
 The shaft we raise to them and thee.

Ralph Waldo Emerson.

Casey at the Bat

It looked extremely rocky for the Mudville nine that day;
The score stood two to four with but an inning left to play;
So, when Cooney died at second, and Burrows did the same,
A pallor wreathed the features of the patrons of the game.

A straggling few got up to go, leaving there the rest,
With that hope which springs eternal within the human breast,
For they thought: "If only Casey could get a whack at that,"
They'd put up even money now, with Casey at the bat.

But Flynn preceded Casey, and likewise so did Blake,
And the former was a puddin', and the latter was a fake;
So on that stricken multitude a deathlike silence sat,
For there seemed but little chance of Casey's getting to the bat.

But Flynn let drive a "single," to the wonderment of all,
And the much-despised Blakey "tore the cover off the ball";
And when the dust had lifted and they saw what had occurred,
There was Blakey safe at second, and Flynn a-huggin' third.

Then, from the gladdened multitude went up a joyous yell,
It rumbled in the mountain-tops, it rattled in the dell;
It struck upon the hillside and rebounded on the flat;
For Casey, mighty Casey, was advancing to the bat.

There was ease in Casey's manner as he stepped into his place,
There was pride in Casey's bearing, and a smile on Casey's face.
And when, responding to the cheers, he lightly doffed his hat,
No stranger in the crowd could doubt 'twas Casey at the bat.

Ten thousand eyes were on him as he rubbed his hands with dirt,
Five thousand tongues applauded when he wiped them on his shirt;
Then while the New York pitcher ground the ball into his hip,
Defiance gleamed in Casey's eye, a sneer curled Casey's lip.

And now the leather-covered sphere came hurtling through the air,
And Casey stood a-watching it in haughty grandeur there.
Close by the sturdy batsman the ball unheeded sped—
"That ain't my style," said Casey. "Strike one," the umpire said.

From the benches, black with people, there went up a muffled roar,
Like the beating of great storm waves on a stern and distant shore.
"Kill him! Kill the umpire!" shouted someone on the stand.
And it's likely they'd have killed him had not Casey raised a hand.

With a smile of Christian charity great Casey's visage shone;
He stilled the rising tumult; he bade the game go on;
He signaled to Sir Timothy, once more the spheroid flew;
But Casey still ignored it, and the umpire said, "Strike two."

"Fraud," cried the maddened thousands, and echo answered "Fraud!"

But one scornful look from Casey and the audience was awed.
They saw his face grow stern and cold, they saw his muscles strain,
And they knew that Casey wouldn't let that ball go by again.

The sneer is gone from Casey's lip, his teeth are clenched in hate;
He pounds with cruel violence his bat upon the plate;
And now the pitcher holds the ball, and now he lets it go,
And now the air is shattered by the force of Casey's blow.

Oh, somewhere in this favored land the sun is shining bright;
The band is playing somewhere, and somewhere hearts are light;
And somewhere men are laughing, and somewhere children shout:
But there is no joy in Mudville—mighty Casey has struck out.

Phineas Thayer.

Casey's Revenge

(*Being a reply to "Casey at the Bat."*)

There were saddened hearts in Mudville for a week or even more;
There were muttered oaths and curses —every fan in town was sore.
"Just think," said one, "how soft it looked with Casey at the bat!
And then to think he'd go and spring a bush league trick like that."

All his past fame was forgotten; he was now a hopeless "shine."
They called him "Strike-out Casey" from the mayor down the line.
And as he came to bat each day his bosom heaved a sigh,
While a look of hopeless fury shone in mighty Casey's eye.

The lane is long, someone has said, that never turns again,
And Fate, though fickle, often gives another chance to men.
And Casey smiled—his rugged face no longer wore a frown;
The pitcher who had started all the trouble came to town.

All Mudville has assembled; ten thousand fans had come
To see the twirler who had put big Casey on the bum;
And when he stepped into the box the multitude went wild.
He doffed his cap in proud disdain—but Casey only smiled.

"Play ball!" the umpire's voice rang out, and then the game began;
But in that throng of thousands there was not a single fan
Who thought that Mudville had a chance; and with the setting sun
Their hopes sank low—the rival team was leading "four to one."

The last half of the ninth came round, with no change in the score;
But when the first man up hit safe the crowd began to roar.
The din increased, the echo of ten thousands shouts was heard
When the pitcher hit the second and gave "four balls" to the third.

Three men on base—nobody out—three runs to tie the game!
A triple meant the highest niche in Mudville's hall of fame.
But here the rally ended and the gloom was deep as night
When the fourth one "fouled to catcher," and the fifth "flew out to right."

A dismal groan in chorus came—a scowl was on each face—

When Casey walked up, bat in hand, and slowly took his place;
His bloodshot eyes in fury gleamed; his teeth were clinched in hate;
He gave his cap a vicious hook and pounded on the plate.

But fame is fleeting as the wind, and glory fades away;
There were no wild and woolly cheers, no glad acclaim this day.
They hissed and groaned and hooted as they clamored, "Strike him out!"
But Casey gave no outward sign that he had heard the shout.

The pitcher smiled and cut one loose; across the plate it spread;
Another hiss, another groan—"Strike one!" the umpire said.
Zip! Like a shot, the second curve broke just below his knee—
"Strike two!" the umpire roared aloud; but Casey made no plea.

No roasting for the umpire now—his was an easy lot.
But here the pitcher twirled again—was that a rifle shot?
A whack; a crack; and out through space the leather pellet flew—
A blot against the distant sky, a speck against the blue.

Above the fence in center field, in rapid whirling flight
The sphere sailed on; the blot grew dim and then was lost to sight.
Ten thousand hats were thrown in air, ten thousand threw a fit;
But no one ever found the ball that mighty Casey hit!

Oh, somewhere in this favored land dark clouds may hide the sun,
And somewhere bands no longer play and children have no fun;
And somewhere over blighted lives there hangs a heavy pall,
But Mudville hearts are happy now—for Casey hit the ball!

James Wilson.

Rock Me to Sleep

Backward, turn backward, O time, in your flight,
Make me a child again just for to-night!
Mother, come back from the echoless shore,
Take me again to your heart as of yore;
Kiss from my forehead the furrows of care,
Smooth the few silver threads out of my hair;
Over my slumbers your loving watch keep;—
Rock me to sleep, mother, rock me to sleep.

Backward, flow backward, O tide of the years!
I am so weary of toil and of tears,—
Toil without recompense, tears all in vain,—
Take them, and give me my childhood again!
I have grown weary of dust and decay,—
Weary of flinging my soul-wealth away;
Weary of sowing for others to reap;—
Rock me to sleep, mother, rock me to sleep.

Tired of the hollow, the base, the untrue,
Mother, O mother, my heart calls for you!
Many a summer the grass has grown green,
Blossomed and faded, our faces between;

Yet with strong yearning and passionate pain
Long I to-night for your presence again.
Come from the silence so long and so deep;—
Rock me to sleep, mother, rock me to sleep.

Over my heart, in the days that are flown,
No love like mother-love ever has shone;
No other worship abides and endures—
Faithful, unselfish and patient, like yours;
None like a mother can charm away pain
From the sick soul and the world-weary brain.
Slumber's soft calms o'er my heavy lids creep;—
Rock me to sleep, mother, rock me to sleep.

Come, let your brown hair, just lighted with gold,
Fall on your shoulders again as of old;
Let it drop over my forehead to-night,
Shading my faint eyes away from the light;
For with its sunny-edged shadows once more
Haply will throng the sweet visions of yore;
Lovingly, softly, its bright billows sweep;—
Rock me to sleep, mother, rock me to sleep.

Mother, dear mother, the years have been long
Since I last listened your lullaby song;
Sing, then, and unto my soul it shall seem
Womanhood's years have been only a dream.
Clasped to your breast in a loving embrace,
With your light lashes just sweeping my face,
Never hereafter to wake or to weep;—
Rock me to sleep, mother, rock me to sleep.

Elizabeth Akers Allen.

An Answer to "Rock Me to Sleep"

My child, ah, my child; thou art weary to-night,
Thy spirit is sad, and dim is the light;
Thou wouldst call me back from the echoless shore
To the trials of life, to thy heart as of yore;
Thou longest again for my fond loving care,
For my kiss on thy cheek, for my hand on thy hair;
But, angels around thee their loving watch keep,
And angels, my darling, will rock thee to sleep.

"Backward?" Nay, onward, ye swift rolling years!
Gird on thy armor, keep back thy tears;
Count not thy trials nor efforts in vain,
They'll bring thee the light of thy childhood again.
Thou shouldst not weary, my child, by the way,
But watch for the light of that brighter day;
Not tired of "Sowing for others to reap,"
For angels, my darling, will rock thee to sleep.

Tired, my child, of the "base, the untrue!"

I have tasted the cup they have given
to you;
I've felt the deep sorrow in the living
green
Of a low mossy grave by the silvery
stream.
But the dear mother I then sought for
in vain
Is an angel presence and with me
again;
And in the still night, from the silence
deep,
Come the bright angels to rock me to
sleep.

Nearer thee now than in days that are
flown,
Purer the love-light encircling thy
home;
Far more enduring the watch for to-
night
Than ever earth worship away from
the light;
Soon the dark shadows will linger no
more,
Nor come to thy call from the opening
door;
But know thou, my child, that the an-
gels watch keep,
And soon, very soon, they'll rock thee
to sleep.

They'll sing thee to sleep with a sooth-
ing song;
And, waking, thou'lt be with a heaven-
ly throng;
And thy life, with its toil and its tears
and pain,
Thou wilt then see has not been in vain.
Thou wilt meet those in bliss whom on
earth thou didst love,
And whom thou hast taught of the
"Mansions above."
"Never hereafter to suffer or weep,"
The angels, my darling, will rock thee
to sleep.

Bay Billy

(*December 15, 1862*)

'Twas the last fight at Fredericks-
burg,—
Perhaps the day you reck,
Our boys, the Twenty-second Maine,
Kept Early's men in check.
Just where Wade Hampton boomed
away
The fight went neck and neck.

All day the weaker wing we held,
And held it with a will.
Five several stubborn times we
charged
The battery on the hill,
And five times beaten back, re-formed,
And kept our column still.

At last from out the center fight
Spurred up a general's aide.
"That battery must silenced be!"
He cried, as past he sped.
Our colonel simply touched his cap,
And then, with measured tread,

To lead the crouching line once more,
The grand old fellow came.
No wounded man but raised his head
And strove to gasp his name,
And those who could not speak nor stir,
"God blessed him" just the same.

For he was all the world to us,
That hero gray and grim;
Right well we knew that fearful slope
We'd climb with none but him,
Though while his white head led the
way
We'd charge hell's portals in.

This time we were not half way up
When, midst the storm of shell,
Our leader, with his sword upraised,
Beneath our bayonets fell,
And as we bore him back, the foe
Set up a joyous yell.

Our hearts went with him. Back we swept,
And when the bugle said,
"Up, charge again!" no man was there
But hung his dogged head.
"We've no one left to lead us now,"
The sullen soldiers said.

Just then before the laggard line
The colonel's horse we spied—
Bay Billy, with his trappings on,
His nostrils swelling wide,
As though still on his gallant back
The master sat astride.

Right royally he took the place
That was of old his wont,
And with a neigh that seemed to say,
Above the battle's brunt,
"How can the Twenty-second charge
If I am not in front?"

Like statues rooted there we stood,
And gazed a little space;
Above that floating mane we missed
The dear familiar face,
But we saw Bay Billy's eye of fire,
And it gave us heart of grace.

No bugle-call could rouse us all
As that brave sight had done.
Down all the battered line we felt
A lightning impulse run.
Up, up the hill we followed Bill,—
And we captured every gun!

And when upon the conquered height
Died out the battle's hum,
Vainly 'mid living and the dead
We sought our leader dumb.
It seemed as if a spectre steed
To win that day had come.

And then the dusk and dew of night
Fell softly o'er the plain,
As though o'er man's dread work of death
The angels wept again,
And drew night's curtain gently round
A thousand beds of pain.

All night the surgeons' torches went
The ghastly rows between,—
All night with solemn step I paced
The torn and bloody green.
But who that fought in the big war
Such dread sights have not seen?

At last the morning broke. The lark
Sang in the merry skies,
As if to e'en the sleepers there
It said "Awake, arise!"
Though naught but that last trump of all
Could ope their heavy eyes.

And then once more, with banners gay,
Stretched out the long brigade.
Trimly upon the furrowed field
The troops stood on parade,
And bravely 'mid the ranks were closed
The gaps the fight had made.

Not half the Twenty-second's men
Were in their place that morn;
And Corporal Dick, who yester-noon
Stood six brave fellows on,
Now touched my elbow in the ranks,
For all between were gone.

Ah! who forgets that weary hour
When, as with misty eyes,
To call the old familiar roll
The solemn sergeant tries,—
One feels that thumping of the heart
As no prompt voice replies.

And as in faltering tone and slow
The last few names were said,
Across the field some missing horse
Toiled up with weary tread.
It caught the sergeant's eye, and quick
Bay Billy's name he read.

Yes! there the old bay hero stood,
All safe from battle's harms,
And ere an order could be heard,
Or the bugle's quick alarms,
Down all the front, from end to end,
The troops presented arms!

Not all the shoulder-straps on earth
Could still our mighty cheer;
And ever from that famous day,
When rang the roll-call clear,
Bay Billy's name was read, and then
The whole line answered, "Here!"

Frank H. Gassaway.

The Legend of the Organ-Builder

Day by day the Organ-builder in his lonely chamber wrought;
Day by day the soft air trembled to the music of his thought;
Till at last the work was ended; and no organ voice so grand
Ever yet had soared responsive to the master's magic hand.

Ay, so rarely was it builded that whenever groom and bride,
Who, in God's sight were well-pleasing, in the church stood side by side,
Without touch or breath the organ of itself began to play,
And the very airs of heaven through the soft gloom seemed to stray.

He was young, the Organ-builder, and o'er all the land his fame
Ran with fleet and eager footsteps, like a swiftly rushing flame.
All the maidens heard the story; all the maidens blushed and smiled,
By his youth and wondrous beauty and his great renown beguiled.

So he sought and won the fairest, and the wedding-day was set:
Happy day—the brightest jewel in the glad year's coronet!
But when they the portal entered, he forgot his lovely bride—
Forgot his love, forgot his God, and his heart swelled high with pride.

"Ah!" thought he, "how great a master am I! When the organ plays,
How the vast cathedral-arches will re-echo with my praise!"
Up the aisle the gay procession moved. The altar shone afar,
With every candle gleaming through soft shadows like a star.

But he listened, listened, listened, with no thought of love or prayer,
For the swelling notes of triumph from his organ standing there.
All was silent. Nothing heard he save the priest's low monotone,
And the bride's robe trailing softly o'er the floor of fretted stone.

Then his lips grew white with anger. Surely God was pleased with him,
Who had built the wondrous organ for His temple vast and dim!
Whose the fault then? Hers—the maiden standing meekly at his side!
Flamed his jealous rage, maintaining she was false to him—his bride.

Vain were all her protestations, vain her innocence and truth;
On that very night he left her to her anguish and her ruth.
Far he wandered to a country wherein no man knew his name:
For ten weary years he dwelt there, nursing still his wrath and shame.

Then his haughty heart grew softer, and he thought by night and day
Of the bride he had deserted, till he hardly dared to pray;

Thought of her, a spotless maiden, fair and beautiful and good;
Thought of his relentless anger, that had cursed her womanhood;

Till his yearning grief and penitence at last were all complete,
And he longed, with bitter longing, just to fall down at her feet.
Ah! how throbbed his heart when, after many a weary day and night,
Rose his native towers before him, with the sunset glow alight!

Through the gates into the city on he pressed with eager tread;
There he met a long procession—mourners following the dead.
"Now why weep ye so, good people? And whom bury ye to-day?
Why do yonder sorrowing maidens scatter flowers along the way?

"Has some saint gone up to heaven?" "Yes," they answered, weeping sore;
"For the Organ-builder's saintly wife our eyes shall see no more;
And because her days were given to the service of God's poor,
From His church we mean to bury her. See! yonder is the door."

No one knew him; no one wondered when he cried out, white with pain;
No one questioned when, with pallid lips, he poured his tears like rain.
" 'Tis someone she has comforted, who mourns with us," they said,
As he made his way unchallenged, and bore the coffin's head;

Bore it through the open portal, bore it up the echoing aisle,
Let it down before the altar, where the lights burned clear the while.

When, oh, hark; the wondrous organ of itself began to play
Strains of rare, unearthly sweetness never heard until that day!

All the vaulted arches rang with music sweet and clear;
All the air was filled with glory, as of angels hovering near;
And ere yet the strain was ended, he who bore the coffin's head,
With the smile of one forgiven, gently sank beside it—dead.

They who raised the body knew him, and they laid him by his bride;
Down the aisle and o'er the threshold they were carried, side by side;
While the organ played a dirge that no man ever heard before,
And then softly sank to silence—silence kept forevermore.

Julia C. R. Dorr.

Our Folks

"Hi! Harry Holly! Halt; and tell
A fellow just a thing or two;
You've had a furlough, been to see
How all the folks in Jersey do.
It's months ago since I was there—
I, and a bullet from Fair Oaks.
When you were home, old comrade, say,
Did you see any of our folks?

"You did? Shake hands—Oh, ain't I glad!
For if I do look grim and rough,
I've got some feelin'—
People think
A soldier's heart is mighty tough;
But, Harry, when the bullets fly,
And hot saltpetre flames and smokes,
While whole battalions lie afield,
One's apt to think about his folks.

"And so you saw them—when? and where?

The old man—is he hearty yet?
And mother—does she fade at all?
Or does she seem to pine and fret
For me? And Sis?—has she grown tall?
And did you see her friend—you know—
That Annie Moss—
(How this pipe chokes!)
Where did you see her?—Tell me, Hal,
A lot of news about our folks.

"You saw them in the church—you say,
It's likely, for they're always there.
Not Sunday? No? A funeral? Who?
Who, Harry? how you shake and stare!
All well, you say, and all were out.
What ails you, Hal? Is this a hoax?
Why don't you tell me like a man
What is the matter with our folks?"

"I said all well, old comrade, true;
I say all well, for He knows best
Who takes the young ones in his arms,
Before the sun goes to the west.
The axe-man Death deals right and left,
And flowers fall as well as oaks;
And so—
Fair Annie blooms no more!
And that's the matter with your folks.

"See, this long curl was kept for you;
And this white blossom from her breast;
And here—your sister Bessie wrote
A letter telling all the rest.
Bear up, old friend."
Nobody speaks;
Only the old camp-raven croaks,
And soldiers whisper, "Boys, be still;
There's some bad news from Granger's folks."

He turns his back—the only foe
That ever saw it—on this grief,
And, as men will, keeps down the tears
Kind nature sends to woe's relief.
Then answers he: "Ah, Hal, I'll try;
But in my throat there's something chokes,
Because, you see, I've thought so long
To count her in among our folks.

"I s'pose she must be happy now,
But still I will keep thinking, too,
I could have kept all trouble off,
By being tender, kind and true.
But maybe not.
She's safe up there,
And when the Hand deals other strokes,
She'll stand by Heaven's gate, I know,
And wait to welcome in our folks."

Ethel Lynn Beers.

The Face upon the Floor

'Twas a balmy summer evening, and a goodly crowd was there,
Which well-nigh filled Joe's bar-room on the corner of the square;
And as songs and witty stories came through the open door,
A vagabond crept slowly in and posed upon the floor.

"Where did it come from?" someone said. "The wind has blown it in."
"What does it want?" another cried. "Some whisky, rum or gin?"
"Here, Toby, seek him, if your stomach's equal to the work—
I wouldn't touch him with a fork, he's as filthy as a Turk."

This badinage the poor wretch took with stoical good grace;
In fact, he smiled as though he thought he'd struck the proper place.
"Come, boys, I know there's kindly hearts among so good a crowd—

To be in such good company would
make a deacon proud.

"Give me a drink—that's what I
want—I'm out of funds, you know;
When I had cash to treat the gang, this
hand was never slow.
What? You laugh as though you
thought this pocket never held a
sou;
I once was fixed as well, my boys, as
any one of you.

"There, thanks; that's braced me nice-
ly; God bless you one and all;
Next time I pass this good saloon, I'll
make another call.
Give you a song? No, I can't do that,
my singing days are past;
My voice is cracked, my throat's worn
out, and my lungs are going fast.

"Say! give me another whisky, and
I'll tell you what I'll do—
I'll tell you a funny story, and a fact,
I promise, too.
That I was ever a decent man, not one
of you would think;
But I was, some four or five years back.
Say, give me another drink.

"Fill her up, Joe, I want to put some
life into my frame—
Such little drinks, to a bum like me, are
miserably tame;
Five fingers—there, that's the scheme
—and corking whisky, too.
Well, here's luck, boys; and landlord,
my best regards to you.

"You've treated me pretty kindly, and
I'd like to tell you how
I came to be the dirty sot you see be-
fore you now.
As I told you, once I was a man, with
muscle, frame and health,
And but for a blunder, ought to have
made considerable wealth.

"I was a painter—not one that daubed
on bricks and wood,
But an artist, and, for my age, was
rated pretty good.
I worked hard at my canvas, and was
bidding fair to rise,
For gradually I saw the star of fame
before my eyes.

"I made a picture, perhaps you've seen,
'tis called the 'Chase of Fame.'
It brought me fifteen hundred pounds,
and added to my name.
And then I met a woman—now comes
the funny part—
With eyes that petrified my brain and
sunk into my heart.

"Why don't you laugh? 'Tis funny
that the vagabond you see
Could ever love a woman, and expect
her love for me;
But 'twas so, and for a month or two
her smiles were freely given,
And when her loving lips touched mine
it carried me to heaven.

"Did you ever see a woman for whom
your soul you'd give,
With a form like the Milo Venus, too
beautiful to live;
With eyes that would beat the Koh-i-
noor, and a wealth of chestnut
hair?
If so, 'twas she, for there never was
another half so fair.

"I was working on a portrait, one af-
ternoon in May,
Of a fair-haired boy, a friend of mine,
who lived across the way;
And Madeline admired it, and, much to
my surprise,
Said that she'd like to know the man
that had such dreamy eyes.

"It didn't take long to know him, and
before the month had flown,

My friend had stolen my darling, and I was left alone;
And ere a year of misery had passed above my head,
The jewel I had treasured so had tarnished, and was dead.

"That's why I took to drink, boys. Why, I never saw you smile,—
I thought you'd be amused, and laughing all the while.
Why, what's the mattter, friend? There's a teardrop in your eye,
Come, laugh, like me; 'tis only babes and women that should cry.

"Say, boys, if you give me just another whisky, I'll be glad,
And I'll draw right here a picture of the face that drove me mad.
Give me that piece of chalk with which you mark the baseball score—
You shall see the lovely Madeline upon the bar-room floor."

Another drink, and, with chalk in hand, the vagabond began
To sketch a face that well might buy the soul of any man.
Then as he placed another lock upon the shapely head,
With a fearful shriek, he leaped, and fell across the picture dead.

H. Antoine D'Arcy.

The Calf Path

One day through the primeval wood,
A calf walked home, as good calves should;
But made a trail all bent askew,
A crooked trail, as all calves do.
Since then three hundred years have fled,
And, I infer, the calf is dead.

But still he left behind his trail,
And thereby hangs a moral tale.
The trail was taken up next day
By a lone dog that passed that way,
And then the wise bell-wether sheep
Pursued the trail o'er vale and steep,
And drew the flock behind him, too,
As good bell-wethers always do.
And from that day, o'er hill and glade,
Through those old woods a path was made.

And many men wound in and out,
And turned and dodged and bent about,
And uttered words of righteous wrath
Because 'twas such a crooked path:
But still they followed—do not laugh—
The first migrations of that calf,
And through this winding woodway stalked
Because he wabbled when he walked.

This forest path became a lane,
That bent and turned and turned again;
This crooked path became a road,
Where many a poor horse, with his load,
Toiled on beneath the burning sun,
And traveled some three miles in one.
And thus a century and a half
They trod the footsteps of that calf.

The years passed on in swiftness fleet,
The road became a village street;
And this, before men were aware,
A city's crowded thoroughfare.
And soon the central street was this
Of a renowned metropolis.
And men two centuries and a half
Trod in the footsteps of that calf!

Each day a hundred thousand rout
Followed the zigzag calf about;
And o'er his crooked journey went
The traffic of a continent.
A hundred thousand men were led
By a calf near three centuries dead.
They followed still his crooked way
And lost one hundred years a day;

For thus such reverence is lent
To well-established precedent.

A moral lesson this might teach
Were I ordained and called to preach;
For men are prone to go it blind,
Along the calf-paths of the mind,
And work away from sun to sun
To do what other men have done.
They follow in the beaten track,
And out and in, and forth and back,
And still their devious course pursue,
To keep the path that others do.
But how the wise wood-gods must laugh,
Who saw the first primeval calf;
Ah, many things this tale might teach—
But I am not ordained to preach.

Sam Walter Foss.

The Ride of Jennie M'Neal

Paul Revere was a rider bold—
Well has his valorous deed been told;
Sheridan's ride was a glorious one—
Often it has been dwelt upon;
But why should men do all the deeds
On which the love of a patriot feeds?
Hearken to me, while I reveal
The dashing ride of Jennie M'Neal.

On a spot as pretty as might be found
In the dangerous length of the Neutral Ground,
In a cottage, cozy, and all their own,
She and her mother lived alone.
Safe were the two, with their frugal store,
From all of the many who passed their door;
For Jennie's mother was strange to fears,
And Jennie was large for fifteen years;
With vim her eyes were glistening,
Her hair was the hue of a blackbird's wing;
And while the friends who knew her well
The sweetness of her heart could tell,
A gun that hung on the kitchen wall
Looked solemnly quick to heed her call;
And they who were evil-minded knew
Her nerve was strong and her aim was true.
So all kind words and acts did deal
To generous, black-eyed Jennie M'Neal.

One night, when the sun had crept to bed,
And rain-clouds lingered overhead,
And sent their surly drops for proof
To drum a tune on the cottage roof,
Close after a knock at the outer door
There entered a dozen dragoons or more.
Their red coats, stained by the muddy road,
That they were British soldiers showed;
The captain his hostess bent to greet,
Saying, "Madam, please give us a bit to eat;
We will pay you well, and, if may be,
This bright-eyed girl for pouring our tea;
Then we must dash ten miles ahead,
To catch a rebel colonel abed.
He is visiting home, as doth appear;
We will make his pleasure cost him dear."
And they fell on the hasty supper with zeal,
Close-watched the while by Jennie M'Neal.

For the gray-haired colonel they hovered near
Had been her true friend, kind and dear;
And oft, in her younger days, had he
Right proudly perched her upon his knee,
And told her stories many a one

Concerning the French war lately done.
And oft together the two friends were,
And many the arts he had taught to her;
She had hunted by his fatherly side,
He had shown her how to fence and ride;
And once had said, "The time may be,
Your skill and courage may stand by me."
So sorrow for him she could but feel,
Brave, grateful-hearted Jennie M'Neal.

With never a thought or a moment more,
Bare-headed she slipped from the cottage door,
Ran out where the horses were left to feed,
Unhitched and mounted the captain's steed,
And down the hilly and rock-strewn way
She urged the fiery horse of gray.
Around her slender and cloakless form
Pattered and moaned the ceaseless storm;
Secure and tight a gloveless hand
Grasped the reins with stern command;
And full and black her long hair streamed,
Whenever the ragged lightning gleamed.
And on she rushed for the colonel's weal,
Brave, lioness-hearted Jennie M'Neal.

Hark! from the hills, a moment mute,
Came a clatter of hoofs in hot pursuit;
And a cry from the foremost trooper said,
"Halt! or your blood be on your head";
She heeded it not, and not in vain
She lashed the horse with the bridle-rein.

So into the night the gray horse strode;
His shoes hewed fire from the rocky road;
And the high-born courage that never dies
Flashed from his rider's coal-black eyes.
The pebbles flew from the fearful race;
The raindrops grasped at her glowing face.
"On, on, brave beast!" with loud appeal,
Cried eager, resolute Jennie M'Neal.

"Halt!" once more came the voice of dread;
"Halt! or your blood be on your head!"
Then, no one answering to the calls,
Sped after her a volley of balls.
They passed her in her rapid flight,
They screamed to her left, they screamed to her right;
But, rushing still o'er the slippery track,
She sent no token of answer back,
Except a silvery laughter-peal,
Brave, merry-hearted Jennie M'Neal.

So on she rushed, at her own good will,
Through wood and valley, o'er plain and hill;
The gray horse did his duty well,
Till all at once he stumbled and fell,
Himself escaping the nets of harm,
But flinging the girl with a broken arm.
Still undismayed by the numbing pain,
She clung to the horse's bridle-rein
And gently bidding him to stand,
Petted him with her able hand;
Then sprung again to the saddle bow,
And shouted, "One more trial now!"
As if ashamed of the heedless fall,
He gathered his strength once more for all,
And, galloping down a hillside steep,
Gained on the troopers at every leap;
No more the high-bred steed did reel,

But ran his best for Jennie M'Neal.

They were a furlong behind, or more,
When the girl burst through the colonel's door,
Her poor arm helpless hanging with pain,
And she all drabbled and drenched with rain,
But her cheeks as red as fire-brands are,
And her eyes as bright as a blazing star,
And shouted, "Quick! be quick, I say!
They come! they come! Away! away!"
Then sunk on the rude white floor of deal,
Poor, brave, exhausted Jennie M'Neal.

The startled colonel sprung, and pressed
The wife and children to his breast,
And turned away from his fireside bright,
And glided into the stormy night;
Then soon and safely made his way
To where the patriot army lay.
But first he bent in the dim firelight,
And kissed the forehead broad and white,
And blessed the girl who had ridden so well
To keep him out of a prison-cell.
The girl roused up at the martial din,
Just as the troopers came rushing in,
And laughed, e'en in the midst of a moan,
Saying, "Good sirs, your bird has flown.
'Tis I who have scared him from his nest;
So deal with me now as you think best."
But the grand young captain bowed, and said,
"Never you hold a moment's dread.
Of womankind I must crown you queen;
So brave a girl I have never seen.
Wear this gold ring as your valor's due;
And when peace comes I will come for you."
But Jennie's face an arch smile wore,
As she said, "There's a lad in Putnam's corps,
Who told me the same, long time ago;
You two would never agree, I know.
I promised my love to be as true as steel,"
Said good, sure-hearted Jennie M'Neal.

Will Carleton.

The Hand That Rules the World

They say that man is mighty, he governs land and sea;
He wields a mighty scepter o'er lesser powers that be;
By a mightier power and stronger, man from his throne is hurled,
And the hand that rocks the cradle is the hand that rules the world.

Blessings on the hand of woman! angels guard its strength and grace,
In the palace, cottage, hovel, oh, no matter where the place!
Would that never storms assailed it, rainbows ever gently curled;
For the hand that rocks the cradle is the hand that rules the world.

Infancy's the tender fountain, power may with beauty flow;
Mother's first to guide the streamlets, from them souls unresting grow;
Grow on for the good or evil, sunshine streamed or darkness hurled;
For the hand that rocks the cradle is the hand that rules the world.

Woman, how divine your mission here upon our natal sod!
Keep, oh, keep the young heart open always to the breath of God!

All true trophies of the ages are from
mother-love impearled,
For the hand that rocks the cradle is
the hand that rules the world.

Blessings on the hand of woman! fathers, sons and daughters cry,
And the sacred song is mingled with
the worship in the sky—
Mingles where no tempest darkens,
rainbows evermore are curled;
For the hand that rocks the cradle is
the hand that rules the world.

William Ross Wallace.

What I Live For

I live for those who love me,
Whose hearts are kind and true,
For the heaven that smiles above me,
And awaits my spirit, too;
For the human ties that bind me,
For the task by God assigned me,
For the bright hopes left behind me,
And the good that I can do.

I live to learn their story
Who've suffered for my sake,
To emulate their glory,
And to follow in their wake;
Bards, patriots, martyrs, sages,
The noble of all ages,
Whose deeds crowd history's pages,
And Time's great volume make.

I live to hold communion
With all that is divine,
To feel there is a union
'Twixt Nature's heart and mine;
To profit by affliction,
Reap truths from fields of fiction,
Grow wiser from conviction,
And fulfill each grand design.

I live to hail that season,
By gifted minds foretold,
When men shall rule by reason,
And not alone by gold;
When man to man united,
And every wrong thing righted,
The whole world shall be lighted
As Eden was of old.

I live for those who love me,
For those who know me true,
For the heaven that smiles above me,
And awaits my spirit, too;
For the cause that lacks assistance,
For the wrong that needs resistance,
For the future in the distance,
And the good that I can do.

George Linnaeus Banks.

My Love Ship

If all the ships I have at sea
Should come a-sailing home to me,
Weighed down with gems, and silk and
gold,
Ah! well, the harbor would not hold
So many ships as there would be,
If all my ships came home from sea.

If half my ships came home from sea,
And brought their precious freight to
me,
Ah! well, I should have wealth as great
As any king that sits in state,
So rich the treasure there would be
In half my ships now out at sea.

If but one ship I have at sea
Should come a-sailing home to me,
Ah! well, the storm clouds then might
frown,
For, if the others all went down,
Still rich and glad and proud I'd be
If that one ship came home to me.

If that one ship went down at sea
And all the others came to me
Weighed down with gems and wealth
untold,
With honor, riches, glory, gold,
The poorest soul on earth I'd be
If that one ship came not to me.

O skies, be calm; O winds, blow free!
Blow all my ships safe home to me,
But if thou sendest some awrack,
To nevermore come sailing back,
Send any, all that skim the sea,
But send my love ship home to me.
Ella Wheeler Wilcox.

The Man With the Hoe

(*Written after seeing Millet's famous painting.*)

God made man in His own image; in the image of God made he him.—GENESIS.

Bowed by the weight of centuries he leans
Upon his hoe and gazes on the ground,
The emptiness of ages in his face,
And on his back the burden of the world.
Who made him dead to rapture and despair,
A thing that grieves not and that never hopes,
Stolid and stunned, a brother to the ox?
Who loosened and let down this brutal jaw?
Whose was the hand that slanted back this brow?
Whose breath blew out the light within this brain?
Is this the Thing the Lord God made and gave
To have dominion over sea and land;
To trace the stars and search the heavens for power;
To feel the passion of Eternity?
Is this the dream He dreamed who shaped the suns
And pillared the blue firmament with light?
Down all the stretch of Hell to its last gulf
There is no shape more terrible than this—
More tongued with censure of the world's blind greed—
More filled with signs and portents for the soul—
More fraught with menace to the universe.

What gulfs between him and the seraphim!
Slave of the wheel of labor, what to him
Are Plato and the swing of Pleiades?
What the long reaches of the peaks of song,
The rift of dawn, the reddening of the rose?
Through this dread shape the suffering ages look;
Time's tragedy is in that aching stoop;
Through this dread shape humanity betrayed,
Plundered, profaned and disinherited,
Cries protest to the judges of the world,
A protest that is also prophecy.

O masters, lords and rulers in all lands,
Is this the handiwork you give to God,
This monstrous thing distorted and soul-quenched?
How will you ever straighten up this shape;
Touch it again with immortality;
Give back the upward looking and the light,
Rebuild it in the music and the dream;
Make right the immemorial infamies, perfidious wrongs, immedicable woes?

O masters, lords and rulers in all lands,
How will the Future reckon with this man?
How answer his brute question in that hour
When whirlwinds of rebellion shake the world?

How will it be with kingdom and with kings—
With those who shaped him to the thing he is—
When this dumb Terror shall reply to God,
After the silence of the centuries?

Edwin Markham.

Poorhouse Nan

Did you say you wished to see me, sir? Step in; 'tis a cheerless place,
But you're heartily welcome all the same; to be poor is no disgrace.
Have I been here long? Oh, yes, sir! 'tis thirty winters gone
Since poor Jim took to crooked ways and left me all alone!
Jim was my son, and a likelier lad you'd never wish to see,
Till evil counsels won his heart and led him away from me.

'Tis the old, sad, pitiful story, sir, of the devil's winding stair,
And men go down—and down—and down—to blackness and despair;
Tossing about like wrecks at sea, with helm and anchor lost,
On and on, through the surging waves, nor caring to count the cost;
I doubt sometimes if the Savior sees, He seems so far away,
How the souls He loved and died for, are drifting—drifting astray!

Indeed, 'tis little wonder, sir, if woman shrinks and cries
When the life-blood on Rum's altar spilled is calling to the skies;
Small wonder if her own heart feels each sacrificial blow,
For isn't each life a part of hers? each pain her hurt and woe?
Read all the records of crime and shame—'tis bitterly, sadly true;
Where manliness and honor die, there some woman's heart dies, too.

I often think, when I hear folks talk so prettily and so fine
Of "alcohol as needful food"; of the "moderate use of wine";
How "the world couldn't do without it, there was clearly no other way
But for a man to drink, or let it alone. as his own strong will might say";
That "to use it, but not abuse it, was the proper thing to do,"
How I wish they'd let old Poorhouse Nan preach her little sermon, too!

I would give them scenes in a woman's life that would make their pulses stir,
For I was a drunkard's child and wife—aye, a drunkard's mother, sir!
I would tell of childish terrors, of childish tears and pain,
Of cruel blows from a father's hand when rum had crazed his brain;
He always said he could drink his fill, or let it alone as well;
Perhaps he might, he was killed one night in a brawl—in a grog-shop hell!

I would tell of years of loveless toil the drunkard's child had passed,
With just one gleam of sunshine, too beautiful to last.
When I married Tom I thought for sure I had nothing more to fear,
That life would come all right at last; the world seemed full of cheer.
But he took to moderate drinking—he allowed 'twas a harmless thing,
So the arrow sped, and my bird of Hope came down with a broken wing.

Tom was only a moderate drinker; ah, sir, do you bear in mind

How the plodding tortoise in the race left the leaping hare behind?
'Twas because he held right on and on, steady and true, if slow,
And that's the way, I'm thinking, that the moderate drinkers go!
Step over step—day after day—with sleepless, tireless pace,
While the toper sometimes looks behind and tarries in the race!

Ah, heavily in the well-worn path poor Tom walked day by day,
For my heart-strings clung about his feet and tangled up the way;
The days were dark, and friends were gone, and life dragged on full slow,
And children came, like reapers, and to a harvest of want and woe!
Two of them died, and I was glad when they lay before me dead;
I had grown so weary of their cries—their pitiful cries for bread.

There came a time when my heart was stone; I could neither hope nor pray;
Poor Tom lay out in the Potter's Field, and my boy had gone astray;
My boy who'd been my idol, while, like hound athirst for blood,
Between my breaking heart and him the liquor seller stood,
And lured him on with pleasant words, his pleasures and his wine;
Ah, God have pity on other hearts as bruised and hurt as mine.

There were whispers of evil-doing, of dishonor, and of shame,
That I cannot bear to think of now, and would not dare to name!
There was hiding away from the light of day, there was creeping about at night,
A hurried word of parting—then a criminal's stealthy flight!

His lips were white with remorse and fright when he gave me a good-by kiss;
And I've never seen my poor lost boy from that black day to this.

Ah, none but a mother can tell you, sir, how a mother's heart will ache,
With the sorrow that comes of a sinning child, with grief for a lost one's sake,
When she knows the feet she trained to walk have gone so far astray,
And the lips grown bold with curses that she taught to sing and pray;
A child may fear—a wife may weep, but of all sad things, none other
Seems half so sorrowful to me as being a drunkard's mother.

They tell me that down in the vilest dens of the city's crime and murk,
There are men with the hearts of angels, doing the angels' work;
That they win back the lost and the straying, that they help the weak to stand,
By the wonderful power of loving words—and the help of God's right hand!
And often and often, the dear Lord knows, I've knelt and prayed to Him,
That somewhere, somehow, 'twould happen that they'd find and save my Jim!

You'll say 'tis a poor old woman's whim; but when I prayed last night,
Right over yon eastern window there shone a wonderful light!
(Leastways it looked that way to me) and out of the light there fell
The softest voice I had ever heard: it rung like a silver bell;

And these were the words, "The prodigal turns, so tired by want and sin,
He seeks his father's open door—he weeps—and enters in."

Why, sir, you're crying as hard as I; what—is it really done?
Have the loving voice and the Helping Hand brought back my wandering son?
Did you kiss me and call me "Mother" —and hold me to your breast,
Or is it one of the taunting dreams that come to mock my rest?
No—no! thank God, 'tis a dream come true! I can die, for He's saved my boy!
And the poor old heart that had lived on grief was broken at last by joy!

Lucy M. Blinn.

Why Should the Spirit of Mortal be Proud!

Oh, why should the spirit of mortal be proud!
Like a swift fleeting meteor, a fast flying cloud,
A flash of the lightning, a break of the wave,
He passes from life to his rest in the grave.

The leaves of the oak and the willows shall fade,
Be scattered around, and together be laid;
And the young and the old, and the low and the high
Shall moulder to dust, and together shall die.

The child whom a mother attended and loved,
The mother that infant's affection who proved,
The husband that mother and infant who blessed,
Each— all are away to their dwelling of rest.

The maid on whose cheek, on whose brow, in whose eye
Shone beauty and pleasure— her triumphs are by;
And the memory of those who loved her and praised
Are alike from the minds of the living erased.

The hand of the king who the scepter hath borne,
The brow of the priest who the mitre hath worn,
The eye of the sage and the heart of the brave
Are hidden and lost in the depths of the grave.

The peasant whose lot was to sow and to reap,
The herdsman who climbed with his goats to the steep,
The beggar who wandered in search of his bread
Have faded away like the grass that we tread.

The saint who enjoyed the communion of heaven,
The sinner who dared to remain unforgiven,
The wise and the foolish, the guilty and just
Have quietly mingled their bones in the dust.

So the multitude goes— like the flower and the weed
That wither away to let others succeed;
So the multitude comes—even those we behold,

To repeat every tale that has often been
told.

For we are the same things that our
fathers have been,
We see the same sights that our fathers
have seen;
We drink the same stream, and we feel
the same sun,
And we run the same course that our
fathers have run.

The thoughts we are thinking our fa-
thers would think,
From the death we are shrinking from,
they too would shrink,
To the life we are clinging to, they too
would cling,
But it speeds from the earth like a bird
on the wing.

They loved— but their story we can-
not enfold,
They scorned— but the heart of the
haughty is cold,
They grieved— but no wail from their
slumbers may come,
They joy'd— but the voice of their
gladness—is dumb.

They died, ay, they died! and we things
that are now,
Who walk on the turf that lies over
their brow,
Who make in their dwellings a tran-
sient abode
Meet the changes they met on their pil-
grimage road.

Yea, hope and despondence, and pleas-
ure and pain,
Are mingled together in sunshine and
rain;
And the smile, and the tear, and the
song and the dirge
Still follow each other like surge upon
surge,

'Tis the wink of an eye, 'tis the draught
of a breath
From the blossoms of health to the
paleness of death;
From the gilded saloon to the bier and
the shroud—
Oh, why should the spirit of mortal be
proud! *William Knox.*

How He Saved St. Michael's

'Twas long ago—ere ever the signal
gun
That blazed before Fort Sumter had
wakened the North as one;
Long ere the wondrous pillar of battle-
cloud and fire
Had marked where the unchained mil-
lions marched on to their heart's
desire.
On roofs and glittering turrets, that
night, as the sun went down,
The mellow glow of the twilight shone
like a jeweled crown,
And, bathed in the living glory, as the
people lifted their eyes,
They saw the pride of the city, the
spire of St. Michael's rise
High over the lesser steeples, tipped
with a golden ball
That hung like a radiant planet caught
in its earthward fall;
First glimpse of home to the sailor who
made the harbor round,
And last slow-fading vision dear to the
outward bound.
The gently gathering shadows shut out
the waning light;
The children prayed at their bedsides
as they were wont each night;
The noise of buyer and seller from the
busy mart was gone,
And in dreams of a peaceful morrow
the city slumbered on.

But another light than sunrise aroused
the sleeping street,

For a cry was heard at midnight, and the rush of trampling feet;
Men stared in each other's faces, thro' mingled fire and smoke,
While the frantic bells went clashing clamorous, stroke on stroke.
By the glare of her blazing roof-tree the houseless mother fled,
With the babe she pressed to her bosom shrieking in nameless dread;
While the fire-king's wild battalions scaled wall and cap-stone high,
And painted their glaring banners against an inky sky.
From the death that raged behind them, and the crush of ruin loud,
To the great square of the city, were driven the surging crowd,
Where yet firm in all the tumult, unscathed by the fiery flood,
With its heavenward pointing finger the church of St. Michael's stood.

But e'en as they gazed upon it there rose a sudden wail,
A cry of horror blended with the roaring of the gale,
On whose scorching wings updriven, a single flaming brand,
Aloft on the towering steeple clung like a bloody hand.
"Will it fade?" the whisper trembled from a thousand whitening lips;
Far out on the lurid harbor they watched it from the ships.
A baleful gleam, that brighter and ever brighter shone,
Like a flickering, trembling will-o'-the-wisp to a steady beacon grown.
"Uncounted gold shall be given to the man whose brave right hand,
For the love of the periled city, plucks down yon burning brand!"
So cried the Mayor of Charleston, that all the people heard,
But they looked each one at his fellow, and no man spoke a word.

Who is it leans from the belfry, with face upturned to the sky—
Clings to a column and measures the dizzy spire with his eye?
Will he dare it, the hero undaunted, that terrible, sickening height,
Or will the hot blood of his courage freeze in his veins at the sight?
But see! he has stepped on the railing, he climbs with his feet and his hands,
And firm on a narrow projection, with the belfry beneath him, he stands!
Now once, and once only, they cheer him—a single tempestuous breath,
And there falls on the multitude gazing a hush like the stillness of death.

Slow, steadily mounting, unheeding aught save the goal of the fire,
Still higher and higher, an atom, he moves on the face of the spire;
He stops! Will he fall? Lo! for answer, a gleam like a meteor's track,
And, hurled on the stones of the pavement, the red brand lies shattered and black!
Once more the shouts of the people have rent the quivering air;
At the church door mayor and council wait with their feet on the stair,
And the eager throng behind them press for a touch of his hand—
The unknown savior whose daring could compass a deed so grand.

But why does a sudden tremor seize on them as they gaze?
And what meaneth that stifled murmur of wonder and amaze?
He stood in the gate of the temple he had periled his life to save,
And the face of the unknown hero was the sable face of a slave!
With folded arms he was speaking in tones that were clear, not loud,

And his eyes, ablaze in their sockets,
burnt into the eyes of the crowd.
"Ye may keep your gold, I scorn it!
but answer me, ye who can,
If the deed I have done before you be
not the deed of a *man?*"

He stepped but a short space backward, and from all the women and
men
There were only sobs for answer, and
the mayor called for a pen,
And the great seal of the city, that he
might read who ran,
And the slave who saved St. Michael's
went out from its door a man.

Mary A. P. Stansbury.

Bingen on the Rhine

A soldier of the Legion lay dying in
Algiers,
There was lack of woman's nursing,
there was dearth of woman's
tears;
But a comrade stood beside him, while
his life-blood ebbed away,
And bent, with pitying glances, to
hear what he might say.
The dying soldier faltered, as he took
that comrade's hand,
And he said, "I never more shall see my
own, my native land;
Take a message, and a token, to some
distant friends of mine,
For I was born at Bingen—at Bingen
on the Rhine!

"Tell my brothers and companions,
when they meet and crowd around
To hear my mournful story in the pleasant vineyard ground,
That we fought the battle bravely, and
when the day was done,
Full many a corpse lay ghastly pale,
beneath the setting sun.
And 'midst the dead and dying, were
some grown old in wars,
The death-wound on their gallant
breasts the last of many scars:
But some were young—and suddenly
beheld life's morn decline;
And one had come from Bingen—fair
Bingen on the Rhine!

"Tell my mother that her other sons
shall comfort her old age,
And I was aye a truant bird, that
thought his home a cage:
For my father was a soldier, and even
as a child
My heart leaped forth to hear him tell
of struggles fierce and wild;
And when he died, and left us to divide
his scanty hoard,
I let them take whate'er they would,
but kept my father's sword,
And with boyish love I hung it where
the bright light used to shine,
On the cottage-wall at Bingen—calm
Bingen on the Rhine!

"Tell my sister not to weep for me, and
sob with drooping head,
When the troops are marching home
again with glad and gallant tread;
But to look upon them proudly, with a
calm and steadfast eye,
For her brother was a soldier too, and
not afraid to die.
And if a comrade seek her love, I ask
her in my name
To listen to him kindly, without regret
or shame;
And to hang the old sword in its place
(my father's sword and mine),
For the honor of old Bingen—dear
Bingen on the Rhine!

"There's another—not a sister; in the
happy days gone by,
You'd have known her by the merriment that sparkled in her eye;
Too innocent for coquetry—too fond
for idle scorning—

Oh, friend! I fear the lightest heart makes sometimes heaviest mourning;
Tell her the last night of my life (for ere the moon be risen
My body will be out of pain—my soul be out of prison),
I dreamed I stood with her, and saw the yellow sunlight shine
On the vine-clad hills of Bingen—fair Bingen on the Rhine!

"I saw the blue Rhine sweep along—I heard, or seemed to hear,
The German songs we used to sing, in chorus sweet and clear;
And down the pleasant river, and up the slanting hill,
The echoing chorus sounded, through the evening calm and still;
And her glad blue eyes were on me as we passed with friendly talk
Down many a path beloved of yore, and well-remembered walk,
And her little hand lay lightly, confidingly in mine:
But we'll meet no more at Bingen—loved Bingen on the Rhine!"

His voice grew faint and hoarser,—his grasp was childish weak,—
His eyes put on a dying look,—he sighed and ceased to speak;
His comrade bent to lift him, but the spark of life had fled,—
The soldier of the Legion, in a foreign land—was dead!
And the soft moon rose up slowly, and calmly she looked down
On the red sand of the battle-field, with bloody corpses strown;
Yea, calmly on that dreadful scene her pale light seemed to shine
As it shone on distant Bingen—fair Bingen on the Rhine!

—*Caroline Norton.*

College Oil Cans

On a board of bright mosaic wrought in many a quaint design,
Gleam a brace of silver goblets wreathed with flowers and filled with wine.
Round the board a group is seated; here and there are threads of white
Which their dark locks lately welcomed; but they're only boys tonight.
Some whose words have thrilled the senate, some who win the critic's praise—
All are "chums" to-night, with voices redolent of college days.

"Boys," said one, "do you remember that old joke about the wine—
How we used to fill our oil cans and repair to 'No. 9'?
But at last the old professor—never long was he outdone—
Opened up our shining oil cans and demolished all our fun!"
In the laugh that rings so gayly through the richly curtained room,
Join they all, save one; Why is it? Does he see the waxen bloom
Tremble in its vase of silver? Does he see the ruddy wine
Shiver in its crystal goblet, or do those grave eyes divine
Something sadder yet? He pauses till their mirth has died away,
Then in measured tones speaks gravely:
"Boys, a story, if I may, I will tell you, though it may not merit worthily your praise,
It is bitter fruitage ripened from our pranks of college days."

Eagerly they claim the story, for they know the LL. D.

With his flexible voice would garnish any tale, whate'er it be.

"Just a year ago to-night, boys, I was in my room alone,
At the San Francisco L— House, when I heard a plaintive moan
Sounding from the room adjoining. Hoping to give some relief
To the suffering one, I entered; but it thrilled my heart with grief
Just to see that wreck of manhood—bloated face, disheveled hair—
Wildly tossing, ever moaning, while his thin hands beat the air.
Broken prayers, vile oaths and curses filled the air as I drew near;
Then in faint and piteous accents, these words I could plainly hear:
'Give me one more chance—one only—let me see my little Belle—
Then I'll follow where they lead me, be it to the depths of hell!'
When he saw me he grew calmer, started strangely — looked me o'er—
Oh, the glory of expression! I had seen those eyes before!
Yes, I knew him; it was Horace, he who won the college prize;
Naught remained of his proud beauty but the splendor of his eyes.
He whom we were all so proud of, lay there in the fading light.
If my years should number fourscore, I shall ne'er forget that sight.
And he knew me—called me 'Albert,' ere a single word I'd said—
We were comrades in the old days; I sat down beside the bed.

"Horace seemed to grow more quiet, but he would not go to sleep;
He kept talking of our boyhood while my hand he still would keep
In his own so white and wasted, and with burning eyes would gaze
On my face, still talking feebly of the dear old college days.
'Ah,' he said, 'life held such promise; but, alas! I am to-day
But a poor degraded outcast—hopes, ambition swept away,
And it dates back to those oil cans that we filled in greatest glee.
Little did I think in those days what the harvest now would be!'

"For a moment he was silent, then a cry whose anguish yet
Wrings my heart, burst from his white lips, though his teeth were tightly set,
And with sudden strength he started—sprang from my detaining arm,
Shrieking wildly, 'Curse the demons; do they think to do me harm?
Back! I say, ye forked-tongued serpents reeking with the filth of hell!
Don't ye see I have her with me—my poor sainted little Belle?'

"When I'd soothed him into quiet, with a trembling arm he drew
My head down, 'Oh, Al,' he whispered, 'such remorse you never knew.'
And again I tried to soothe him, but my eyes o'erbrimmed with tears;
His were dry and clear, as brilliant as they were in college years.
All the flush had left his features, he lay white as marble now;
Tenderly I smoothed his pillow, wiped the moisture from his brow.
Though I begged him to be quiet, he would talk of those old days,
Brokenly at times, but always of 'the boys' with loving praise.

"Once I asked him of Lorena—the sweet girl whom he had wed—
You remember Rena Barstow. When I asked if she were dead,

'No,' he said, his poor voice faltering, 'she is far beyond the Rhine,
But I wish, to God, it were so, and I still might call her mine.
She's divorced—she's mine no longer,' here his voice grew weak and hoarse
'But although I am a drunkard, *I have one they can't divorce.*
I've a little girl in heaven, playing round the Savior's knee,
Always patient and so faithful that at last she died for me.

" 'I had drank so much, so often, that my brain was going wild;
Every one had lost hope in me but my faithful little child.
She would say, "Now stop, dear papa, for I know you can stop *now.*"
I would promise, kiss my darling, and the next day break my vow.
So it went until one Christmas, dark and stormy, cold and drear;
Out I started, just as usual, for the cursed rum shop near,
And my darling followed after, in the storm of rain and sleet,
With no covering wrapped about her, naught but slippers on her feet;
No one knew it, no one missed her, till there came with solemn tread,
Stern-faced men unto our dwelling, bringing back our darling—*dead!*
They had found her cold and lifeless, like, they said, an angel fair,
Leaning 'gainst the grog shop window —oh, she thought that *I was there!*'
Then he raised his arms toward heaven, called aloud unto the dead,
For his mind again was wandering: 'Belle, my precious Belle!' he said,
'Papa's treasure—papa's darling! oh, my baby—did—you—come
All the way—alone—my darling—just to lead—poor—papa—home?'
And he surely had an answer, for a silence o'er him fell.
And I sat alone and lonely—death had come with little Belle."

Silence in that princely parlor—head of every guest is bowed.
They still see the red wine sparkle, but 'tis through a misty cloud.
Said the host at last, arising, "I have scorned the pledge to sign,
Laughed at temperance all my life long. Never more shall drop of wine
Touch my lips. The fruit *was* bitter, boys; 'twas I proposed it first—
That foul joke from which poor Horace ever bore a life accurst!
Let us pledge ourselves to-night, boys, never more by word, or deed,
In our own fair homes, or elsewhere, help to plant the poison seed."

Silence once again, but only for a moment's space, and then,
In one voice they all responded with a low and firm "Amen."

Will Victor McGuire.

God's Judgment on a Wicked Bishop

The summer and autumn had been so wet,
That in winter the corn was growing yet.
'Twas a piteous sight to see all round
The grain lie rotting on the ground.

Every day the starving poor
Crowded round Bishop Hatto's door,
For he had a plentiful last year's store,
And all the neighborhood could tell
His granaries were furnish'd well.

At last Bishop Hatto appointed a day
To quiet the poor without delay;

He bade them to his great barn repair,
And they should have food for the winter there.

Rejoiced the tidings good to hear,
The poor folk flock'd from far and near;
The great barn was full as it could hold
Of women and children, and young and old.

Then, when he saw it could hold no more,
Bishop Hatto he made fast the door,
And while for mercy on Christ they call,
He set fire to the barn and burnt them all.

"I' faith, 'tis an excellent bonfire!" quoth he,
"And the country is greatly obliged to me
For ridding it, in these times forlorn,
Of rats that only consume the corn."

So then to his palace returned he,
And he sat down to supper merrily,
And he slept that night like an innocent man;
But Bishop Hatto never slept again.

In the morning, as he enter'd the hall
Where his picture hung against the wall,
A sweat like death all over him came,
For the rats had eaten it out of the frame.

As he look'd, there came a man from his farm,
He had a countenance white with alarm:
"My lord, I open'd your granaries this morn,
And the rats had eaten all your corn."

Another came running presently,
And he was pale as pale could be.
"Fly, my lord bishop, fly!" quoth he,
"Ten thousand rats are coming this way,
The Lord forgive you for yesterday!"

"I'll go to my tower on the Rhine," replied he;
" 'Tis the safest place in Germany;
The walls are high, and the shores are steep
And the stream is strong, and the water deep."

Bishop Hatto fearfully hasten'd away,
And he cross'd the Rhine without delay,
And reach'd his tower and barr'd with care
All the winaows, doors, and loopholes there.

He laid him down and closed his eyes,
But soon a scream made him arise;
He started, and saw two eyes of flame
On his pillow, from whence the screaming came.

He listen'd and look'd,—it was only the cat,
But the bishop he grew more fearful for that,
For she sat screaming, mad with fear
At the army of rats that were drawing near.

For they have swum over the river so deep,
And they have climb'd the shores so steep,
And up the tower their way is bent,
To do the work for which they were sent.

They are not to be told by the dozen or score;
By thousands they come, and by myriads and more;
Such numbers had never been heard of before,

Such a judgment had never been witness'd of yore.

Down on his knees the bishop fell,
And faster and faster his beads did he tell,
As louder and louder, drawing near,
The gnawing of their teeth he could hear.

And in at the window, and in at the door,
And through the walls helter-skelter they pour;
And down from the ceiling and up through the floor,

From the right and the left, from behind and before,
From within and without, from above and below,—
And all at once to the bishop they go.

They have whetted their teeth against the stones,
And now they pick the bishop's bones;
They gnaw'd the flesh from every limb,
For they were sent to do judgment on him! *Robert Southey.*

The Last Hymn

The Sabbath day was ending in a village by the sea,
The uttered benediction touched the people tenderly,
And they rose to face the sunset in the glowing, lighted west,
And then hastened to their dwellings for God's blessed boon of rest.

But they looked across the waters, and a storm was raging there;
A fierce spirit moved above them—the wild spirit of the air—
And it lashed and shook and tore them till they thundered, groaned and boomed,
And, alas! for any vessel in their yawning gulfs entombed.

Very anxious were the people on that rocky coast of Wales,
Lest the dawn of coming morrow should be telling awful tales,
When the sea had spent its passion and should cast upon the shore
Bits of wreck and swollen victims as it had done heretofore.

With the rough winds blowing round her, a brave woman strained her eyes,
As she saw along the billows a large vessel fall and rise.
Oh, it did not need a prophet to tell what the end must be,
For no ship could ride in safety near that shore on such a sea!

Then the pitying people hurried from their homes and thronged the beach.
Oh, for power to cross the waters and the perishing to reach!
Helpless hands were wrung in terror, tender hearts grew cold with dread,
And the ship, urged by the tempest, to the fatal rock-shore sped.

"She's parted in the middle! Oh, the half of her goes down!"
"God have mercy! Is his heaven far to seek for those who drown?"
Lo! when next the white, shocked faces looked with terror on the sea,
Only one last clinging figure on a spar was seen to be.

Nearer to the trembling watchers came the wreck tossed by the wave,
And the man still clung and floated, though no power on earth could save.

"Could we send him a short message?
Here's a trumpet. Shout away!"
'Twas the preacher's hand that took it,
and he wondered what to say.

Any memory of his sermon? Firstly?
Secondly? Ah, no!
There was but one thing to utter in
that awful hour of woe.
So he shouted through the trumpet,
"Look to Jesus!
Can you hear?" And "Aye, aye, sir,"
rang the answer o'er the waters
loud and clear.

Then they listened,—"He is singing,
'Jesus, lover of my soul.'"
And the winds brought back the echo,
"While the nearer waters roll."
Strange, indeed, it was to hear him,—
"Till the storm of life is past,"
Singing bravely o'er the waters, "Oh,
receive my soul at last!"

He could have no other refuge,—
"Hangs my helpless soul on thee."
"Leave, ah! leave me not"—the singer
dropped at last into the sea.
And the watchers, looking homeward,
through their eyes by tears made
dim,
Said, "He passed to be with Jesus in
the singing of that hymn."

Marianne Faringham.

A Fence or an Ambulance

'Twas a dangerous cliff, as they freely
confessed,
Though to walk near its crest was so
pleasant;
But over its terrible edge there had
slipped
A duke and full many a peasant.
So the people said something would
have to be done,
But their projects did not at all
tally;
Some said, "Put a fence around the
edge of the cliff,"
Some, "An ambulance down in the
valley."

But the cry for the ambulance carried
the day,
For it spread through the neighbor-
ing city;
A fence may be useful or not, it is true,
But each heart became brimful of
pity
For those who slipped over that dan-
gerous cliff;
And the dwellers in highway and al-
ley
Gave pounds or gave pence, not to put
up a fence,
But an ambulance down in the valley.

"For the cliff is all right, if you're care-
ful," they said,
"And, if folks even slip and are
dropping,
It isn't the slipping that hurts them so
much,
As the shock down below when
they're stopping."
So day after day, as these mishaps
occurred,
Quick forth would these rescuers
sally
To pick up the victims who fell off the
cliff,
With their ambulance down in the
valley.

Then an old sage remarked: "It's a
marvel to me
That people give far more attention
To repairing results than to stopping
the cause,
When they'd much better aim at pre-
vention.

Let us stop at its source all this mischief," cried he,
"Come, neighbors and friends, let us rally,
If the cliff we will fence, we might almost dispense
With the ambulance down in the valley."

"Oh, he's a fanatic," the others rejoined,
"Dispense with the ambulance? Never!
He'd dispense with all charities, too, if he could;
No! No! We'll support them forever.
Aren't we picking up folks just as fast as they fall?
And shall this man dictate to us? Shall he?
Why should people of sense stop to put up a fence,
While the ambulance works in the valley?"

But a sensible few, who are practical too,
Will not bear with such nonsense much longer;
They believe that prevention is better than cure,
And their party will soon be the stronger.
Encourage them then, with your purse, voice, and pen,
And while other philanthropists dally,
They will scorn all pretense and put up a stout fence
On the cliff that hangs over the valley.

Better guide well the young than reclaim them when old,
For the voice of true wisdom is calling,
"To rescue the fallen is good, but 'tis best
To prevent other people from falling."
Better close up the source of temptation and crime,
Than deliver from dungeon or galley;
Better put a strong fence 'round the top of the cliff
Than an ambulance down in the valley."

Joseph Malins.

The Smack in School

A district school, not far away,
'Mid Berkshire hills, one winter's day,
Was humming with its wonted noise
Of three-score mingled girls and boys;
Some few upon their tasks intent,
But more on furtive mischief bent.
The while the master's downward look
Was fastened on a copy-book;
When suddenly, behind his back,
Rose sharp and clear a rousing smack!
As 'twere a battery of bliss
Let off in one tremendous kiss!
"What's that?" the startled master cries;
"That, thir," a little imp replies,
"Wath William Willith, if you pleathe,
I thaw him kith Thuthanna Peathe!"
With frown to make a statue thrill,
The master thundered, "Hither, Will!"
Like wretch o'ertaken in his track
With stolen chattels on his back,
Will hung his head in fear and shame,
And to the awful presence came,—
A great, green, bashful simpleton,
The butt of all good-natured fun,
With smile suppressed, and birch upraised
The threatener faltered, "I'm amazed
That you, my biggest pupil, should
Be guilty of an act so rude—
Before the whole set school to boot—
What evil genius put you to 't?"

" 'Twas she, herself, sir," sobbed the lad;
"I did not mean to be so bad;
But when Susanna shook her curls,
And whispered I was 'fraid of girls,
And dursn't kiss a baby's doll,
I couldn't stand it, sir, at all,
But up and kissed her on the spot!
I know—boo-hoo—I ought to not,
But, somehow, from her looks—boo-hoo—
I thought she kind o' wished me to!"

William Pitt Palmer.

A Woman's Question

Do you know you have asked for the costliest thing
Ever made by the Hand above—
A woman's heart and a woman's life,
And a woman's wonderful love?

Do you know you have asked for this priceless thing
As a child might ask for a toy;
Demanding what others have died to win,
With the reckless dash of a boy?

You have written my lesson of duty out,
Man-like you have questioned me—
Now stand at the bar of my woman's soul,
Until I shall question thee.

You require your mutton shall always be hot,
Your socks and your shirts shall be whole.
I require your heart to be true as God's stars,
And pure as heaven your soul.

You require a cook for your mutton and beef;
I require a far better thing—
A seamstress you're wanting for stockings and shirts—
I look for a man and a king.

A king for a beautiful realm called home,
And a man that the Maker, God,
Shall look upon as He did the first,
And say, "It is very good."

I am fair and young, but the rose will fade
From my soft, young cheek one day—
Will you love then, 'mid the falling leaves,
As you did 'mid the bloom of May?

Is your heart an ocean so strong and deep
I may launch my all on its tide?
A loving woman finds heaven or hell
On the day she is made a bride.

I require all things that are grand and true,
All things that a man should be;
If you give this all, I would stake my life
To be all you demand of me.

If you cannot do this, a laundress and cook
You can hire with little to pay;
But a woman's heart and a woman's life
Are not to be won that way.

Lena Lathrop.

Lasca

I want free life and I want fresh air;
And I sigh for the canter after the cattle,
The crack of the whips like shots in battle,
The mellay of horns, and hoofs, and heads
That wars, and wrangles, and scatters, and spreads;
The green beneath and the blue above,
And dash and danger, and life and love;
And Lasca!

Lasca used to ride
On a mouse-gray mustang, close to my side,
With blue *serape* and bright-belled spur;
I laughed with joy as I looked at her!
Little knew she of books or creeds;
An *Ave Maria* sufficed her needs;
Little she cared, save to be by my side,
To ride with me, and ever to ride,
From San Saba's shore to Lavaca's tide.
She was as bold as the billows that beat,
She was as wild as the breezes that blow;
From her little head to her little feet
She was swayed, in her suppleness, to and fro
By each gust of passion; a sapling pine,
That grows on the edge of a Kansas bluff
And wars with the wind when the weather is rough,
Is like this Lasca, this love of mine.
She would hunger that I might eat,
Would take the bitter and leave me the sweet;
But once, when I made her jealous for fun,
At something I'd whispered, or looked, or done,
One Sunday, in San Antonio,
To a glorious girl on the Alamo,
She drew from her girdle a dear little dagger,
And—sting of a wasp!—it made me stagger!
An inch to the left or an inch to the right,
And I shouldn't be maundering here to-night;
But she sobbed, and, sobbing, so swiftly bound
Her torn *rebosa* about the wound
That I quite forgave her. Scratches don't count
In Texas, down by the Rio Grande.

Her eye was brown,—a deep, deep brown;
Her hair was darker than her eye;
And something in her smile and frown,
Curled crimson lip, and instep high,
Showed that there ran in each blue vein,
Mixed with the milder Aztec strain,
The vigorous vintage of old Spain.
She was alive in every limb
With feeling, to the finger tips;
And when the sun is like a fire,
And sky one shining, soft sapphire,
One does not drink in little sips.

The air was heavy, the night was hot,
I sat by her side, and forgot—forgot;
Forgot the herd that were taking their rest;
Forgot that the air was close opprest;
That the Texas norther comes sudden and soon,
In the dead of night or the blaze of noon;
That once let the herd at its breath take fright,
That nothing on earth can stop the flight;
And woe to the rider, and woe to the steed,
Who falls in front of their mad stampede!
Was that thunder? No, by the Lord!
I sprang to my saddle without a word,
One foot on mine, and she clung behind.
Away on a hot chase down the wind!
But never was fox-hunt half so hard,
And never was steed so little spared,
For we rode for our lives. You shall hear how we fared
In Texas, down by the Rio Grande.

The mustang flew, and we urged him on;
There was one chance left, and you have but one;
Halt, jump to the ground, and shoot your horse;
Crouch under his carcass, and take your chance;
And if the steers, in their frantic course,
Don't batter you both to pieces at once,
You may thank your star; if not, good-by
To the quickening kiss and the long-drawn sigh,
And the open air and the open sky,
In Texas, down by the Rio Grande.

The cattle gained on us, and just as I felt
For my old six-shooter, behind in my belt,
Down came the mustang, and down came we,
Clinging together, and—what was the rest?
A body that spread itself on my breast,
Two arms that shielded my dizzy head,
Two lips that hard on my lips were pressed;
Then came thunder in my ears,
As over us surged the sea of steers,
Blows that beat blood into my eyes,
And when I could rise,
Lasca was dead!

I gouged out a grave a few feet deep,
And there in Earth's arms I laid her to sleep!
And there she is lying, and no one knows,
And the summer shines and the winter snows;
For many a day the flowers have spread
A pall of petals over her head;
And the little gray hawk hangs aloft in the air,
And the sly coyote trots here and there,
And the black snake glides, and glitters, and slides
Into the rift in a cotton-wood tree;
And the buzzard sails on,
And comes and is gone,
Stately and still like a ship at sea;
And I wonder why I do not care
For the things that are like the things that were.
Does half my heart lie buried there
In Texas, down by the Rio Grande?

Frank Desprez.

Over the Hill to the Poor-House

Over the hill to the poor-house I'm trudgin' my weary way—
I, a woman of seventy, and only a trifle gray—
I, who am smart an' chipper, for all the years I've told,
As many another woman that's only half as old.

Over the hill to the poor-house—I can't quite make it clear!
Over the hill to the poor-house—it seems so horrid queer!
Many a step I've taken a-toiling to and fro,
But this is a sort of journey I never thought to go.

What is the use of heapin' on me a pauper's shame?
Am I lazy or crazy? Am I blind or lame?
True, I am not so supple, nor yet so awful stout;
But charity ain't no favor, if one can live without.

I am willin' and anxious an' ready any day

To work for a decent livin', an' pay my honest way;
For I can earn my victuals, an' more too, I'll be bound,
If anybody only is willin' to have me round.

Once I was young an' han'some—I was upon my soul—
Once my cheeks was roses, my eyes as black as coal;
And I can't remember, in them days, of hearin' people say,
For any kind of a reason, that I was in their way.

'Tain't no use of boastin', or talkin' over-free,
But many a house an' home was open then to me;
Many a han'some offer I had from likely men,
And nobody ever hinted that I was a burden then.

And when to John I was married, sure he was good and smart,
But he and all the neighbors would own I done my part;
For life was all before me, an' I was young an' strong,
And I worked the best that I could in tryin' to get along.

And so we worked together: and life was hard, but gay,
With now and then a baby for to cheer us on our way;
Till we had half a dozen, an' all growed clean an' neat,
An' went to school like others, an' had enough to eat.

So we worked for the childr'n, and raised 'em every one,
Worked for 'em summer and winter just as we ought to 've done;
Only, perhaps, we humored 'em, which some good folks condemn—
But every couple's childr'n's a heap the best to them.

Strange how much we think of our blessed little ones!
I'd have died for my daughters, I'd have died for my sons;
And God he made that rule of love; but when we're old and gray,
I've noticed it sometimes, somehow, fails to work the other way.

Strange, another thing: when our boys an' girls was grown,
And when, exceptin' Charley, they'd left us there alone;
When John he nearer an' nearer come, an' dearer seemed to be,
The Lord of Hosts he come one day, an' took him away from me.

Still I was bound to struggle, an' never to cringe or fall—
Still I worked for Charley, for Charley was now my all;
And Charley was pretty good to me, with scarce a word or frown,
Till at last he went a-courtin', and brought a wife from town.

She was somewhat dressy, an' hadn't a pleasant smile—
She was quite conceity, and carried a heap o' style;
But if ever I tried to be friends, I did with her, I know;
But she was hard and proud, an' I couldn't make it go.

She had an edication, an' that was good for her;
But when she twitted me on mine 'twas carryin' things too fur;
An' I told her once, 'fore company (an it almost made her sick),

That I never swallowed a grammar, or eat a 'rithmetic.

So 'twas only a few days before the thing was done—
They was a family of themselves, and I another one;
And a very little cottage one family will do,
But I never have seen a house that was big enough for two.

An' I never could speak to suit her, never could please her eye,
An' it made me independent, an' then I didn't try;
But I was terribly staggered, an' felt it like a blow,
When Charley turn'd agin me, an' told me I could go.

I went to live with Susan, but Susan's house was small,
And she was always a-hintin' how snug it was for us all;
And what with her husband's sisters, and what with childr'n three,
'Twas easy to discover that there wasn't room for me.

An' then I went to Thomas, the oldest son I've got,
For Thomas's buildings 'd cover the half of an acre lot;
But all the childr'n was on me—I couldn't stand their sauce—
And Thomas said I needn't think I was comin' there to boss.

An' then I wrote Rebecca, my girl who lives out West,
And to Isaac, not far from her—some twenty miles, at best;
And one of 'em said 'twas too warm there for any one so old,
And t'other had an opinion the climate was too cold.

So they have shirked and slighted me, an' shifted me about—
So they have well-nigh soured me, an' wore my old heart out;
But still I've borne up pretty well, an' wasn't much put down,
Till Charley went to the poor-master, an' put me on the town.

Over the hill to the poor-house—my childr'n dear, good-by!
Many a night I've watched you when only God was nigh;
And God'll judge between us; but I will always pray
That you shall never suffer the half I do to-day.

Will Carleton.

The American Flag

When Freedom from her mountain height
Unfurled her standard to the air,
She tore the azure robe of night,
And set the stars of glory there.
She mingled with its gorgeous dyes
The milky baldric of the skies,
And striped its pure celestial white
With streakings of the morning light;
Then from his mansion in the sun
She called her eagle bearer down,
And gave into his mighty hand
The symbol of her chosen land.

Majestic monarch of the cloud,
Who rear'st aloft thy regal form,
To hear the tempest trumpings loud
And see the lightning lances driven,
When strive the warriors of the storm,
And rolls the thunder-drum of heaven,
Child of the sun! to thee 'tis given
To guard the banner of the free,
To hover in the sulphur smoke,
To ward away the battle stroke,
And bid its blendings shine afar,
Like rainbows on the cloud of war,
The harbingers of victory!

Flag of the brave! thy folds shall fly,
The sign of hope and triumph high,
When speaks the signal trumpet tone,
And the long line comes gleaming on.
Ere yet the lifeblood, warm and wet,
Has dimmed the glistening bayonet,
Each soldier eye shall brightly turn
To where thy sky-born glories burn,
And, as his springing steps advance,
Catch war and vengeance from the glance.

And when the cannon-mouthings loud
Heave in wild wreaths the battle shroud,
And gory sabres rise and fall
Like shoots of flame on midnight's pall,
Then shall thy meteor glances glow,
And cowering foes shall shrink beneath
Each gallant arm that strikes below
That lovely messenger of death.

Flag of the seas! on ocean wave
Thy stars shall glitter o'er the brave;
When death, careering on the gale,
Sweeps darkly 'round the bellied sail,
And frighted waves rush wildly back
Before the broadside's reeling rack,
Each dying wanderer of the sea
Shall look at once to heaven and thee,
And smile to see thy splendors fly
In triumph o'er his closing eye.

Flag of the free heart's hope and home!
By angel hands to valor given;
Thy stars have lit the welkin dome,
And all thy hues were born in heaven.
Forever float that standard sheet!
Where breathes the foe but falls before us,
With Freedom's soil beneath our feet,
And Freedom's banner streaming o'er us?

Joseph Rodman Drake.

Golden Keys

A bunch of golden keys is mine
To make each day with gladness shine

"Good morning!" that's the golden key
That unlocks every door for me.

When evening comes, "Good night!" I say,
And close the door of each glad day.

When at the table "If you please"
I take from off my bunch of keys.

When friends give anything to me,
I'll use the little "Thank you" key.

"Excuse me," "Beg your pardon," too
When by mistake some harm I do.

Or if unkindly harm I've given,
With "Forgive me" key I'll be forgiven

On a golden ring these keys I'll bind,
This is its motto: "Be ye kind."

I'll often use each golden key,
And so a happy child I'll be.

The Four-leaf Clover

I know a place where the sun is like gold,
And the cherry blooms burst like snow;
And down underneath is the loveliest nook,
Where the four-leaf clovers grow.

One leaf is for faith, and one is for hope,
And one is for love, you know;
And God put another one in for luck—
If you search, you will find where they grow.

But you must have faith and you must have hope,
You must love and be strong, and so
If you work, if you wait, you will find the place
Where the four-leaf clovers grow.

Ella Higginson.

Telling the Bees

NOTE: A remarkable custom, brought from the Old Country, formerly prevailed in the rural districts of New England. On the death of a member of the family, the bees were at once informed of the event, and their hives dressed in mourning. This ceremonial was supposed to be necessary to prevent the swarms from leaving their hives and seeking a new home.

Here is the place; right over the hill
Runs the path I took;
You can see the gap in the old wall still.
And the stepping-stones in the shallow brook.

There is the house, with the gate red-barred,
And the poplars tall;
And the barn's brown length, and the cattle-yard,
And the white horns tossing above the wall.

There are the beehives ranged in the sun;
And down by the brink
Of the brook are her poor flowers, weed-o'errun,
Pansy and daffodil, rose and pink.

A year has gone, as the tortoise goes,
Heavy and slow;
And the same rose blows, and the same sun glows,
And the same brook sings of a year ago.

There's the same sweet clover-smell in the breeze;
And the June sun warm
Tangles his wings of fire in the trees,
Setting, as then, over Fernside farm.

I mind me how with a lover's care
From my Sunday coat
I brushed off the burs, and smoothed my hair,
And cooled at the brookside my brow and throat.

Since we parted, a month had passed,—
To love, a year;
Down through the beeches I looked at last
On the little red gate and the well-sweep near.

I can see it all now,—the slantwise rain
Of light through the leaves,
The sundown's blaze on her window-pane,
The bloom of her roses under the eaves.

Just the same as a month before,—
The house and the trees,
The barn's brown gable, the vine by the door,—
Nothing changed but the hives of bees.

Before them, under the garden wall,
Forward and back,
Went drearily singing the chore-girl small,
Draping each hive with a shred of black.

Trembling, I listened; the summer sun
Had the chill of snow;
For I knew she was telling the bees of one
Gone on the journey we all must go!

Then I said to myself, "My Mary weeps
For the dead to-day:
Haply her blind grandsire sleeps
The fret and pain of his age away."

But her dog whined low; on the door-way sill,
With his cane to his chin,
The old man sat; and the chore-girl still
Sung to the bees stealing out and in.

And the song she was singing ever
since
In my ear sounds on:—
"Stay at home, pretty bees, fly not
hence!
Mistress Mary is dead and gone!"

John G. Whittier.

"Not Understood"

Not understood, we move along asunder,
Our paths grow wider as the seasons creep
Along the years. We marvel and we wonder,
Why life is life, and then we fall asleep,
Not understood.

Not understood, we gather false impressions,
And hug them closer as the years go by,
Till virtues often seem to us transgressions;
And thus men rise and fall and live and die,
Not understood.

Not understood, poor souls with stunted visions
Often measure giants by their narrow gauge;
The poisoned shafts of falsehood and derision
Are oft impelled 'gainst those who mould the age,
Not understood.

Not understood, the secret springs of action
Which lie beneath the surface and the show
Are disregarded; with self-satisfaction
We judge our neighbors, and they often go
Not understood.

Not understood, how trifles often change us—
The thoughtless sentence or the fancied slight—
Destroy long years of friendship and estrange us,
And on our souls there falls a freezing blight—
Not understood.

Not understood, how many hearts are aching
For lack of sympathy! Ah! day by day
How many cheerless, lonely hearts are breaking,
How many noble spirits pass away
Not understood.

O God! that men would see a little clearer,
Or judge less hardly when they cannot see!
O God! that men would draw a little nearer
To one another! They'd be nearer Thee,
And understood.

Somebody's Mother

The woman was old, and ragged, and gray,
And bent with the chill of a winter's day;
The streets were white with a recent snow,
And the woman's feet with age were slow.

At the crowded crossing she waited long,
Jostled aside by the careless throng
Of human beings who passed her by,
Unheeding the glance of her anxious eye.

Down the street with laughter and shout,
Glad in the freedom of "school let out,"
Come happy boys, like a flock of sheep,
Hailing the snow piled white and deep;
Past the woman, so old and gray,
Hastened the children on their way.

None offered a helping hand to her,
So weak and timid, afraid to stir,
Lest the carriage wheels or the horses' feet
Should trample her down in the slippery street.

At last came out of the merry troop
The gayest boy of all the group;
He paused beside her, and whispered low,
"I'll help you across, if you wish to go."

Her aged hand on his strong young arm
She placed, and so without hurt or harm,
He guided the trembling feet along,
Proud that his own were young and strong;
Then back again to his friends he went,
His young heart happy and well content.

"She's somebody's mother, boys, you know,
For all she's aged, and poor, and slow;
And some one, some time, may lend a hand
To help my mother—you understand?—
If ever she's poor, and old, and gray,
And her own dear boy is far away."

"Somebody's mother" bowed low her head,
In her home that night, and the prayer she said
Was: "God, be kind to that noble boy,
Who is somebody's son, and pride and joy."

Faint was the voice, and worn and weak,
But the Father hears when His children speak;
Angels caught the faltering word,
And "Somebody's Mother's" prayer was heard.

To a Waterfowl

Whither, midst falling dew,
While glow the heavens with the last steps of day,
Far, through their rosy depths, dost thou pursue
Thy solitary way?

Vainly the fowler's eye
Might mark thy distant flight to do thee wrong,
As, darkly seen against the crimson sky,
Thy figure floats along.

Seek'st thou the plashy brink
Of weedy lake, or marge of river wide,
Or where the rocking billows rise and sink
On the chafed ocean-side?

There is a Power whose care
Teaches thy way along that pathless coast—
The desert and illimitable air—
Lone wandering, but not lost.

All day thy wings have fanned,
At that far height, the cold, thin atmosphere;

Yet stoop not, weary, to the welcome land,
Though the dark night is near.

And soon that toil shall end;
Soon shalt thou find a summer home, and rest,
And scream among thy fellows; reeds shall bend,
Soon, o'er thy sheltered nest.

Thou'rt gone, the abyss of heaven
Hath swallowed up thy form; yet, on my heart
Deeply hath sunk the lesson thou hast given,
And shall not soon depart.

He who, from zone to zone,
Guides through the boundless sky thy certain flight,
In the long way that I must tread alone,
Will lead my steps aright.

William Cullen Bryant.

My Mother

Who fed me from her gentle breast
And hushed me in her arms to rest,
And on my cheek sweet kisses prest?
My mother.

When sleep forsook my open eye,
Who was it sung sweet lullaby
And rocked me that I should not cry?
My mother.

Who sat and watched my infant head
When sleeping in my cradle bed,
And tears of sweet affection shed?
My mother.

When pain and sickness made me cry,
Who gazed upon my heavy eye,
And wept, for fear that I should die?
My mother.

Who ran to help me when I fell
And would some pretty story tell,
Or kiss the part to make it well?
My mother.

Who taught my infant lips to pray,
To love God's holy word and day,
And walk in wisdom's pleasant way?
My mother.

And can I ever cease to be
Affectionate and kind to thee
Who wast so very kind to me,—
My mother.

Oh, no, the thought I cannot bear;
And if God please my life to spare
I hope I shall reward thy care,
My mother.

When thou art feeble, old and gray,
My healthy arms shall be thy stay,
And I will soothe thy pains away,
My mother.

And when I see thee hang thy head,
'Twill be my turn to watch thy bed,
And tears of sweet affection shed,—
My mother.

The Walrus and the Carpenter

The sun was shining on the sea,
Shining with all his might:
He did his very best to make
The billows smooth and bright—
And this was odd, because it was
The middle of the night.

The moon was shining sulkily,
Because she thought the sun
Had got no business to be there
After the day was done—
"It's very rude of him," she said,
"To come and spoil the fun!"

The sea was wet as wet could be,
The sands were dry as dry.
You could not see a cloud, because

No cloud was in the sky:
No birds were flying overhead—
There were no birds to fly.

The Walrus and the Carpenter
Were walking close at hand:
They wept like anything to see
Such quantities of sand:
"If this were only cleared away,"
They said, "it would be grand!"

"If seven maids with seven mops
Swept it for half a year,
Do you suppose," the Walrus said,
"That they could get it clear?"
"I doubt it," said the Carpenter,
And shed a bitter tear.

"O Oysters, come and walk with us!"
The Walrus did beseech.
"A pleasant walk, a pleasant talk,
Along the briny beach:
We cannot do with more than four,
To give a hand to each."

The eldest Oyster looked at him,
But never a word he said:
The eldest Oyster winked his eye,
And shook his heavy head—
Meaning to say he did not choose
To leave the oyster-bed.

But four young Oysters hurried up,
All eager for the treat:
Their coats were brushed, their faces washed,
Their shoes were clean and neat—
And this was odd, because, you know,
They hadn't any feet.

Four other Oysters followed them,
And yet another four;
And thick and fast they came at last,
And more, and more, and more—
All hopping through the frothy waves,
And scrambling to the shore.

The Walrus and the Carpenter
Walked on a mile or so,
And then they rested on a rock
Conveniently low:
And all the little Oysters stood
And waited in a row.

"The time has come," the Walrus said,
"To talk of many things:
Of shoes—and ships—and sealing-wax—
Of cabbages and kings—
And why the sea is boiling hot—
And whether pigs have wings."

"But wait a bit," the Oysters cried,
"Before we have our chat;
For some of us are out of breath,
And all of us are fat!"
"No hurry!" said the Carpenter.
They thanked him much for that.

"A loaf of bread," the Walrus said,
"Is what we chiefly need:
Pepper and vinegar besides
Are very good indeed—
Now, if you're ready, Oysters dear,
We can begin to feed."

"But not on us!" the Oysters cried,
Turning a little blue.
"After such kindness, that would be
A dismal thing to do!"
"The night is fine," the Walrus said,
"Do you admire the view?

"It was so kind of you to come!
And you are very nice!"
The Carpenter said nothing but
"Cut us another slice.
I wish you were not quite so deaf—
I've had to ask you twice!"

"It seems a shame," the Walrus said,
"To play them such a trick.
After we've brought them out so far,

And made them trot so quick!"
The Carpenter said nothing but
"The butter's spread too thick!"

"I weep for you," the Walrus said:
"I deeply sympathize."
With sobs and tears he sorted out
Those of the largest size,
Holding his pocket-handkerchief
Before his streaming eyes.

"O Oysters," said the Carpenter,
"You've had a pleasant run!
Shall we be trotting home again?"
But answer came there none—
And this was scarcely odd, because
They'd eaten every one.

Lewis Carroll.

The Teacher's Dream

The weary teacher sat alone
While twilight gathered on:
And not a sound was heard around,—
The boys and girls were gone.

The weary teacher sat alone;
Unnerved and pale was he;
Bowed 'neath a yoke of care, he spoke
In sad soliloquy:

"Another round, another round
Of labor thrown away,
Another chain of toil and pain
Dragged through a tedious day.

"Of no avail is constant zeal,
Love's sacrifice is lost,
The hopes of morn, so golden, turn,
Each evening, into dross.
"I squander on a barren field
My strength, my life, my all:

The seeds I sow will never grow,—
They perish where they fall."
He sighed, and low upon his hands
His aching brow he pressed;
And o'er his frame ere long there came
A soothing sense of rest.

And then he lifted up his face,
But started back aghast,—
The room, by strange and sudden change,
Assumed proportions vast.

It seemed a Senate-hall, and one
Addressed a listening throng;
Each burning word all bosoms stirred,
Applause rose loud and long.

The 'wildered teacher thought he knew
The speaker's voice and look,
"And for his name," said he, "the same
Is in my record book."

The stately Senate-hall dissolved,
A church rose in its place,
Wherein there stood a man of God,
Dispensing words of grace.

And though he spoke in solemn tone,
And though his hair was gray,
The teacher's thought was strangely wrought—
"I whipped that boy to-day."

The church, a phantom, vanished soon;
What saw the teacher then?
In classic gloom of alcoved room
An author plied his pen.

"My idlest lad!" the teacher said,
Filled with a new surprise;
"Shall I behold his name enrolled
Among the great and wise?"

The vision of a cottage home
The teacher now descried;
A mother's face illumed the place
Her influence sanctified.

"A miracle! a miracle!
This matron, well I know,

Was but a wild and careless child,
  Not half an hour ago.

"And when she to her children speaks
  Of duty's golden rule,
Her lips repeat in accents sweet,
  My words to her at school."

The scene was changed again, and lo!
  The schoolhouse rude and old;
Upon the wall did darkness fall,
  The evening air was cold.

"A dream!" the sleeper, waking, said,
  Then paced along the floor,
And, whistling slow and soft and low,
  He locked the schoolhouse door.

And, walking home, his heart was full
  Of peace and trust and praise;
And singing slow and soft and low,
  Said, "After many days."

W. H. Venable.

A Legend of Bregenz

Girt round with rugged mountains, the fair Lake Constance lies;
In her blue heart reflected shine back the starry skies;
And watching each white cloudlet float silently and slow,
You think a piece of heaven lies on our earth below!

Midnight is there: and silence, enthroned in heaven, looks down
Upon her own calm mirror, upon a sleeping town:
For Bregenz, that quaint city upon the Tyrol shore,
Has stood above Lake Constance a thousand years and more.

Her battlement and towers, from off their rocky steep,
Have cast their trembling shadow for ages on the deep;
Mountain, and lake, and valley, a sacred legend know,
Of how the town was saved, one night three hundred years ago.

Far from her home and kindred, a Tyrol maid had fled,
To serve in the Swiss valleys, and toil for daily bread;
And every year that fleeted so silently and fast,
Seemed to bear farther from her the memory of the past.

She served kind, gentle masters, nor asked for rest or change;
Her friends seemed no more new ones, their speech seemed no more strange;
And when she led her cattle to pasture every day,
She ceased to look and wonder on which side Bregenz lay.

She spoke no more of Bregenz, with longing and with tears;
Her Tyrol home seemed faded in a deep mist of years;
She heeded not the rumors of Austrian war and strife;
Each day she rose, contented, to the calm toils of life.

Yet when her master's children would clustering round her stand,
She sang them ancient ballads of her own native land;
And when at morn and evening she knelt before God's throne,
The accents of her childhood rose to her lips alone.

And so she dwelt: the valley more peaceful year by year;
When suddenly strange portents of some great deed seemed near.

The golden corn was bending upon its fragile stock,
While farmers, heedless of their fields, paced up and down in talk.

The men seemed stern and altered, with looks cast on the ground;
With anxious faces, one by one, the women gathered round;
All talk of flax, or spinning, or work, was put away;
The very children seemed afraid to go alone to play.

One day, out in the meadow with strangers from the town,
Some secret plan discussing, the men walked up and down.
Yet now and then seemed watching a strange uncertain gleam,
That looked like lances 'mid the trees that stood below the stream.

At eve they all assembled, then care and doubt were fled;
With jovial laugh they feasted, the board was nobly spread.
The elder of the village rose up, his glass in hand,
And cried, "We drink the downfall of an accursed land!

"The night is growing darker,—ere one more day is flown,
Bregenz, our foeman's stronghold, Bregenz shall be our own!"
The women shrank in terror, (yet Pride, too, had her part,)
But one poor Tyrol maiden felt death within her heart.

Before her stood fair Bregenz, once more her towers arose;
What were the friends beside her? Only her country's foes!
The faces of her kinsfolk, the days of childhood flown,
The echoes of her mountains, reclaimed her as their own!

Nothing she heard around her, (though shouts rang forth again,)
Gone were the green Swiss valleys, the pasture, and the plain;
Before her eyes one vision, and in her heart one cry,
That said, "Go forth, save Bregenz, and then, if need be, die!"

With trembling haste and breathless, with noiseless step, she sped;
Horses and weary cattle were standing in the shed;
She loosed the strong white charger, that fed from out her hand,
She mounted, and she turned his head towards her native land.

Out—out into the darkness—faster, and still more fast;
The smooth grass flies behind her, the chestnut wood is past;
She looks up; clouds are heavy: Why is her steed so slow?—
Scarcely the wind beside them can pass them as they go.

"Faster!" she cries. "Oh, faster!" Eleven the church-bells chime;
"O God," she cries, "help Bregenz, and bring me there in time!"
But louder than bells' ringing, or lowing of the kine,
Grows nearer in the midnight the rushing of the Rhine.

Shall not the roaring waters their headlong gallop check?
The steed draws back in terror, she leans upon his neck
To watch the flowing darkness,—the bank is high and steep;
One pause—he staggers forward, and plunges in the deep.

She strives to pierce the blackness, and looser throws the rein;
Her steed must breast the waters that dash above his mane.
How gallantly, how nobly, he struggles through the foam,
And see—in the far distance shine out the lights of home!

Up the steep bank he bears her, and now they rush again
Toward the heights of Bregenz, that tower above the plain.
They reach the gate of Bregenz, just as the midnight rings,
And out come serf and soldier to meet the news she brings.

Bregenz is saved! Ere daylight her battlements are manned;
Defiance greets the army that marches on the land.
And if to deeds heroic should endless fame be paid,
Bregenz does well to honor the noble Tyrol maid.

Three hundred years are vanished, and yet upon the hill
An old stone gateway rises, to do her honor still.
And there, when Bregenz women sit spinning in the shade,
They see in quaint old carving the charger and the maid.

And when, to guard old Bregenz, by gateway, street, and tower,
The warder paces all night long, and calls each passing hour:
"Nine," "ten," "eleven," he cries aloud, and then (O crown of fame!)
When midnight pauses in the skies he calls the maiden's name!

Adelaide A. Procter.

Better Than Gold

Better than grandeur, better than gold,
Than rank and title a thousand fold,
Is a healthy body, a mind at ease,
And simple pleasures that always please;
A heart that can feel for a neighbor's woe
And share his joys with a genial glow,—
With sympathies large enough to enfold
All men as brothers,—is better than gold.

Better than gold is a conscience clear,
Though toiling for bread in an humble sphere:
Doubly blest with content and health,
Untried by the lusts or cares of wealth.
Lowly living and lofty thought
Adorn and ennoble a poor man's cot;
For mind and morals, in Nature's plan,
Are the genuine test of a gentleman.

Better than gold is the sweet repose
Of the sons of toil when their labors close;
Better than gold is the poor man's sleep,
And the balm that drops on his slumbers deep.
Bring sleeping draughts to the downy bed,
Where luxury pillows his aching head;
His simple opiate labor deems
A shorter road to the land of dreams.

Better than gold is a thinking mind
That in the realm of books can find
A treasure surpassing Australian ore,
And live with the great and good of yore.
The sage's lore and the poet's lay,
The glories of empires pass'd away,

The world's great drama will thus unfold
And yield a pleasure better than gold.

Better than gold is a peaceful home,
Where all the fireside charities come;—
The shrine of love and the heaven of life,
Hallowed by mother, or sister, or wife.
However humble the home may be,
Or tried with sorrow by Heaven's decree,
The blessings that never were bought or sold,
And center there, are better than gold.

Alexander Smart.

October's Bright Blue Weather

O suns and skies and clouds of June,
And flowers of June together,
Ye cannot rival for one hour
October's bright blue weather;

When loud the bumblebee makes haste,
Belated, thriftless vagrant,
And goldenrod is dying fast,
And lanes with grapes are fragrant;

When gentians roll their fringes tight
To save them for the morning,
And chestnuts fall from satin burrs
Without a sound of warning;

When on the ground red apples lie
In piles like jewels shining,
And redder still on old stone walls
Are leaves of woodbine twining;

When all the lovely wayside things
Their white-winged seeds are sowing,
And in the fields, still green and fair,
Late aftermaths are growing;

When springs run low, and on the brooks,
In idle, golden freighting,
Bright leaves sink noiseless in the hush
Of woods, for winter waiting;

When comrades seek sweet country haunts,
By twos and threes together,
And count like misers hour by hour,
October's bright blue weather.

O suns and skies and flowers of June,
Count all your boasts together,
Love loveth best of all the year
October's bright blue weather.

Helen Hunt Jackson.

Brier-Rose

Said Brier-Rose's mother to the naughty Brier-Rose:
"What *will* become of you, my child, the Lord Almighty knows.
You will not scrub the kettles, and you will not touch the broom;
You never sit a minute still at spinning-wheel or loom."

Thus grumbled in the morning, and grumbled late at eve,
The good-wife as she bustled with pot and tray and sieve;
But Brier-Rose, she laughed and she cocked her dainty head:
"Why, I shall marry, mother dear," full merrily she said.

"*You* marry; saucy Brier-Rose! The man, he is not found
To marry such a worthless wench, these seven leagues around."
But Brier-Rose, she laughed and she trilled a merry lay:
"Perhaps he'll come, my mother dear, from eight leagues away."

The good-wife with a "humph" and a sigh forsook the battle,
And flung her pots and pails about with much vindictive rattle:

"O Lord, what sin did I commit in youthful days, and wild,
That thou hast punished me in age with such a wayward child?"

Up stole the girl on tiptoe, so that none her step could hear,
And laughing pressed an airy kiss behind the good-wife's ear.
And she, as e'er relenting, sighed: "Oh, Heaven only knows
Whatever will become of you, my naughty Brier-Rose!"

The sun was high and summer sounds were teeming in the air;
The clank of scythes, the cricket's whir, and swelling woodnotes rare,
From fields and copse and meadow; and through the open door
Sweet, fragrant whiffs of new-mown hay the idle breezes bore.

Then Brier-Rose grew pensive, like a bird of thoughtful mien,
Whose little life has problems among the branches green.
She heard the river brawling where the tide was swift and strong,
She heard the summer singing its strange, alluring song.

And out she skipped the meadows o'er and gazed into the sky;
Her heart o'erbrimmed with gladness, she scarce herself knew why,
And to a merry tune she hummed, "Oh, Heaven only knows
Whatever will become of the naughty Brier-Rose!"

Whene'er a thrifty matron this idle maid espied,
She shook her head in warning, and scarce her wrath could hide;
For girls were made for housewives, for spinning-wheel and loom,
And not to drink the sunshine and wild flower's sweet perfume.

And oft the maidens cried, when the Brier-Rose went by,
"You cannot knit a stocking, and you cannot make a pie."
But Brier-Rose, as was her wont, she cocked her curly head:
"But I can sing a pretty song," full merrily she said.

And oft the young lads shouted, when they saw the maid at play:
"Ho, good-for-nothing Brier-Rose, how do you do to-day?"
Then she shook her tiny fist; to her cheeks the color flew:
"However much you coax me, I'll *never* dance with you."

Thus flew the years light winged over Brier-Rose's head,
Till she was twenty summers old and yet remained unwed.
And all the parish wondered: "The Lord Almighty knows
Whatever will become of that naughty Brier-Rose!"

And while they wondered came the spring a-dancing o'er the hills;
Her breath was warmer than of yore, and all the mountain rills,
With their tinkling and their rippling and their rushing, filled the air,
And the misty sounds of water forth-welling everywhere.

And in the valley's depth, like a lusty beast of prey,
The river leaped and roared aloud and tossed its mane of spray;

Then hushed again its voice to a softly plashing croon,
As dark it rolled beneath the sun and white beneath the moon.

It was a merry sight to see the lumber as it whirled
Adown the tawny eddies that hissed and seethed and swirled,
Now shooting through the rapids and, with a reeling swing,
Into the foam-crests diving like an animated thing.

But in the narrows of the rocks, where o'er a steep incline
The waters plunged, and wreathed in foam the dark boughs of the pine,
The lads kept watch with shout and song, and sent each straggling beam
A-spinning down the rapids, lest it should lock the stream.

And yet—methinks I hear it now—wild voices in the night,
A rush of feet, a dog's harsh bark, a torch's flaring light,
And wandering gusts of dampness, and round us far and nigh,
A throbbing boom of water like a pulse-beat in the sky.

The dawn just pierced the pallid east with spears of gold and red,
As we, with boat-hooks in our hands, toward the narrows sped.
And terror smote us; for we heard the mighty tree-tops sway,
And thunder, as of chariots, and hissing showers of spray.

"Now, lads," the sheriff shouted, "you are strong, like Norway's rock:
A hundred crowns I give to him who breaks the lumber lock!
For if another hour go by, the angry waters' spoil
Our homes will be, and fields, and our weary years of toil."

We looked each at the other; each hoped his neighbor would
Brave death and danger for his home, as valiant Norsemen should.
But at our feet the brawling tide expanded like a lake,
And whirling beams came shooting on, and made the firm rock quake.

"Two hundred crowns!" the sheriff cried, and breathless stood the crowd.
"Two hundred crowns, my bonny lads!" in anxious tones and loud.
But not a man came forward, and no one spoke or stirred,
And nothing save the thunder of the cataract was heard.

But as with trembling hands and with fainting hearts we stood,
We spied a little curly head emerging from the wood.
We heard a little snatch of a merry little song,
And saw the dainty Brier-Rose come dancing through the throng.

An angry murmur rose from the people round about.
"Fling her into the river," we heard the matrons shout;
"Chase her away, the silly thing; for God himself scarce knows
Why ever he created that worthless Brier-Rose."

Sweet Brier-Rose, she heard their cries; a little pensive smile
Across her fair face flitted that might a stone beguile;

And then she gave her pretty head a
roguish little cock:
"Hand me a boat-hook, lads," she said;
"I think I'll break the lock."

Derisive shouts of laughter broke from
throats of young and old:
"Ho! good-for-nothing Brier-Rose, your
tongue was ever bold."
And, mockingly, a boat-hook into her
hands was flung,
When, lo! into the river's midst with
daring leaps she sprung!

We saw her dimly through a mist of
dense and blinding spray;
From beam to beam she skipped, like
a water-sprite at play.
And now and then faint gleams we
caught of color through the mist:
A crimson waist, a golden head, a little
dainty wrist.

In terror pressed the people to the margin of the hill,
A hundred breaths were bated, a hundred hearts stood still.
For, hark! from out the rapids came a
strange and creaking sound,
And then a crash of thunder which
shook the very ground.

The waters hurled the lumber mass
down o'er the rocky steep.
We heard a muffled rumbling and a
rolling in the deep;
We saw a tiny form which the torrent
swiftly bore
And flung into the wild abyss, where
it was seen no more.

Ah, little naughty Brier-Rose, thou
couldst not weave nor spin;
Yet thou couldst do a nobler deed than
all thy mocking kin;
For thou hadst courage e'en to die, and
by thy death to save
A thousand farms and lives from the
fury of the wave.

And yet the adage lives, in the valley
of thy birth,
When wayward children spend their
days in heedless play and mirth,
Oft mothers say, half smiling, half
sighing, "Heaven knows
Whatever will become of the naughty
Brier-Rose!"

Hjalmar Hjorth Boyesen.

King Robert of Sicily

Robert of Sicily, brother of Pope Urbane
And Valmond, Emperor of Allemaine,
Appareled in magnificent attire
With retinue of many a knight and
squire,
On St. John's eve, at vespers, proudly
sat
And heard the priests chant the Magnificat.
And as he listened, o'er and o'er again
Repeated, like a burden or refrain,
He caught the words, "*Deposuit potentes*
De sede, et exaltavit humiles";
And slowly lifting up his kingly head,
He to a learned clerk beside him said,
"What mean those words?" The clerk
made answer meet,
"He has put down the mighty from
their seat,
And has exalted them of low degree."
Thereat King Robert muttered scornfully,
" 'Tis well that such seditious words
are sung
Only by priests, and in the Latin
tongue;
For unto priests, and people be it
known,

There is no power can push me from my throne,"
And leaning back he yawned and fell asleep,
Lulled by the chant monotonous and deep.

When he awoke, it was already night;
The church was empty, and there was no light,
Save where the lamps, that glimmered few and faint,
Lighted a little space before some saint.
He started from his seat and gazed around,
But saw no living thing and heard no sound.
He groped towards the door, but it was locked;
He cried aloud, and listened, and then knocked,
And uttered awful threatenings and complaints,
And imprecations upon men and saints.
The sounds re-echoed from the roof and walls
As if dead priests were laughing in their stalls.

At length the sexton, hearing from without
The tumult of the knocking and the shout,
And thinking thieves were in the house of prayer,
Came with his lantern, asking, "Who is there?"
Half choked with rage, King Robert fiercely said,
"Open; 'tis I, the king! Art thou afraid?"
The frightened sexton, muttering with a curse,
"This is some drunken vagabond, or worse!"
Turned the great key and flung the portal wide;
A man rushed by him at a single stride,
Haggard, half-naked, without hat or cloak,
Who neither turned, nor looked at him, nor spoke,
But leaped into the blackness of the night,
And vanished like a spectre from his sight.

Robert of Sicily, brother of Pope Urbane
And Valmond, Emperor of Allemaine,
Despoiled of his magnificent attire,
Bare-headed, breathless, and besprent with mire,
With sense of wrong and outrage desperate,
Strode on and thundered at the palace gate;
Rushed through the court-yard, thrusting in his rage
To right and left each seneschal and page,
And hurried up the broad and sounding stair,
His white face ghastly in the torches' glare.
From hall to hall he passed with breathless speed;
Voices and cries he heard, but did not heed,
Until at last he reached the banquet-room,
Blazing with light, and breathing with perfume.

There on the dais sat another king,
Wearing his robes, his crown, his signet ring—
King Robert's self in features, form, and height,
But all transfigured with angelic light!

It was an angel; and his presence there
With a divine effulgence filled the air,
An exaltation, piercing the disguise,
Though none the hidden angel recognize.

A moment speechless, motionless, amazed,
The throneless monarch on the angel gazed,
Who met his look of anger and surprise
With the divine compassion of his eyes!
Then said, "Who art thou, and why com'st thou here?"
To which King Robert answered with a sneer,
"I am the king, and come to claim my own
From an impostor, who usurps my throne!"
And suddenly, at these audacious words,
Up sprang the angry guests, and drew their swords;
The angel answered with unruffled brow,
"Nay, not the king, but the king's jester; thou
Henceforth shalt wear the bells and scalloped cape
And for thy counselor shalt lead an ape;
Thou shalt obey my servants when they call,
And wait upon my henchmen in the hall!"

Deaf to King Robert's threats and cries and prayers,
They thrust him from the hall and down the stairs;
A group of tittering pages ran before,
And as they opened wide the folding door,
His heart failed, for he heard, with strange alarms,
The boisterous laughter of the men-at-arms,
And all the vaulted chamber roar and ring
With the mock plaudits of "Long live the king!"

Next morning, waking with the day's first beam,
He said within himself, "It was a dream!"
But the straw rustled as he turned his head,
There were the cap and bells beside his bed;
Around him rose the bare, discolored walls,
Close by, the steeds were champing in their stalls,
And in the corner, a revolting shape,
Shivering and chattering, sat the wretched ape.
It was no dream; the world he loved so much
Had turned to dust and ashes at his touch!

Days came and went; and now returned again
To Sicily the old Saturnian reign;
Under the angel's governance benign
The happy island danced with corn and wine,
And deep within the mountain's burning breast
Enceladus, the giant, was at rest.

Meanwhile King Robert yielded to his fate,
Sullen and silent and disconsolate.
Dressed in the motley garb that jesters wear,

With look bewildered, and a vacant stare,
Close shaven above the ears, as monks are shorn,
By courtiers mocked, by pages laughed to scorn,
His only friend the ape, his only food
What others left—he still was unsubdued.
And when the angel met him on his way,
And half in earnest, half in jest, would say,
Sternly, though tenderly, that he might feel
The velvet scabbard held a sword of steel,
"Art thou the king?" the passion of his woe
Burst from him in resistless overflow,
And lifting high his forehead, he would fling
The haughty answer back, "I am, I am the king!"

Almost three years were ended, when there came
Ambassadors of great repute and name
From Valmond, Emperor of Allemaine,
Unto King Robert, saying that Pope Urbane
By letter summoned them forthwith to come
On Holy Thursday to his City of Rome.
The angel with great joy received his guests,
And gave them presents of embroidered vests,
And velvet mantles with rich ermine lined,
And rings and jewels of the rarest kind.
Then he departed with them o'er the sea
Into the lovely land of Italy,
Whose loveliness was more resplendent made
By the mere passing of that cavalcade
With plumes, and cloaks, and housings, and the stir
Of jeweled bridle and of golden spur.

And lo! among the menials, in mock state,
Upon a piebald steed, with shambling gait,
His cloak of foxtails flapping in the wind,
The solemn ape demurely perched behind,
King Robert rode, making huge merriment
In all the country towns through which they went.

The Pope received them with great pomp, and blare
Of bannered trumpets, on St. Peter's Square,
Giving his benediction and embrace,
Fervent, and full of apostolic grace.
While with congratulations and with prayers
He entertained the angel unawares,
Robert, the jester, bursting through the crowd,
Into their presence rushed, and cried aloud:
"I am the king! Look and behold in me
Robert, your brother, King of Sicily!
This man, who wears my semblance to your eyes,
Is an impostor in a king's disguise.
Do you not know me? Does no voice within
Answer my cry, and say we are akin?"
The Pope in silence, but with troubled mien,
Gazed at the angel's countenance serene;

The Emperor, laughing, said, "It is strange sport
To keep a mad man for thy fool at court!"
And the poor, baffled jester, in disgrace
Was hustled back among the populace.

In solemn state the holy week went by,
And Easter Sunday gleamed upon the sky;
The presence of the angel, with its light,
Before the sun rose, made the city bright,
And with new fervor filled the hearts of men,
Who felt that Christ indeed had risen again.
Even the jester, on his bed of straw,
With haggard eyes the unwonted splendor saw;
He felt within a power unfelt before,
And kneeling humbly on his chamber floor,
He heard the rustling garments of the Lord
Sweep through the silent air, ascending heavenward.

And now the visit ending, and once more
Valmond returning to the Danube's shore,
Homeward the angel journeyed, and again
The land was made resplendent with his train,
Flashing along the towns of Italy
Unto Salerno, and from thence by sea.
And when once more within Palermo's wall,
And, seated on the throne in his great hall,
He heard the Angelus from convent towers,
As if the better world conversed with ours,
He beckoned to King Robert to draw nigher,
And with a gesture bade the rest retire.
And when they were alone, the angel said,
"Art thou the king?" Then, bowing down his head,
King Robert crossed both hands upon his breast,
And meekly answered him, "Thou knowest best!
My sins as scarlet are; let me go hence,
And in some cloister's school of penitence,
Across those stones that pave the way to heaven
Walk barefoot till my guilty soul be shriven!"

The angel smiled, and from his radiant face
A holy light illumined all the place,
And through the open window, loud and clear,
They heard the monks chant in the chapel near,
Above the stir and tumult of the street,
"He has put down the mighty from their seat,
And has exalted them of low degree!"
And through the chant a second melody
Rose like the throbbing of a single string:
"I am an angel, and thou art the king!"

King Robert, who was standing near the throne,
Lifted his eyes, and lo! he was alone!
But all appareled as in days of old,

With ermined mantle and with cloth of gold;
And when his courtiers came they found him there,
Kneeling upon the floor, absorbed in silent prayer. *H. W. Longfellow.*

The Huskers

It was late in mild October, and the long autumnal rain
Had left the summer harvest-fields all green with grass again;
The first sharp frosts had fallen, leaving all the woodlands gay
With the hues of summer's rainbow, or the meadow-flowers of May.

Through a thin, dry mist, that morning, the sun rose broad and red,
At first a rayless disk of fire, he brightened as he sped;
Yet, even his noontide glory fell chastened and subdued,
On the cornfields and the orchards, and softly pictured wood.

And all that quiet afternoon, slow sloping to the night,
He wove with golden shuttle the haze with yellow light;
Slanting through the painted beeches, he glorified the hill;
And beneath it, pond and meadow lay brighter, greener still.

And shouting boys in woodland haunts caught glimpses of that sky,
Flecked by the many-tinted leaves, and laughed, they knew not why;
And schoolgirls, gay with aster-flowers, beside the meadow brooks,
Mingled the glow of autumn with the sunshine of sweet looks.

From spire and ball looked westerly the patient weathercock,
But even the birches on the hill stood motionless as rocks.
No sound was in the woodlands, save the squirrel's dropping shell,
And the yellow leaves among the boughs, low rustling as they fell.

The summer grains were harvested; the stubble-fields lay dry,
Where June winds rolled, in light and shade, the pale green waves of rye;
But still, on gentle hill-slopes, in valleys fringed with wood,
Ungathered, bleaching in the sun, the heavy corn crop stood.

Bent low, by autumn's wind and rain, through husks that, dry and sere,
Unfolded by their ripened charge, shone out the yellow ear;
Beneath, the turnip lay concealed, in many a verdant fold,
And glistened in the slanting light the pumpkin's sphere of gold.

There wrought the busy harvesters; and many a creaking wain
Bore slowly to the long barn-floor its load of husk and grain;
Till broad and red, as when he rose, the sun sank down, at last,
And like a merry guest's farewell, the day in brightness passed.

And lo! as through the western pines on meadow, stream, and pond,
Flamed the red radiance of a sky, set all afire beyond,
Slowly o'er the eastern sea-bluffs a milder glory shone,
And the sunset and the moonrise were mingled into one!

As thus into the quiet night the twilight lapsed away,
And deeper in the brightening moon the tranquil shadows lay;

From many a brown old farm-house, and hamlet without name,
Their milking and their home-tasks done, the merry huskers came.

Swung o'er the heaped-up harvest, from pitchforks in the mow,
Shone dimly down the lanterns on the pleasant scene below;
The growing pile of husks behind, the golden ears before,
And laughing eyes and busy hands and brown cheeks glimmering o'er.

Half hidden in a quiet nook, serene of look and heart,
Talking their old times over, the old men sat apart;
While, up and down the unhusked pile, or nestling in its shade,
At hide-and-seek, with laugh and shout, the happy children played.

Urged by the good host's daughter, a maiden young and fair,
Lifting to light her sweet blue eyes and pride of soft brown hair,
The master of the village school, sleek of hair and smooth of tongue,
To the quaint tune of some old psalm, a husking-ballad sung.

John G. Whittier.

Darius Green and His Flying Machine

If ever there lived a Yankee lad,
Wise or otherwise, good or bad,
Who, seeing the birds fly, didn't jump
With flapping arms from stake or stump,
Or, spreading the tail
Of his coat for a sail,
Take a soaring leap from post or rail,
And wonder why
He couldn't fly,
And flap and flutter and wish and try—
If ever you knew a country dunce
Who didn't try that as often as once,
All I can say is, that's a sign
He never would do for a hero of mine.

An aspiring genius was D. Green:
The son of a farmer,—age fourteen;
His body was long and lank and lean,—
Just right for flying, as will be seen;
He had two eyes, each bright as a bean,
And a freckled nose that grew between,
A little awry,—for I must mention
That he had riveted his attention
Upon his wonderful invention,
Twisting his tongue as he twisted the strings,
Working his face as he worked the wings,
And with every turn of gimlet and screw
Turning and screwing his mouth round, too,
Till his nose seemed bent
To catch the scent,
Around some corner, of new-baked pies,
And his wrinkled cheeks and his squinting eyes
Grew puckered into a queer grimace,
That made him look very droll in the face,
And also very wise.

And wise he must have been, to do more
Than ever a genius did before,
Excepting Dædalus of yore
And his son Icarus, who wore
Upon their backs
Those wings of wax
He had read of in the old almanacs.
Darius was clearly of the opinion
That the air is also man's dominion,
And that, with paddle or fin or pinion,
We soon or late

Shall navigate
The azure as now we sail the sea.
The thing looks simple enough to me;
And if you doubt it,
Hear how Darius reasoned about it.

"Birds can fly,
An' why can't I?
Must we give in,"
Says he with a grin,
" 'T the bluebird an' phœbe
Are smarter'n we be?
Jest fold our hands an' see the swaller,
An' blackbird an' catbird beat us holler?
Does the leetle, chatterin', sassy wren,
No bigger'n my thumb, know more than men?
Jest show me that!
Er prove 't the bat
Has got more brains than's in my hat,
An' I'll back down, an' not till then!"

He argued further: "Ner I can't see
What's th' use o' wings to a bumblebee,
Fer to git a livin' with, more'n to me;—
Ain't my business
Important's his'n is?
That Icarus
Was a silly cuss,—
Him an' his daddy Dædalus.
They might 'a' knowed wings made o' wax
Wouldn't stan' sun-heat an' hard whacks.
I'll make mine o' luther,
Er suthin' er other."

And he said to himself, as he tinkered and planned:
"But I ain't goin' to show my hand
To mummies that never can understand
The fust idee that's big an' grand.
They'd 'a' laft an' made fun
O' Creation itself afore 't was done!"
So he kept his secret from all the rest
Safely buttoned within his vest;
And in the loft above the shed
Himself he locks, with thimble and thread
And wax and hammer and buckles and screws,
And all such things as geniuses use;—
Two bats for patterns, curious fellows!
A charcoal-pot and a pair of bellows;
An old hoop-skirt or two, as well as
Some wire and several old umbrellas;
A carriage-cover, for tail and wings;
A piece of harness; and straps and strings;
And a big strong box,
In which he locks
These and a hundred other things.

His grinning brothers, Reuben and Burke
And Nathan and Jotham and Solomon, lurk
Around the corner to see him work,—
Sitting cross-legged, like a Turk,
Drawing the waxed end through with a jerk,
And boring the holes with a comical quirk
Of his wise old head, and a knowing smirk.
But vainly they mounted each other's backs,
And poked through knot-holes and pried through cracks;
With wood from the pile and straw from the stacks
He plugged the knot-holes and calked the cracks;
And a bucket of water, which one would think
He had brought up into the loft to drink
When he chanced to be dry,
Stood always nigh,
For Darius was sly!

And whenever at work he happened to spy
At chink or crevice a blinking eye,
He let a dipper of water fly.
"Take that! an' ef ever ye get a peep,
Guess ye'll ketch a weasel asleep!"
And he sings as he locks
His big strong box:—

"The weasel's head is small an' trim,
An' he is leetle an' long an' slim,
An' quick of motion an' nimble of limb,
An' ef yeou'll be
Advised by me
Keep wide awake when ye're ketchin' him!"
So day after day
He stitched and tinkered and hammered away,
Till at last 'twas done,—
The greatest invention under the sun!
"An' now," says Darius, "hooray fer some fun!"

'Twas the Fourth of July,
And the weather was dry,
And not a cloud was on all the sky,
Save a few light fleeces, which here and there,
Half mist, half air,
Like foam on the ocean went floating by:
Just as lovely a morning as ever was seen
For a nice little trip in a flying-machine.

Thought cunning Darius: "Now I sha'n't go
Along 'ith the fellers to see the show.
I'll say I've got sich a terrible cough!
An' then, when the folks 'ave all gone off
I'll hev full swing
For to try the thing,
An' practyse a leetle on the wing."

"Ain't goin' to see the celebration?"
Says Brother Nate. "No; botheration!
I've got sich a cold—a toothache—I—
My gracious!—feel's though I should fly!"

Said Jotham, "Sho!
Guess ye better go."
But Darius said, "No!
Shouldn't wonder 'f yeou might see me, though,
'Long 'bout noon, ef I git red
O' this jumpin', thumpin' pain 'n my head."
For all the while to himself he said:—
"I'll tell ye what!
I'll fly a few times around the lot,
To see how 't seems, then soon's I've got
The hang o' the thing, ez likely's not,
I'll astonish the nation,
And all creation,
By flyin' over the celebration!
Over their heads I'll sail like an eagle;
I'll balance myself on my wings like a sea-gull;
I'll dance on the chimbleys; I'll stan' on the steeple;
I'll flop up to winders an' scare the people!
I'll light on the libbe'ty-pole, an' crow;
An' I'll say to the gawpin' fools below,
'What world's this 'ere
That I've come near?'
Fer I'll make 'em believe I'm a chap f'm the moon!
An' I'll try a race 'ith their ol' bulloon."
He crept from his bed;
And, seeing the others were gone, he said,
I'm a-gittin' over the cold 'n my head."
And away he sped,
To open the wonderful box in the shed.

His brothers had walked but a little way
When Jotham to Nathan chanced to say,
"What on airth is he up to, hey?"
"Don'o,—the' 's suthin' er other to pay,
Er he wouldn't 'a' stayed to hum to-day."
Says Burke, "His toothache's all 'n his eye!
He never'd miss a Fo'th-o'-July,
Ef he hedn't some machine to try.
Le's hurry back and hide in the barn,
An' pay him fer tellin' us that yarn!"
"Agreed!" Through the orchard they creep back,
Along by the fences, behind the stack,
And one by one, through a hole in the wall,
In under the dusty barn they crawl,
Dressed in their Sunday garments all;
And a very astonishing sight was that,
When each in his cobwebbed coat and hat
Came up through the floor like an ancient rat.
And there they hid;
And Reuben slid
The fastenings back, and the door undid.
"Keep dark!" said he,
"While I squint an' see what the' is to see."

As knights of old put on their mail,—
From head to foot
An iron suit,
Iron jacket and iron boot,
Iron breeches, and on the head
No hat, but an iron pot instead,
And under the chin the bail,—
I believe they called the thing a helm;
And the lid they carried they called a shield;
And, thus accoutred, they took the field,
Sallying forth to overwhelm
The dragons and pagans that plagued the realm:—
So this modern knight
Prepared for flight,
Put on his wings and strapped them tight;
Jointed and jaunty, strong and light;
Buckled them fast to shoulder and hip,—
Ten feet they measured from tip to tip!
And a helm had he, but that he wore,
Not on his head like those of yore,
But more like the helm of a ship.

"Hush!" Reuben said,
"He's up in the shed!
He's opened the winder,—I see his head!
He stretches it out,
An' pokes it about,
Lookin' to see 'f the coast is clear,
An' nobody near;—
Guess he don'o' who's hid in here!
He's riggin' a spring-board over the sill!
Stop laffin', Solomon! Burke, keep still!
He's a climbin' out now—of all the things!
What's he got on? I van, it's wings!
An' that t'other thing? I vum, it's a tail!
An' there he sets like a hawk on a rail!
Steppin' careful, he travels the length
Of his spring-board, and teeters to try its strength.
Now he stretches his wings, like a monstrous bat;
Peeks over his shoulder, this way an' that,
Fer to see 'f the' 's anyone passin' by;
But the' 's on'y a ca'f an' a goslin' nigh.
They turn up at him a wonderin' eye,
To see—The dragon! he's goin' to fly!
Away he goes! Jimminy! what a jump!

Flop—flop—an' plump
To the ground with a thump!
Flutt'rin an' flound'rin', all in a lump!"

As a demon is hurled by an angel's spear,
Heels over head, to his proper sphere,—
Heels over head, and head over heels,
Dizzily down the abyss he wheels,—
So fell Darius. Upon his crown,
In the midst of the barnyard, he came down,
In a wonderful whirl of tangled strings,
Broken braces and broken springs,
Broken tail and broken wings,
Shooting-stars, and various things!
Away with a bellow fled the calf,
And what was that? Did the gosling laugh?
'Tis a merry roar
From the old barn-door,
And he hears the voice of Jotham crying,
"Say, D'rius! how de yeou like flyin'?
Slowly, ruefully, where he lay,
Darius just turned and looked that way,
As he stanched his sorrowful nose with his cuff.
"Wall, I like flyin' well enough,"
He said; "but the' ain't sich a thunderin' sight
O' fun in 't when ye come to light."

MORAL

I just have room for the moral here:
And this is the moral,—Stick to your sphere.
Or if you insist, as you have the right,
On spreading your wings for a loftier flight,
The moral is,—Take care how you light.

John T. Trowbridge.

Song of the Shirt

With fingers weary and worn,
With eyelids heavy and red,
A woman sat, in unwomanly rags,
Plying her needle and thread—
Stitch! stitch! stitch!
In poverty, hunger and dirt,
And still with a voice of dolorous pitch
She sang the "Song of the Shirt!"

"Work! work! work!
While the cock is crowing aloof!
And work—work—work,
Till the stars shine through the roof!
It's oh! to be a slave
Along with the barbarous Turk,
Where a woman has never a soul to save,
If this is Christian work!

"Work—work—work,
Till the brain begins to swim;
Work—work—work,
Till the eyes are heavy and dim!
Seam, and gusset, and band,
Band, and gusset, and seam,
Till over the buttons I fall asleep,
And sew them on in a dream!

"O men, with sisters dear!
O men, with mothers and wives!
It is not linen you're wearing out,
But human creatures' lives!
Stitch—stitch—stitch!
In poverty, hunger, and dirt,—
Sewing at once, with a double thread,
A shroud as well as a shirt!

"But why do I talk of Death,—
That phantom of grisly bone?
I hardly fear his terrible shape,
It seems so like my own,—
It seems so like my own,
Because of the fasts I keep;
O God! that bread should be so dear,
And flesh and blood so cheap!

"Work! work! work!
My labor never flags;
And what are its wages? A bed of straw,
A crust of bread—and rags,
That shattered roof—this naked floor—
A table—a broken chair—
And a wall so blank, my shadow I thank
For sometimes falling there!

"Work—work—work!
From weary chime to chime!
Work—work—work!
As prisoners work for crime!
Band, and gusset, and seam,
Seam, and gusset, and band,—
Till the heart is sick and the brain benumbed,
As well as the weary hand.

"Work—work—work!
In the dull December light!
And work—work—work!
When the weather is warm and bright!
While underneath the eaves
The brooding swallows cling,
As if to show me their sunny backs,
And twit me with the spring.

"Oh, but to breathe the breath
Of the cowslip and primrose sweet,—
With the sky above my head,
And the grass beneath my feet!
For only one short hour
To feel as I used to feel,
Before I knew the woes of want
And the walk that costs a meal!

"Oh, but for one short hour,—
A respite, however brief!
No blessed leisure for love or hope,
But only time for grief!
A little weeping would ease my heart;
But in their briny bed
My tears must stop, for every drop
Hinders needle and thread!"

With fingers weary and worn,
With eyelids heavy and red,
A woman sat, in unwomanly rags,
Plying her needle and thread,—
Stitch! stitch! stitch!
In poverty, hunger and dirt;
And still with a voice of dolorous pitch—
Would that its tone could reach the rich!—
She sang this "Song of the Shirt."

Thomas Hood.

Christmas Everywhere

Everywhere, everywhere, Christmas to-night!
Christmas in lands of the fir-tree and pine,
Christmas in lands of the palm-tree and vine,
Christmas where snow-peaks stand solemn and white,
Christmas where corn-fields lie sunny and bright,
Everywhere, everywhere, Christmas to-night!

Christmas where children are hopeful and gay,
Christmas where old men are patient and gray,
Christmas where peace, like a dove in its flight,
Broods o'er brave men in the thick of the fight;
Everywhere, everywhere, Christmas to-night!

For the Christ-child who comes is the Master of all,
No palace too great and no cottage too small,

The angels who welcome Him sing from the height:
"In the city of David, a King in his might."
Everywhere, everywhere, Christmas to-night!

Then let every heart keep its Christmas within,
Christ's pity for sorrow, Christ's hatred of sin,
Christ's care for the weakest, Christ's courage for right,
Christ's dread of the darkness, Christ's love of the light.
Everywhere, everywhere, Christmas to-night!

So the stars of the midnight which compass us round
Shall see a strange glory, and hear a sweet sound,
And cry, "Look! the earth is aflame with delight,
O sons of the morning, rejoice at the sight."
Everywhere, everywhere, Christmas to-night!

Phillips Brooks.

The Cloud

I bring fresh showers for the thirsting flowers,
From the seas and the streams;
I bear light shade for the leaves when laid
In their noon-day dreams.
From my wings are shaken the dews that waken
The sweet buds every one,
When rocked to rest on their mother's breast,
As she dances about the sun.
I wield the flail of the lashing hail,
And whiten the green plains under,
And then again I dissolve it in rain,
And laugh as I pass in thunder.

I sift the snow on the mountains below,
And their great pines groan aghast;
And all the night 'tis my pillow white,
While I sleep in the arms of the blast.
Sublime on the towers of my skyey bowers,
Lightning my pilot sits,
In a cavern under is fettered the thunder,
It struggles and howls at fits;
Over earth and ocean, with gentle motion,
This pilot is guiding me,
Lured by the love of the genii that move
In the depths of the purple sea;
Over the rills, and the crags, and the hills,
Over the lakes and the plains,
Wherever he dream, under mountain or stream,
The Spirit he loves remains;
And I all the while bask in heaven's blue smile,
Whilst he is dissolving in rains.

The sanguine sunrise, with his meteor eyes,
And his burning plumes outspread,
Leaps on the back of my sailing rack,
When the morning star shines dead;
As on the jag of a mountain crag,
Which an earthquake rocks and swings,
An eagle alit one moment may sit
In the light of its golden wings.
And when sunset may breathe, from the lit sea beneath,
Its ardors of rest and of love,
And the crimson pall of eve may fall
From the depth of heaven above,
With wings folded I rest, on mine airy nest,
As still as a brooding dove.

That orbed maiden, with white fire laden,
Whom mortals call the moon,
Glides glimmering o'er my fleece-like floor,
By the midnight breezes strewn;
And wherever the beat of her unseen feet,
Which only the angels hear,
May have broken the woof of my tent's thin roof,
The stars peep behind her and peer;
And I laugh to see them whirl and flee,
Like a swarm of golden bees,
When I widen the rent in my windbuilt tent,
Till the calm rivers, lakes, and seas,
Like strips of the sky fallen thro' me on high,
Are each paved with the moon and these.

I bind the sun's throne with a burning zone,
And the moon's with a girdle of pearl;
The volcanoes are dim, and the stars reel and swim,
When the whirlwinds my banner unfurl.
From cape to cape, with a bridge-like shape,
Over a torrent sea,
Sunbeam-proof, I hang like a roof,
The mountains its columns be.
The triumphal arch thro' which I march,
With hurricane, fire, and snow,
When the powers of the air are chained to my chair,
Is the million-colored bow;
The sphere-fire above its soft colors wove,
Whilst the moist earth was laughing below.

I am the daughter of earth and water,
And the nursling of the sky;
I pass thro' the pores of the ocean and shores;
I change, but I cannot die.
For after the rain, when with never a stain
The pavilion of heaven is bare,
And the winds and sunbeams with their convex gleams
Build up the blue dome of air,
I silently laugh at my own cenotaph,
And out of the caverns of rain,
Like a child from the womb, like a ghost from the tomb,
I arise and unbuild it again.

Percy Bysshe Shelley.

To a Skylark

Hail to thee, blithe spirit!
Bird thou never wert,
That from heaven, or near it,
Pourest thy full heart
In profuse strains of unpremeditated art.

Higher still and higher
From the earth thou springest
Like a cloud of fire;
The blue deep thou wingest,
And singing still dost soar, and soaring ever singest.

In the golden lightning
of the sunken sun,
O'er which clouds are bright'ning,
Thou dost float and run,
Like an unbodied joy whose race is just begun.

The pale purple even
Melts around thy flight;
Like a star of heaven,
In the broad daylight
Thou art unseen, but yet I hear thy shrill delight:

Keen as are the arrows
Of that silver sphere
Whose intense lamp narrows
In the white dawn clear,
Until we hardly see, we feel, that it is there.

All the earth and air
With thy voice is loud,
As, when night is bare,
From one lonely cloud
The moon rains out her beams, and heaven is overflowed.

What thou art we know not;
What is most like thee?
From rainbow clouds there flow not
Drops so bright to see,
As from thy presence showers a rain of melody:—

Like a poet hidden
In the light of thought,
Singing hymns unbidden,
Till the world is wrought
To sympathy with hopes and fears it heeded not:

Like a high-born maiden
In a palace-tower,
Soothing her love-laden
Soul in secret hour
With music sweet as love, which overflows her bower:

Like a glow-worm golden
In a dell of dew,
Scattering unbeholden
Its aerial hue
Among the flowers and grass, which screen it from the view:

Like a rose embowered
In its own green leaves,
By warm winds deflowered,
Till the scent it gives
Makes faint with too much sweet these heavy-winged thieves:

Sound of vernal showers
On the twinkling grass,
Rain-awakened flowers,
All that ever was
Joyous, and clear, and fresh, thy music doth surpass.

Teach us, sprite or bird,
What sweet thoughts are thine:
I have never heard
Praise of love or wine
That panted forth a flood of rapture so divine.

Chorus Hymeneal,
Or triumphal chaunt,
Matched with thine would be all
But an empty vaunt,
A thing wherein we feel there is some hidden want.

What objects are the fountains
Of thy happy strain?
What fields, or waves, or mountains?
What shapes of sky or plain?
What love of thine own kind? what ignorance of pain?

With thy clear keen joyance
Languor cannot be:
Shadow of annoyance
Never came near thee:
Thou lovest: but ne'er knew love's sad satiety.

Waking or asleep,
Thou of death must deem
Things more true and deep
Than we mortals dream,
Or how could thy notes flow in such a crystal stream?

We look before and after
And pine for what is not:
Our sincerest laughter
With some pain is fraught;
Our sweetest songs are those that tell of saddest thought.

Yet if we could scorn
Hate, and pride, and fear;
If we were things born
Not to a shed a tear,
I know not how thy joy we ever should come near.

Better than all measures
Of delightful sound,
Better than all treasures
That in books are found,
Thy skill to poet were, thou scorner of the ground!

Teach me half the gladness
That thy brain must know,
Such harmonious madness
From my lips would flow,
The world should listen then, as I am listening now.

Percy Bysshe Shelley.

The Brook

I come from haunts of coot and hern,
I make a sudden sally,
And sparkle out among the fern,
To bicker down a valley.

By thirty hills I hurry down,
Or slip between the ridges,
By twenty thorps, a little town,
And half a hundred bridges.

Till last by Philip's farm I flow
To join the brimming river,
For men may come and men may go,
But I go on forever.

I chatter over stony ways,
In little sharps and trebles,
I bubble into eddying bays,
I babble on the pebbles.

With many a curve my banks I fret
By many a field and fallow,
And many a fairy foreland set
With willow-weed and mallow.

I chatter, chatter as I flow
To join the brimming river,
For men may come and men may go,
But I go on forever.

I wind about, and in and out,
With here a blossom sailing,
And here and there a lusty trout,
And here and there a grayling,

And here and there a foamy flake
Upon me as I travel
With many a silvery waterbreak
Above the golden gravel,

And draw them all along, and flow
To join the brimming river,
For men may come and men may go,
But I go on forever.

I steal by lawns and grassy plots,
I slide by hazel covers;
I move the sweet forget-me-nots
That grow for happy lovers.

I slip, I slide, I gloom, I glance,
Among my skimming swallows;
I make the netted sunbeam dance
Against my sandy shallows.

I murmur under moon and stars,
In brambly wildernesses;
I linger by my shingly bars;
I loiter round my cresses;

And out again I curve and flow
To join the brimming river,
For men may come and men may go,
But I go on forever.

Alfred, Lord Tennyson.

June

(From "The Vision of Sir Launfal")

No price is set on the lavish summer,
June may be had by the poorest comer.

And what is so rare as a day in June?
Then, if ever, come perfect days;
Then Heaven tries earth if it be in tune,
And over it softly her warm ear lays;
Whether we look, or whether we listen,
We hear life murmur, or see it glisten;
Every clod feels a stir of might,
An instinct within it that reaches and towers,
And, groping blindly above it for light,
Climbs to a soul in grass and flowers;
The flush of life may well be seen
Thrilling back over hills and valleys;
The cowslip startles in meadows green,
The buttercup catches the sun in its chalice,
And there's never a leaf nor a blade too mean
To be some happy creature's palace;
The little bird sits at his door in the sun,
Atilt like a blossom among the leaves,
And lets his illumined being o'errun
With the deluge of summer it receives;
His mate feels the eggs beneath her wings,
And the heart in her dumb breast flutters and sings;
He sings to the wide world, and she to her nest,—
In the nice ear of Nature, which song is the best?

Now is the high-tide of the year,
And whatever of life hath ebbed away
Comes flooding back, with a ripply cheer,
Into every bare inlet and creek and bay;
Now the heart is so full that a drop overfills it,
We are happy now because God wills it;
No matter how barren the past may have been,
'T is enough for us now that the leaves are green;
We sit in the warm shade and feel right well
How the sap creeps up and the blossoms swell;
We may shut our eyes, but we cannot help knowing
That skies are clear and grass is growing;
The breeze comes whispering in our ear,
That dandelions are blossoming near,
That maize has sprouted, that streams are flowing,
That the river is bluer than the sky,
That the robin is plastering his house hard by;
And if the breeze kept the good news back,
For other couriers we should not lack;
We could guess it all by yon heifer's lowing,—
And hark! how clear bold chanticleer,
Warmed with the new wine of the year,
Tells all in his lusty crowing!

Joy comes, grief goes, we know not how;
Everything is happy now,
Everything is upward striving;
'T is as easy now for the heart to be true
As for grass to be green or skies to be blue,—
'T is the natural way of living.

Who knows whither the clouds have fled?
In the unscarred heaven they leave no wake,
And the eyes forget the tears they have shed,
The heart forgets its sorrow and ache;
The soul partakes the season's youth,
And the sulphurous rifts of passion and woe
Lie deep 'neath a silence pure and smooth,
Like burnt-out craters healed with snow.

James Russell Lowell.

The Planting of the Apple-Tree

Come, let us plant the apple-tree.
Cleave the tough greensward with the spade;
Wide let its hollow bed be made;
There gently lay the roots, and there
Sift the dark mould with kindly care,
And press it o'er them tenderly,
As round the sleeping infant's feet
We softly fold the cradle-sheet;
So plant we the apple tree.

What plant we in this apple-tree?
Buds, which the breath of summer days
Shall lengthen into leafy sprays;
Boughs where the thrush with crimson breast
Shall haunt, and sing, and hide her nest;
We plant, upon the sunny lea,
A shadow for the noontide hour,
A shelter from the summer shower,
When we plant the apple-tree.

What plant we in this apple-tree?
Sweets for a hundred flowery springs,
To load the May-wind's restless wings,
When, from the orchard row, he pours
Its fragrance through our open doors;
A world of blossoms for the bee,
Flowers for the sick girl's silent room,
For the glad infant sprigs of bloom,
We plant with the apple-tree.

What plant we in this apple-tree?
Fruits that shall swell in sunny June,
And redden in the August noon,
And drop, when gentle airs come by,
That fan the blue September sky.
While children come, with cries of glee,
And seek them where the fragrant grass
Betrays their bed to those who pass,
At the foot of the apple tree.

And when, above this apple tree,
The winter stars are quivering bright,
And winds go howling through the night,
Girls, whose young eyes o'erflow with mirth,
Shall peel its fruit by cottage hearth,
And guests in prouder homes shall see,
Heaped with the grape of Cintra's vine
And golden orange of the Line,
The fruit of the apple-tree.

The fruitage of this apple-tree
Winds, and our flag of stripe and sta[r]
Shall bear to coasts that lie afar,
Where men shall wonder at the view,
And ask in what fair groves they grew
And sojourners beyond the sea
Shall think of childhood's careless da[y]
And long, long hours of summer play,
In the shade of the apple-tree.

Each year shall give this apple-tre[e]
A broader flush of roseate bloom,
A deeper maze of verdurous gloom,
And loosen, when the frost-cloud[s]
lower,
The crisp brown leaves in thicke[r]
shower.

The years shall come and pass, but we
Shall hear no longer, where we lie,
The summer's songs, the autumn's sigh,
In the boughs of the apple-tree.

And time shall waste this apple tree.
Oh, when its aged branches throw
Thin shadows on the ground below,
Shall fraud and force and iron will
Oppress the weak and helpless still?
What shall the tasks of mercy be,
Amid the toils, the strifes, the tears
Of those who live when length of years
Is wasting this apple-tree?

"Who planted this old apple-tree?"
The children of that distant day
Thus to some aged man shall say;
And, gazing on its mossy stem,
The gray-haired man shall answer them:
"A poet of the land was he,
Born in the rude but good old times;
'Tis said he made some quaint old rhymes
On planting the apple-tree."

William Cullen Bryant.

Character of the Happy Warrior

Who is the happy Warrior? Who is he
That every man in arms should wish to be?
—It is the generous Spirit, who, when brought
Among the tasks of real life, hath wrought
Upon the plan that pleased his boyish thought:
Whose high endeavors are an inward light
That makes the path before him always bright:
Who, with a natural instinct to discern
What knowledge can perform, is diligent to learn;
Abides by this resolve, and stops not there,
But makes his moral being his prime care;
Who, doomed to go in company with Pain,
And Fear, and Bloodshed, miserable train!
Turns his necessity to glorious gain;
In face of these doth exercise a power
Which is our human nature's highest dower;
Controls them and subdues, transmutes, bereaves
Of their bad influence, and their good receives:
By objects, which might force the soul to abate
Her feeling, rendered more compassionate;
Is placable—because occasions rise
So often that demand such sacrifice;
More skillful in self-knowledge, even more pure,
As tempted more; more able to endure,
As more exposed to suffering and distress;
Thence also, more alive to tenderness.
—'Tis he whose law is reason; who depends
Upon that law as on the best of friends;
Whence, in a state where men are tempted still
To evil for a guard against worse ill,
And what in quality or act is best
Doth seldom on a right foundation rest,
He labors good on good to fix, and owes
To virtue every triumph that he knows:
—Who, if he rise to station of command,
Rises by open means; and there will stand
On honorable terms, or else retire,
And in himself possess his own desire;
Who comprehends his trust, and to the same

Keeps faithful with a singleness of aim;
And therefore does not stoop, nor lie in wait
For wealth, or honors, or for worldly state;
Whom they must follow; on whose head must fall,
Like showers of manna, if they come at all:
Whose powers shed round him in the common strife,
Or mild concerns of ordinary life,
A constant influence, a peculiar grace;
But who, if he be called upon to face
Some awful moment to which Heaven has joined
Great issues, good or bad for human kind,
Is happy as a Lover; and attired
With sudden brightness, like a Man inspired;
And, through the heat of conflict, keeps the law
In calmness made, and sees what he foresaw;
Or if an unexpected call succeed,
Come when it will, is equal to the need:
—He who, though thus endued as with a sense
And faculty for storm and turbulence,
Is yet a Soul whose master-bias leans
To homefelt pleasures and to gentle scenes;
Sweet images! which, wheresoe'er he be,
Are at his heart; and such fidelity
It is his darling passion to approve;
More brave for this, that he hath much to love:—
'Tis, finally, the Man who lifted high,
Conspicuous object in a Nation's eye,
Or left unthought-of in obscurity,—
Who, with a toward or untoward lot,
Prosperous or adverse, to his wish or not—
Plays, in the many games of life, that one
Where what he most doth value must be won:
Whom neither shape of danger can dismay,
Nor thought of tender happiness betray;
Who, not content that former worth stand fast,
Looks forward, persevering to the last,
From well to better, daily self-surpast:
Who, whether praise of him must walk the earth
Forever, and to noble deeds give birth,
Or he must fall, to sleep without his fame,
And leave a dead unprofitable name—
Finds comfort in himself and in his cause;
And, while the mortal mist is gathering, draws
His breath in confidence of Heaven's applause:
This is the happy Warrior; this is He
That every Man in arms should wish to be.

William Wordsworth.

The Charge of the Light Brigade

Half a league, half a league,
Half a league onward,
All in the valley of Death
Rode the six hundred.
"Forward, the Light Brigade!
Charge for the guns," he said:
Into the valley of Death
Rode the six hundred.

"Forward, the Light Brigade!"
Was there a man dismay'd?
Not tho' the soldier knew
Some one had blunder'd:
Theirs not to make reply,

Theirs not to reason why,
Theirs but to do and die:
Into the valley of Death
  Rode the six hundred.

Cannon to right of them,
Cannon to left of them,
Cannon in front of them
  Volley'd and thunder'd;
Storm'd at with shot and shell,
Boldly they rode and well,
Into the jaws of Death,
Into the mouth of Hell
  Rode the six hundred.

Flash'd all their sabres bare,
Flash'd as they turn'd in air,
Sabring the gunners there,
Charging an army, while
  All the world wonder'd:
Plung'd in the battery-smoke
Right thro' the line they broke;
Cossack and Russian
Reel'd from the sabre-stroke
  Shatter'd and sunder'd.
Then they rode back, but not,—
  Not the six hundred.

Cannon to right of them,
Cannon to left of them,
Cannon behind them
  Volley'd and thunder'd;
Storm'd at with shot and shell,
While horse and hero fell,
They that had fought so well
Came thro' the jaws of Death,
Back from the mouth of Hell,
All that was left of them,
  Left of six hundred.

When can their glory fade?
O the wild charge they made!
  All the world wonder'd.
Honor the charge they made!
Honor the Light Brigade,
  Noble six hundred!

Alfred, Lord Tennyson.

Sheridan's Ride

October 19, 1864

Up from the South at break of day,
Bringing to Winchester fresh dismay,
The affrighted air with a shudder bore,
Like a herald in haste, to the chieftain's door,
The terrible grumble, and rumble, and roar,
Telling the battle was on once more,
And Sheridan—twenty miles away.

And wider still those billows of war
Thundered along the horizon's bar;
And louder yet into Winchester rolled
The roar of that red sea uncontrolled,
Making the blood of the listener cold
As he thought of the stake in that fiery fray,
And Sheridan—twenty miles away.

But there is a road from Winchester town,
A good broad highway leading down;
And there, through the flush of the morning light,
A steed, as black as the steeds of night,
Was seen to pass, as with eagle flight;
As if he knew the terrible need,
He stretched away with the utmost speed;
Hills rose and fell—but his heart was gay,
With Sheridan fifteen miles away.

Still sprung from those swift hoofs, thundering South,
The dust, like smoke from the cannon's mouth;
Or the trail of a comet, sweeping faster and faster,
Foreboding to foemen the doom of disaster.
The heart of the steed and the heart of the master

Were beating like prisoners assaulting
their walls,
Impatient to be where the battle-field
calls;
Every nerve of the charger was
strained to full play,
With Sheridan only ten miles away.

Under his spurning feet the road
Like an arrowy Alpine river flowed,
And the landscape sped away behind
Like an ocean flying before the wind;
And the steed, like a bark fed with
furnace ire,
Swept on, with his wild eyes full of fire.
But lo! he is nearing his heart's de-
sire—
He is snuffing the smoke of the roaring
fray,
With Sheridan only five miles away.

The first that the General saw were
the groups
Of stragglers, and then the retreating
troops.
What was done? what to do? a glance
told him both,
Then striking his spurs, with a terrible
oath,
He dashed down the line 'mid a storm
of huzzas,
And the wave of retreat checked its
course there, because
The sight of the master compelled it to
pause.
With foam and with dust the black
charger was gray;
By the flash of his eye and the red nos-
tril's play
He seemed to the whole great army to
say,
"I have brought you Sheridan all the
way
From Winchester down to save the
day!"

Hurrah, hurrah for Sheridan!
Hurrah, hurrah for horse and man!
And when their statues are placed on
high,
Under the dome of the Union sky—
The American soldier's Temple of
Fame—
There, with the glorious General's
name,
Be it said in letters both bold and
bright:
"Here is the steed that saved the
day,
By carrying Sheridan into the fight,
From Winchester—twenty miles
away!"

Thomas Buchanan Read.

O Little Town of Bethlehem

O little town of Bethlehem,
How still we see thee lie!
Above thy deep and dreamless sleep
The silent stars go by;
Yet in thy dark streets shineth
The everlasting Light;
The hopes and fears of all the years
Are met in thee to-night.

For Christ is born of Mary,
And, gathered all above,
While mortals sleep, the angels keep
Their watch of wondering love.
O morning stars, together
Proclaim the holy birth!
And praises sing to God the King,
And peace to men on earth.

How silently, how silently,
The wondrous gift is given!
So God imparts to human hearts
The blessings of His heaven.
No ear may hear His coming,
But in this world of sin,
Where meek souls will receive Him
still,
The dear Christ enters in.

O holy Child of Bethlehem!
Descend to us, we pray;
Cast out our sin, and enter in,
Be born in us to-day.
We hear the Christmas angels
The great glad tidings tell;
Oh, come to us, abide with us,
Our Lord Emmanuel!

Phillips Brooks.

The Chambered Nautilus

This is the ship of pearl, which, poets feign,
Sails the unshadowed main,—
The venturous bark that flings
On the sweet summer wind its purpled wings
In gulfs enchanted, where the Siren sings,
And coral reefs lie bare,
Where the cold sea-maids rise to sun their streaming hair.

Its webs of living gauze no more unfurl;
Wrecked is the ship of pearl!
And every chambered cell,
Where its dim dreaming life was wont to dwell,
As the frail tenant shaped his growing shell,
Before thee lies revealed,—
Its irised ceiling rent, its sunless crypt unsealed!

Year after year beheld the silent toil
That spread his lustrous coil;
Still, as the spiral grew,
He left the past year's dwelling for the new,
Stole with soft step its shining archway through,
Built up its idle door,
Stretched in his last-found home, and knew the old no more.

Thanks for the heavenly message brought by thee,
Child of the wandering sea,
Cast from her lap, forlorn!
From thy dead lips a clearer note is born
Than ever Triton blew from wreathed horn!
While on mine ear it rings,
Through the deep caves of thought I hear a voice that sings:—

Build thee more stately mansions, O my soul,
As the swift seasons roll!
Leave thy low-vaulted past!
Let each new temple, nobler than the last,
Shut thee from heaven with a dome more vast,
Till thou at length art free,
Leaving thine outgrown shell by life's unresting sea!

Oliver Wendell Holmes.

Nobility

True worth is in *being*, not *seeming*,—
In doing, each day that goes by,
Some little good—not in dreaming
Of great things to do by and by.
For whatever men say in their blindness,
And spite of the fancies of youth,
There's nothing so kingly as kindness,
And nothing so royal as truth.

We get back our mete as we measure—
We cannot do wrong and feel right,
Nor can we give pain and gain pleasure,
For justice avenges each slight.
The air for the wing of the sparrow,
The bush for the robin and wren,
But alway the path that is narrow
And straight, for the children of men.

'Tis not in the pages of story
The heart of its ills to beguile,
Though he who makes courtship to glory
Gives all that he hath for her smile.
For when from her heights he has won her,
Alas! it is only to prove
That nothing's so sacred as honor,
And nothing so loyal as love!

We cannot make bargains for blisses,
Nor catch them like fishes in nets;
And sometimes the thing our life misses
Helps more than the thing which it gets.
For good lieth not in pursuing,
Nor gaining of great nor of small,
But just in the doing, and doing
As we would be done by, is all.

Through envy, through malice, through hating,
Against the world, early and late,
No jot of our courage abating—
Our part is to work and to wait.
And slight is the sting of his trouble
Whose winnings are less than his worth;
For he who is honest is noble,
Whatever his fortunes or birth.

Alice Cary.

The Wind

Who has seen the wind?
Neither I nor you:
But when the leaves hang trembling,
The wind is passing through.

Who has seen the wind?
Neither you nor I:
But when the trees bow down their heads,
The wind is passing by.

Christina G. Rossetti.

The Owl and The Pussy-Cat

The Owl and the Pussy-Cat went to sea
In a beautiful pea-green boat;
They took some honey, and plenty of money,
Wrapped up in a five-pound note.
The Owl looked up to the moon above
And sang to a small guitar,
"O lovely Pussy! O Pussy, my love!
What a beautiful Pussy you are,—
You are,
What a beautiful Pussy you are!"

Pussy said to the Owl, "You elegant fowl!
How wonderful sweet you sing!
Oh, let us be married,—too long we have tarried,—
But what shall we do for a ring?"
They sailed away for a year and a day
To the land where the Bong-tree grows,
And there in a wood, a piggy-wig stood
With a ring in the end of his nose,—
His nose,
With a ring in the end of his nose.

"Dear Pig, are you willing to sell for one shilling
Your ring?" Said the Piggy, "I will."
So they took it away, and were married next day
By the turkey who lives on the hill.
They dined upon mince and slices of quince
Which they ate with a runcible spoon,
And hand in hand on the edge of the sand
They danced by the light of the moon,—
The moon,
They danced by the light of the moon.

Edward Lear.

The Frost

The Frost looked forth one still, clear night,
And whispered, "Now I shall be out of sight;
So through the valley and over the height
In silence I'll take my way.
I will not go on like that blustering train,
The wind and the snow, the hail and the rain,
That make so much bustle and noise in vain,
But I'll be as busy as they!"

So he flew to the mountain, and powdered its crest;
He lit on the trees, and their boughs he drest
In diamond beads—and over the breast
Of the quivering lake he spread
A coat of mail, that it need not fear
The downward point of many a spear
That he hung on its margin, far and near,
Where a rock could rear its head.

He went to the windows of those who slept,
And over each pane like a fairy crept;
Wherever he breathed, wherever he stepped,
By the light of the morn were seen
Most beautiful things; there were flowers and trees;
There were bevies of birds and swarms of bees;
There were cities with temples and towers; and these
All pictured in silver sheen!

But he did one thing that was hardly fair,—
He peeped in the cupboard, and finding there
That all had forgotten for him to prepare,
"Now, just to set them a-thinking,
I'll bite this basket of fruit," said he;
"This costly pitcher I'll burst in three;
And the glass of water they've left for me
Shall 'tchick!' to tell them I'm drinking!"

Hannah F. Gould.

The Corn Song

Heap high the farmer's wintry hoard!
Heap high the golden corn!
No richer gift has Autumn poured
From out her lavish horn!

Let other lands, exulting, glean
The apple from the pine,
The orange from its glossy green,
The cluster from the vine;

We better love the hardy gift
Our rugged vales bestow,
To cheer us when the storm shall drift
Our harvest-fields with snow.

Through vales of grass and meads of flowers,
Our plows their furrows made,
While on the hills the sun and showers
Of changeful April played.

We dropped the seed o'er hill and plain,
Beneath the sun of May,
And frightened from our sprouting grain
The robber crows away.

All through the long, bright days of June,
Its leaves grew green and fair,
And waved in hot midsummer's noon
Its soft and yellow hair.

And now, with Autumn's moonlit eves,
Its harvest time has come,

We pluck away the frosted leaves
And bear the treasure home.

There, richer than the fabled gift
Apollo showered of old,
Fair hands the broken grain shall sift,
And knead its meal of gold.

Let vapid idlers loll in silk,
Around their costly board;
Give us the bowl of samp and milk,
By homespun beauty poured!

Where'er the wide old kitchen hearth
Sends up its smoky curls,
Who will not thank the kindly earth,
And bless our farmer girls!

Then shame on all the proud and vain,
Whose folly laughs to scorn
The blessing of our hardy grain,
Our wealth of golden corn!

Let earth withhold her goodly root,
Let mildew blight her rye,
Give to the worm the orchard's fruit,
The wheat-field to the fly:

But let the good old crop adorn
The hills our fathers trod;
Still let us, for His golden corn,
Send up our thanks to God!

John G. Whittier.

On His Blindness

When I consider how my light is spent
Ere half my days, in this dark world and wide,
And that one talent which is death to hide,
Lodged with me useless, though my soul more bent
To serve therewith my Maker, and present
My true account, lest He, returning, chide;
"Doth God exact day-labor, light denied?"
I fondly ask. But Patience, to prevent
That murmur, soon replies, "God doth not need
Either man's work or His own gifts. Who best
Bear His mild yoke, they serve Him best. His state
Is kingly: thousands at his bidding speed,
And post o'er land and ocean without rest;
They also serve who only stand and wait."

John Milton.

A Boy's Song

Where the pools are bright and deep,
Where the gray trout lies asleep,
Up the river and o'er the lea,
That's the way for Billy and me.

Where the blackbird sings the latest,
Where the hawthorn blooms the sweetest,
Where the nestlings chirp and flee,
That's the way for Billy and me.

Where the mowers mow the cleanest,
Where the hay lies thick and greenest;
There to trace the homeward bee,
That's the way for Billy and me.

Where the hazel bank is steepest,
Where the shadow falls the deepest,
Where the clustering nuts fall free,
That's the way for Billy and me.

Why the boys should drive away
Little sweet maidens from their play,
Or love to banter and fight so well,
That's the thing I never could tell.

But this I know, I love to play,
Through the meadow, among the hay,
Up the water and o'er the lea,
That's the way for Billy and me.

James Hogg.

November

The leaves are fading and falling,
  The winds are rough and wild,
The birds have ceased their calling,
  But let me tell you, my child,

Though day by day, as it closes,
  Doth darker and colder grow,
The roots of the bright red roses
  Will keep alive in the snow.

And when the winter is over,
  The boughs will get new leaves,
The quail come back to the clover,
  And the swallow back to the eaves.

There must be rough, cold weather,
  And winds and rains so wild;
Not all good things together
  Come to us here, my child.

So, when some dear joy loses
  Its beauteous summer glow,
Think how the roots of the roses
  Are kept alive in the snow.

Alice Cary.

Little Birdie

What does little birdie say,
In her nest at peep of day?
"Let me fly," says little birdie—
  "Mother, let me fly away."
"Birdie, rest a little longer,
Till the little wings are stronger."
So she rests a little longer,
  Then she flies away.

What does little baby say
In her bed at peep of day?
Baby says, like little birdie,
  "Let me rise and fly away."
"Baby, sleep a little longer,
Till the little limbs are stronger.
If she sleeps a little longer,
  Baby, too, shall fly away."

Alfred, Lord Tennyson.

The Fairies

Up the airy mountain,
  Down the rushy glen,
We daren't go a-hunting
  For fear of little men;
Wee folk, good folk,
  Trooping all together;
Green jacket, red cap,
  And white owl's feather!

Down along the rocky shore
  Some make their home;
They live on crispy pancakes
  Of yellow tide foam;
Some in the reeds
  Of the black mountain-lake,
With frogs for their watch dogs,
  All night awake.

High on the hill-top
  The old King sits;
He is now so old and gray
  He's nigh lost his wits.
With a bridge of white mist
  Columbkill he crosses,
On his stately journeys
  From Slieveleague to Rosses;
Or going up with music
  On cold, starry nights,
To sup with the Queen
  Of the gay Northern Lights.

By the craggy hillside,
  Through the mosses bare,
They have planted thorn trees
  For pleasure here and there;
Is any man so daring,
  As dig them up in spite?
He shall find their sharpest thorns
  In his bed at night.

Up the airy mountain,
  Down the rushy glen,
We daren't go a-hunting
  For fear of little men;

Wee folk, good folk,
  Trooping all together;
Green jacket, red cap,
  And white owl's feather.

William Allingham.

The Wonderful World

Great, wide, beautiful, wonderful World,
With the wonderful water round you curled,
And the wonderful grass upon your breast,
World, you are beautifully drest.

The wonderful air is over me,
And the wonderful wind is shaking the tree—
It walks on the water, and whirls the mills,
And talks to itself on the top of the hills.

You friendly Earth, how far do you go,
With the wheat-fields that nod and the rivers that flow,
With cities and gardens, and cliffs and isles,
And people upon you for thousands of miles?

Ah! you are so great, and I am so small,
I hardly can think of you, World, at all;
And yet, when I said my prayers to-day,
A whisper within me seemed to say:
"You are more than the Earth, though you are such a dot!
You can love and think, and the Earth can not."

William Brighty Rands.

Be Strong

Be strong!
We are not here to play, to dream, to drift;
We have hard work to do, and loads to lift;
Shun not the struggle—face it; 'tis God's gift.

Be strong!
Say not, "The days are evil. Who's to blame?"
And fold the hands and acquiesce—oh shame!
Stand up, speak out, and bravely, in God's name.

Be strong!
It matters not how deep intrenched the wrong,
How hard the battle goes, the day how long;
Faint not—fight on! To-morrow comes the song.

Maltbie Davenport Babcock.

Song: The Owl

When cats run home and light is come,
  And dew is cold upon the ground,
And the far-off stream is dumb,
  And the whirring sail goes round,
  And the whirring sail goes round,
    Alone and warming his five wits,
    The white owl in the belfry sits.

When merry milkmaids click the latch,
  And rarely smells the new-mown hay,
And the cock hath sung beneath the thatch
  Twice or thrice his roundelay,
  Twice or thrice his roundelay;
    Alone and warming his five wits,
    The white owl in the belfry sits.

Alfred, Lord Tennyson.

Opportunity

Master of human destinies am I!
Fame, love and fortune on my footsteps wait.
Cities and fields I walk: I penetrate
Deserts and fields remote, and, passing by
Hovel and mart and palace, soon or late
I knock unbidden once at every gate!
If sleeping, wake: if feasting, rise before
I turn away. It is the hour of fate,
And they who follow me reach every state
Mortals desire, and conquer every foe
Save death; but those who doubt or hesitate,
Condemned to failure, penury and woe,
Seek me in vain and uselessly implore—
I answer not, and I return no more.

John J. Ingalls.

Opportunity

They do me wrong who say I come no more
When once I knock and fail to find you in;
For every day I stand outside your door
And bid you wake and rise to fight and win.

Wail not for precious chances passed away!
Weep not for golden ages on the wane!
Each night I burn the records of the day;
At sunrise every soul is born again.

Laugh like a boy at splendors that have sped;
To vanished joys be blind and deaf and dumb;
My judgments seal the dead past with its dead,
But never bind a moment yet to come.

Though deep in mire, wring not your hands and weep;
I lend an arm to all who say: "I can!"
No shamefac'd outcast ever sank so deep
But yet might rise and be again a man.

Dost thou behold thy lost youth all aghast?
Dost reel from righteous retribution's blow?
Then turn from blotted archives of the past
And find the future's pages white as snow!

Art thou a mourner? Rouse thee from thy spell;
Art thou a sinner? Sins may be forgiven!
Each morning gives thee wings to flee from hell;
Each night a star to guide thy feet to Heaven.

Walter Malone.

Sweet and Low

(*From "The Princess"*)

Sweet and low, sweet and low,
Wind of the western sea,
Low, low, breathe and blow,
Wind of the western sea!
Over the rolling waters go,
Come from the dying moon, and blow,
Blow him again to me;
While my little one, while my pretty one, sleeps.

Sleep and rest, sleep and rest,
  Father will come to thee soon;
Rest, rest, on mother's breast,
  Father will come to thee soon;
Father will come to his babe in the nest,
Silver sails all out of the west
  Under the silver moon:
Sleep, my little one, sleep, my pretty
    one, sleep.

Alfred, Lord Tennyson.

The Barefoot Boy

Blessings on thee, little man,
Barefoot boy, with cheek of tan!
With thy turned-up pantaloons,
And thy merry whistled tunes;
With thy red lip, redder still
Kissed by strawberries on the hill;
With the sunshine on thy face,
Through thy torn brim's jaunty grace:
From my heart I give thee joy,—
I was once a barefoot boy!
Prince thou art,—the grown-up man
Only is republican.
Let the million-dollared ride!
Barefoot, trudging at his side,
Thou hast more than he can buy
In the reach of ear and eye,—
Outward sunshine, inward joy:
Blessings on thee, barefoot boy!

O for boyhood's painless play,
Sleep that wakes in laughing day,
Health that mocks the doctor's rules,
Knowledge never learned of schools,
Of the wild bee's morning chase,
Of the wild-flower's time and place.
Flight of fowl and habitude
Of the tenants of the wood;
How the tortoise bears his shell,
How the woodchuck digs his cell,
And the ground-mole sinks his well;
How the robin feeds her young,
How the oriole's nest is hung;
Where the whitest lilies blow,
Where the freshest berries grow,
Where the groundnut trails its vine,
Where the wood-grape's clusters shine;
Of the black wasp's cunning way,
Mason of his walls of clay,
And the architectural plans
Of gray hornet artisans!—
For, eschewing books and tasks,
Nature answers all he asks;
Hand in hand with her he walks,
Face to face with her he talks,
Part and parcel of her joy,—
Blessings on the barefoot boy!

O for boyhood's time of June,
Crowding years in one brief moon,
When all things I heard or saw,
Me, their master, waited for.
I was rich in flowers and trees,
Humming-birds and honey-bees;
For my sport the squirrel played,
Plied the snouted mole his spade;
For my taste the blackberry cone
Purpled over hedge and stone;
Laughed the brook for my delight
Through the day and through the night,
Whispering at the garden wall,
Talked with me from fall to fall;
Mine the sand-rimmed pickerel pond,
Mine the walnut slopes beyond,
Mine, on bending orchard trees,
Apples of Hesperides!
Still as my horizon grew,
Larger grew my riches too;
All the world I saw or knew
Seemed a complex Chinese toy,
Fashioned for a barefoot boy!

O for festal dainties spread,
Like my bowl of milk and bread,—
Pewter spoon and bowl of wood,
On the door-stone, gray and rude!
O'er me, like a regal tent,
Cloudy-ribbed, the sunset bent,
Purple-curtained, fringed with gold,
Looped in many a wind-swung fold;
While for music came the play

Of the pied frogs' orchestra;
And, to light the noisy choir,
Lit the fly his lamp of fire.
I was monarch: pomp and joy
Waited on the barefoot boy!

Cheerily, then, my little man,
Live and laugh, as boyhood can!
Though the flinty slopes be hard,
Stubble-speared the new-mown sward,
Every morn shall lead thee through
Fresh baptisms of the dew;
Every evening from thy feet
Shall the cool wind kiss the heat:
All too soon these feet must hide
In the prison cells of pride,
Lose the freedom of the sod,
Like a colt's for work be shod,
Made to tread the mills of toil,
Up and down in ceaseless moil:
Happy if their track be found
Never on forbidden ground,
Happy if they sink not in
Quick and treacherous sands of sin.
Ah! that thou couldst know thy joy,
Ere it passes, barefoot boy!

John Greenleaf Whittier.

Polonius' Advice to Laertes

(*From "Hamlet"*)

There,—my blessing with you!
And these few precepts in thy memory
See thou character.—Give thy thoughts no tongue,
Nor any unproportion'd thought his act.
Be thou familiar, but by no means vulgar.
The friends thou hast, and their adoption tried,
Grapple them to thy soul with hoops of steel;
But do not dull thy palm with entertainment
Of each new-hatched, unfledged comrade. Beware
Of entrance to a quarrel; but being in,
Bear't that the opposed may beware of thee.
Give every man thine ear, but few thy voice:
Take each man's censure, but reserve thy judgment.
Costly thy habit as thy purse can buy,
But not expressed in fancy; rich, not gaudy:
For the apparel oft proclaims the man.
Neither a borrower nor a lender be,
For loan oft loses both itself and friend,
And borrowing dulls the edge of husbandry.
This above all: to thine own self be true,
And it must follow, as the night the day,
Thou canst not then be false to any man.

William Shakespeare.

A Fable

The mountain and the squirrel
Had a quarrel,
And the former called the latter "Little Prig."
Bun replied,
"You are doubtless very big;
But all sorts of things and weather
Must be taken in together,
To make up a year
And a sphere.
And I think it no disgrace
To occupy my place.
If I'm not so large as you,
You are not so small as I,
And not half as spry.
I'll not deny you make
A very pretty squirrel track;
Talents differ; all is well and wisely put;
If I cannot carry forests on my back,
Neither can you crack a nut."

Ralph Waldo Emerson.

Suppose

Suppose, my little lady,
  Your doll should break her head,
Could you make it whole by crying
  Till your eyes and nose are red?
And wouldn't it be pleasanter
  To treat it as a joke,
And say you're glad "'Twas Dolly's
  And not your head that broke"?

Suppose you're dressed for walking,
  And the rain comes pouring down,
Will it clear off any sooner
  Because you scold and frown?
And wouldn't it be nicer
  For you to smile than pout,
And so make sunshine in the house
  When there is none without?

Suppose your task, my little man,
  Is very hard to get,
Will it make it any easier
  For you to sit and fret?
And wouldn't it be wiser
  Than waiting like a dunce,
To go to work in earnest
  And learn the thing at once?

Suppose that some boys have a horse,
  And some a coach and pair,
Will it tire you less while walking
  To say, "It isn't fair"?
And wouldn't it be nobler
  To keep your temper sweet,
And in your heart be thankful
  You can walk upon your feet?

And suppose the world don't please
  you,
  Nor the way some people do,
Do you think the whole creation
  Will be altered just for you?
And isn't it, my boy or girl,
  The wisest, bravest plan,
Whatever comes, or doesn't come,
  To do the best you can?

Phoebe Cary.

I Like Little Pussy

I like little Pussy,
  Her coat is so warm;
And if I don't hurt her
  She'll do me no harm.
So I'll not pull her tail,
  Nor drive her away,
But Pussy and I
  Very gently will play;
She shall sit by my side,
  And I'll give her some food;
And she'll love me because
  I am gentle and good.

I'll pat little Pussy,
  And then she will purr,
And thus show her thanks
  For my kindness to her;
I'll not pinch her ears,
  Nor tread on her paw,
Lest I should provoke her
  To use her sharp claw;
I never will vex her,
  Nor make her displeased,
For Pussy don't like
  To be worried or teased.

Jane Taylor.

Thanksgiving-Day

Over the river and through the wood,
  To Grandfather's house we go;
    The horse knows the way
    To carry the sleigh
  Through the white and drifted snow.

Over the river and through the wood,—
  Oh, how the wind does blow!
    It stings the toes,
    And bites the nose,
  As over the ground we go.

Over the river and through the wood,
  Trot fast, my dapple-gray!
    Spring over the ground,
    Like a hunting hound,
  For this is Thanksgiving-Day.

Over the river and through the wood,
And straight through the barnyard gate!
We seem to go
Extremely slow,—
It is so hard to wait!

Over the river and through the wood;
Now Grandmother's cap I spy!
Hurrah for the fun!
Is the pudding done?
Hurrah for the pumpkin pie!

Lydia Maria Child.

Daffodils

I wandered lonely as a cloud
That floats on high o'er vales and hills,
When all at once I saw a crowd,
A host, of golden daffodils;
Beside the lake, beneath the trees,
Fluttering and dancing in the breeze.

Continuous as the stars that shine
And twinkle on the milky way,
They stretched in never-ending line
Along the margin of a bay;
Ten thousand saw I at a glance,
Tossing their heads in sprightly dance.

The waves beside them danced; but they
Outdid the sparkling waves in glee;
A poet could not but be gay
In such a jocund company;
I gazed—and gazed—but little thought
What wealth the show to me had brought.

For oft, when on my couch I lie
In vacant or in pensive mood,
They flash upon that inward eye
Which is the bliss of solitude;
And then my heart with pleasure fills,
And dances with the daffodils.

William Wordsworth.

To a Butterfly

I've watched you now a full half-hour,
Self-poised upon that yellow flower;
And, little Butterfly! indeed
I know not if you sleep or feed.
More motionless! and then
How motionless!—not frozen seas
What joy awaits you, when the breeze
Hath found you out among the trees,
And calls you forth again;
This plot of orchard-ground is ours;
My trees they are, my Sister's flowers;
Here rest your wings when they are weary;
Here lodge as in a sanctuary!
Come often to us, fear no wrong;
Sit near us on the bough!
We'll talk of sunshine and of song,
And summer days when we were young;
Sweet childish days, that were as long
As twenty days are now.

William Wordsworth.

To The Fringed Gentian

Thou blossom bright with autumn dew,
And colored with the heaven's own blue,
That openest when the quiet light
Succeeds the keen and frosty night,

Thou comest not when violets lean
O'er wandering brooks and springs unseen,
Or columbines, in purple dressed,
Nod o'er the ground-bird's hidden nest.

Thou waitest late and com'st alone,
When woods are bare and birds are flown,
And frosts and shortening days portend
The aged Year is near his end.

Then doth thy sweet and quiet eye
Look through its fringes to the sky,

Blue—blue—as if that sky let fall
A flower from its cerulean wall.

I would that thus, when I shall see
The hour of death draw near to me,
Hope, blossoming within my heart,
May look to heaven as I depart.

William Cullen Bryant.

The Song of the Camp

"Give us a song!" the soldiers cried,
The outer trenches guarding,
When the heated guns of the camps allied
Grew weary of bombarding.

The dark Redan, in silent scoff,
Lay, grim and threatening, under;
And the tawny mound of the Malakoff
No longer belched its thunder.

There was a pause. A guardsman said,
"We storm the forts to-morrow;
Sing while we may, another day
Will bring enough of sorrow."

They lay along the battery's side
Below the smoking cannon:
Brave hearts, from Severn and from Clyde,
And from the banks of Shannon.

They sang of love, and not of fame;
Forgot was Britain's glory:
Each heart recalled a different name,
But all sang "Annie Laurie."

Voice after voice caught up the song,
Until its tender passion
Rose like an anthem, rich and strong,—
Their battle-eve confession.

Dear girl, her name he dared not speak,
But, as the song grew louder,
Something upon the soldier's cheek
Washed off the stains of powder.

Beyond the darkening ocean burned
The bloody sunset's embers,
While the Crimean valleys learned
How English love remembers.

And once again a fire of hell
Rained on the Russian quarters,
With scream of shot, and burst of shell,
And bellowing of the mortars!

And Irish Nora's eyes are dim
For a singer, dumb and gory;
And English Mary mourns for him
Who sang of "Annie Laurie."

Sleep, soldiers! still in honored rest
Your truth and valor wearing:
The bravest are the tenderest,—
The loving are the daring.

Bayard Taylor.

She Walks in Beauty

She walks in beauty, like the night
Of cloudless climes and starry skies;
And all that's best of dark and bright
Meet in her aspect and her eyes:
Thus mellowed to that tender light
Which heaven to gaudy day denies.

One shade the more, one ray the less,
Had half impaired the nameless grace
Which waves in every raven tress,
Or softly lightens o'er her face;
Where thoughts serenely sweet express
How pure, how dear their dwelling-place.

And on that cheek, and o'er that brow,
So soft, so calm, yet eloquent,
The smiles that win, the tints that glow,
But tell of days in goodness spent,
A mind at peace with all below,
A heart whose love is innocent!

Lord Byron.

The Builders

All are architects of Fate,
Working in these walls of Time;
Some with massive deeds and great,
Some with ornaments of rhyme.

Nothing useless is, or low;
Each thing in its place is best;
And what seems but idle show
Strengthens and supports the rest.

For the structure that we raise,
Time is with materials filled;
Our to-days and yesterdays
Are the blocks with which we build.

Truly shape and fashion these;
Leave no yawning gaps between;
Think not, because no man sees,
Such things will remain unseen.

In the elder days of Art,
Builders wrought with greatest care
Each minute and unseen part;
For the Gods see everywhere.

Let us do our work as well,
Both the unseen and the seen!
Make the house, where Gods may dwell,
Beautiful, entire, and clean.

Else our lives are incomplete,
Standing in these walls of Time,
Broken stairways, where the feet
Stumble as they seek to climb.

Build to-day, then, strong and sure,
With a firm and ample base;
And ascending and secure
Shall to-morrow find its place.

Thus alone can we attain
To those turrets, where the eye
Sees the world as one vast plain,
And one boundless reach of sky.

Henry W. Longfellow.

The Brown Thrush

There's a merry brown thrush sitting up in the tree,
He's singing to me! He's singing to me!
And what does he say, little girl, little boy?
"Oh, the world's running over with joy!
Don't you hear? don't you see?
Hush! Look! In my tree,
I'm as happy as happy can be!"

And the brown thrush keeps singing,
"A nest do you see,
And five eggs hid by me in the juniper tree?
Don't meddle! don't touch! little girl, little boy,
Or the world will lose some of its joy!
Now I'm glad! now I'm free!
And I always shall be,
If you never bring sorrow to me."

So the merry brown thrush sings away in the tree,
To you and to me, to you and to me;
And he sings all the day, little girl, little boy,
"Oh, the world's running over with joy;
But long it won't be,
Don't you know? don't you see?
Unless we are as good as can be!"

Lucy Larcom.

The Quality of Mercy

(*From "The Merchant of Venice"*)

The quality of mercy is not strain'd.
It droppeth as the gentle rain from heaven
Upon the place beneath. It is twice bless'd:
It blesseth him that gives and him that takes.
'Tis mightiest in the mightiest; it becomes

The throned monarch better than his
crown.
His sceptre shows the force of temporal power,
The attribute to awe and majesty,
Wherein doth sit the dread and fear of kings;
But mercy is above this sceptred sway;
It is enthroned in the hearts of kings;
It is an attribute to God himself,
And earthly power doth then show likest God's
When mercy seasons justice. Therefore, Jew,
Though justice be thy plea, consider this,
That, in the course of justice, none of us
Should see salvation: we do pray for mercy;
And that same prayer doth teach us all to render
The deeds of mercy.

William Shakespeare.

Don't Give Up

If you've tried and have not won,
Never stop for crying;
All's that's great and good is done
Just by patient trying.

Though young birds, in flying, fall,
Still their wings grow stronger;
And the next time they can keep
Up a little longer.

Though the sturdy oak has known
Many a blast that bowed her,
She has risen again, and grown
Loftier and prouder.

If by easy work you beat,
Who the more will prize you?
Gaining victory from defeat,—
That's the test that tries you!

Phoebe Cary.

Incident of the French Camp

You know we French stormed Ratisbon:
A mile or so away
On a little mound, Napoleon
Stood on our storming-day;
With neck out-thrust, you fancy how,
Legs wide, arms locked behind,
As if to balance the prone brow,
Oppressive with its mind.
Just as perhaps he mused, "My plans
That soar, to earth may fall,
Let once my army-leader Lannes
Waver at yonder wall,"—
Out 'twixt the battery-smokes there flew
A rider, bound on bound
Full-galloping; nor bridle drew
Until he reached the mound.

Then off there flung in smiling joy,
And held himself erect
By just his horse's mane, a boy:
You hardly could suspect—
(So tight he kept his lips compressed,
Scarce any blood came through)
You looked twice ere you saw his breast
Was all but shot in two.

"Well," cried he, "Emperor, by God's grace
We've got you Ratisbon!
The Marshall's in the market-place,
And you'll be there anon
To see your flag-bird flap his vans
Where I, to heart's desire,
Perched him!" The chief's eye flashed; his plans
Soared up again like fire.

The chief's eye flashed; but presently
Softened itself, as sheathes
A film the mother-eagle's eye
When her bruised eaglet breathes:

"You're wounded!" "Nay," his soldier's pride
Touched to the quick, he said:
"I'm killed, Sire!" And his chief beside,
Smiling, the boy fell dead.

Robert Browning.

The Bugle Song

(*From "The Princess"*)

The splendor falls on castle walls
And snowy summits old in story:
The long light shakes across the lakes,
And the wild cataract leaps in glory.
Blow, bugle, blow, set the wild echoes flying,
Blow, bugle; answer, echoes, dying, dying, dying.

O hark, O hear! how thin and clear,
And thinner, clearer, farther going!
O sweet and far from cliff and scar*
The horns of Elfland faintly blowing!
Blow, let us hear the purple glens replying:
Blow, bugle; answer, echoes, dying, dying, dying.

O love, they die in yon rich sky,
They faint on hill or field or river:
Our echoes roll from soul to soul,
And grow for ever and for ever.
Blow bugle, blow, set the wild echoes flying,
And answer, echoes, answer, dying, dying, dying.

Alfred, Lord Tennyson.

* Scar, a deep bank.

A Child's Thought of God

They say that God lives very high;
But if you look above the pines
You cannot see our God; and why?

And if you dig down in the mines,
You never see him in the gold,
Though from Him all that's glory shines.

God is so good, He wears a fold
Of heaven and earth across His face,
Like secrets kept for love untold.

But still I feel that His embrace
Slides down by thrills through all things made,
Through sight and sound of every place;

As if my tender mother laid
On my shut lips her kisses' pressure,
Half waking me at night, and said,
"Who kissed you through the dark, dear guesser?"

Elizabeth Barrett Browning.

The Blue and The Gray

By the flow of the inland river,
Where the fleets of iron have fled,
Where the blades of grave grass quiver,
Asleep are the ranks of the dead;
Under the sod and the dew,
Waiting the judgment day—
Under the one, the Blue;
Under the other, the Gray.

These in the robings of glory,
Those in the gloom of defeat,
All, with the battle blood gory,
In the dusk of eternity meet;
Under the sod and the dew,—
Waiting the judgment day—
Under the laurel, the Blue;
Under the willow, the Gray.

From the silence of sorrowful hours
The desolate mourners go,
Lovingly laden with flowers
Alike for the friend and the foe;
Under the sod and the dew,
Waiting the judgment day—
Under the roses, the Blue;
Under the lilies, the Gray.

So with an equal splendor
The morning sun-rays fall,
With a touch impartially tender,
On the blossoms blooming for all;
Under the sod and the dew,
Waiting the judgment day—
'Broidered with gold, the Blue;
Mellowed with gold, the Gray.

So, when the summer calleth,
On forest and field of grain
With an equal murmur falleth
The cooling drip of the rain;
Under the sod and the dew,
Waiting the judgment day—
Wet with the rain, the Blue;
Wet with the rain, the Gray.

Sadly, but not with upbraiding,
The generous deed was done;
In the storm of the years that are fading,
No braver battle was won;
Under the sod and the dew,
Waiting the judgment day—
Under the blossoms, the Blue;
Under the garlands, the Gray.

No more shall the war-cry sever,
Or the winding rivers be red;
They banish our anger forever
When they laurel the graves of our dead!
Under the sod and the dew,
Waiting the judgment day—
Love and tears for the Blue;
Tears and love for the Gray.

Francis Miles Finch.

Good Night and Good Morning

A fair little girl sat under a tree,
Sewing as long as her eyes could see,
Then smoothed her work, and folded it right,
And said, "Dear work, good night, good night!"

Such a number of rooks came over her head,
Crying "Caw, caw," on their way to bed;
She said, as she watched their curious flight,
"Little black things, good night, good night!"

The horses neighed, and the oxen lowed,
The sheep's "bleat, bleat" came over the road,
And all seemed to say, with a quiet delight,
"Good little girl, good night, good night!"

She did not say to the sun "Good night,"
Tho' she saw him there like a ball of light;
For she knew he had God's own time to keep
All over the world, and never could sleep.

The tall pink foxglove bowed his head,
The violets curtseyed and went to bed;
And good little Lucy tied up her hair,
And said, on her knees, her favorite prayer.

And, while on her pillow she softly lay,
She knew nothing more till again it was day;
And all things said to the beautiful sun,
"Good morning, good morning, our work is begun!"

Lord Houghton.

Lady Moon

"Lady Moon, Lady Moon, where are you roving?"
"Over the sea."
"Lady Moon, Lady Moon, whom are you loving?"
"All that love me."

"Are you not tired with rolling and never
Resting to sleep?
Why look so pale and so sad, as for ever
Wishing to weep?"

"Ask me not this, little child, if you love me;
You are too bold
I must obey my dear Father above me,
And do as I'm told."

"Lady Moon, Lady Moon, where are you roving?"
"Over the sea."
"Lady Moon, Lady Moon, whom are you loving?"
"All that love me."

Lord Houghton.

Breathes There the Man With Soul So Dead?

(*From "The Lay of the Last Minstrel"*)

Breathes there the man with soul so dead
Who never to himself hath said,
This is my own, my native land?
Whose heart hath ne'er within him burned,
As home his footsteps he hath turned
From wandering on a foreign strand?
If such there breathe, go, mark him well;
For him no minstrel raptures swell;
High though his titles, proud his name,
Boundless his wealth as wish can claim,—
Despite those titles, power, and pelf,
The wretch, concentred all in self,
Living, shall forfeit fair renown,
And, doubly dying, shall go down
To the vile dust from whence he sprung,
Unwept, unhonored and unsung.

Sir Walter Scott.

Pippa's Song

The year's at the spring,
And day's at the morn;
Morning's at seven;
The hillside's dew-pearled;
The lark's on the wing;
The snail's on the thorn;
God's in His heaven—
All's right with the world!

Robert Browning.

Twinkle, Twinkle, Little Star

Twinkle, twinkle, little star;
How I wonder what you are!
Up above the world so high,
Like a diamond in the sky.

When the glorious sun is set,
When the grass with dew is wet,
Then you show your little light,
Twinkle, twinkle, all the night.

In the dark blue sky you keep,
And often through my curtains peep;
For you never shut your eye
Till the sun is in the sky.

As your bright and tiny spark
Lights the traveler in the dark,
Though I know not what you are,
Twinkle, twinkle, little star.

Jane Taylor.

Crossing the Bar

Sunset and evening star,
And one clear call for me!
And may there be no moaning of the bar,
When I put out to sea,

But such a tide as moving seems asleep,
Too full for sound and foam,
When that which drew from out the boundless deep
Turns again home.

Twilight and evening bell,
And after that the dark!
And may there be no sadness of farewell,
When I embark;

For tho' from out our bourne of Time and Place
The flood may bear me far,
I hope to see my Pilot face to face
When I have crost the bar.

Alfred, Lord Tennyson.

The Tree

The Tree's early leaf buds were bursting their brown;
"Shall I take them away?" said the Frost, sweeping down.
"No, leave them alone
Till the blossoms have grown,"
Prayed the Tree, while he trembled from rootlet to crown.

The Tree bore his blossoms, and all the birds sung:
"Shall I take them away?" said the Wind, as he swung.
"No, leave them alone
Till the blossoms have grown,"
Said the Tree, while his leaflets quivering hung.

The Tree bore his fruit in the midsummer glow:
Said the child, "May I gather thy berries now?"
"Yes, all thou canst see:
Take them; all are for thee,"
Said the Tree, while he bent down his laden boughs low.

Bjornstjerne Bjornson.

The Fountain

Into the sunshine,
Full of the light,
Leaping and flashing
From morn till night;

Into the moonlight,
Whiter than snow,
Waving so flower-like
When the winds blow;

Into the starlight
Rushing in spray,
Happy at midnight,
Happy by day;

Ever in motion,
Blithesome and cheery,
Still climbing heavenward,
Never aweary;

Glad of all weathers,
Still seeming best,
Upward or downward,
Motion thy rest;

Full of a nature
Nothing can tame,
Changed every moment,
Ever the same;

Ceaseless aspiring,
Ceaseless content,
Darkness or sunshine
Thy element;

Glorious fountain,
  Let my heart be
Fresh, changeful, constant,
  Upward, like thee!
      James Russell Lowell.

The Leak in the Dike

The good dame looked from her cottage
  At the close of the pleasant day,
And cheerily called to her little son,
  Outside the door at play:
"Come, Peter, come! I want you to go,
  While there is light to see,
To the hut of the blind old man who lives
  Across the dike, for me;
And take these cakes I made for him—
  They are hot and smoking yet;
You have time enough to go and come
  Before the sun is set."

Then the good-wife turned to her labor,
  Humming a simple song,
And thought of her husband, working hard
  At the sluices all day long;
And set the turf a-blazing,
  And brought the coarse black bread,
That he might find a fire at night
  And find the table spread.

And Peter left the brother
  With whom all day he had played,
And the sister who had watched their sports
  In the willow's tender shade;
And told them they'd see him back before
  They saw a star in sight,
Though he wouldn't be afraid to go
  In the very darkest night!
For he was a brave, bright fellow,
  With eye and conscience clear;
He could do whatever a boy might do,
  And he had not learned to fear.
Why, he wouldn't have robbed a bird's nest,
  Nor brought a stork to harm,
Though never a law in Holland
  Had stood to stay his arm!

And now with his face all glowing,
  And eyes as bright as the day
With the thoughts of his pleasant errand,
  He trudged along the way;
And soon his joyous prattle
  Made glad a lonesome place—
Alas! if only the blind old man
  Could have seen that happy face!
Yet he somehow caught the brightness
  Which his voice and presence lent;
And he felt the sunshine come and go
  As Peter came and went.

And now, as the day was sinking,
  And the winds began to rise,
The mother looked from her door again,
  Shading her anxious eyes,
And saw the shadows deepen
  And birds to their homes come back,
But never a sign of Peter
  Along the level track.
But she said, "He will come at morning,
  So I need not fret nor grieve—
Though it isn't like my boy at all
  To stay without my leave."

But where was the child delaying?
  On the homeward way was he,
Across the dike while the sun was up
  An hour above the sea.
He was stopping now to gather flowers,
  Now listening to the sound,
As the angry waters dashed themselves
  Against their narrow bound.
"Ah! well for us," said Peter,
  "That the gates are good and strong,
And my father tends them carefully,
  Or they would not hold you long!

You're a wicked sea," said Peter;
"I know why you fret and chafe;
You would like to spoil our lands and homes,
But our sluices keep you safe!

But hark! Through the noise of waters
Comes a low, clear, trickling sound;
And the child's face pales with terror,
And his blossoms drop to the ground.
He is up the bank in a moment,
And, stealing through the sand,
He sees a stream not yet so large
As his slender, childish hand.
'Tis a leak in the dike! He is but a boy,
Unusued to fearful scenes;
But, young as he is, he has learned to know
The dreadful thing that means.
A leak in the dike! The stoutest heart
Grows faint that cry to hear,
And the bravest man in all the land
Turns white with mortal fear;
For he knows the smallest leak may grow
To a flood in a single night;
And he knows the strength of the cruel sea
When loosed in its angry might.

And the boy! He has seen the danger
And shouting a wild alarm,
He forces back the weight of the sea
With the strength of his single arm!
He listens for the joyful sound
Of a footstep passing nigh;
And lays his ear to the ground, to catch
The answer to his cry.
And he hears the rough winds blowing,
And the waters rise and fall,
But never an answer comes to him
Save the echo of his call.

He sees no hope, no succor,
His feeble voice is lost;
Yet what shall he do but watch and wait,
Though he perish at his post!
So, faintly calling and crying
Till the sun is under the sea;
Crying and moaning till the stars
Come out for company;
He thinks of his brother and sister,
Asleep in their safe warm bed;
He thinks of his father and mother,
Of himself as dying—and dead;
And of how, when the night is over,
They must come and find him at last;
But he never thinks he can leave the place
Where duty holds him fast.

The good dame in the cottage
Is up and astir with the light,
For the thought of her little Peter
Has been with her all night.
And now she watches the pathway,
As yester eve she had done;
But what does she see so strange and black
Against the rising sun?
Her neighbors are bearing between them
Something straight to her door;
Her child is coming home, but not
As he ever came before!

"He is dead!" she cries, "my darling!"
And the startled father hears,
And comes and looks the way she looks,
And fears the thing she fears;
Till a glad shout from the bearers
Thrills the stricken man and wife—
"Give thanks, for your son has saved our land,
And God has saved his life!"
So, there in the morning sunshine
They knelt about the boy;
And every head was bared and bent
In tearful, reverent joy.

'Tis many a year since then, but still,
When the sea roars like a flood,
Their boys are taught what a boy can do
Who is brave and true and good;
For every man in that country
Takes his son by the hand,
And tells him of little Peter
Whose courage saved the land.
They have many a valiant hero
Remembered through the years;
But never one whose name so oft
Is named with loving tears;
And his deed shall be sung by the cradle,
And told to the child on the knee,
So long as the dikes of Holland
Divide the land from the sea!

Phoebe Cary.

Robert of Lincoln

Merrily swinging on briar and weed,
Near to the nest of his little dame,
Over the mountain-side or mead,
Robert of Lincoln is telling his name:
Bob-o'-link, bob-o'-link,
Spink, spank, spink;
Snug and safe is that nest of ours,
Hidden among the summer flowers.
Chee, chee, chee.

Robert of Lincoln is gaily drest,
Wearing a bright black wedding coat;
White are his shoulders and white his crest,
Hear him call in his merry note:
Bob-o'-link, bob-o'-link,
Spink, spank, spink;
Look, what a nice new coat is mine,
Sure there was never a bird so fine.
Chee, chee, chee.

Robert of Lincoln's Quaker wife,
Pretty and quiet, with plain brown wings,
Passing at home a patient life,
Broods in the grass while her husband sings:
Bob-o'-link, bob-o'-link,
Spink, spank, spink;
Brood, kind creature; you need not fear
Thieves and robbers while I am here.
Chee, chee, chee.

Modest and shy as a nun is she;
One weak chirp is her only note.
Braggart and prince of braggarts is he,
Pouring boasts from his little throat:
Bob-o'-link, bob-o'-link,
Spink, spank, spink;
Never was I afraid of man;
Catch me, cowardly knaves, if you can.
Chee, chee, chee.

Six white eggs on a bed of hay,
Flecked with purple, a pretty sight!
There as the mother sits all day,
Robert is singing with all his might:
Bob-o'-link, bob-o'-link,
Spink, spank, spink;
Nice, good wife, that never goes out,
Keeping the house while I frolic about.
Chee, chee, chee.

Soon as the little ones chip the shell
Six wide mouths are open for food;
Robert of Lincoln bestirs him well,
Gathering seeds for the hungry brood.
Bob-o'-link, bob-o'-link,
Spink, spank, spink;
This new life is likely to be
Hard for a gay young fellow like me.
Chee, chee, chee.

Robert of Lincoln at length is made
Sober with work, and silent with care;
Off is his holiday garment laid,
Half forgotten that merry air,

Bob-o'-link, bob-o'-link,
Spink, spank, spink;
Nobody knows but my mate and I
Where our nest and our nestlings lie.
Chee, chee, chee.

Summer wanes; the children are grown;
Fun and frolic no more he knows;
Robert of Lincoln's a humdrum crone;
Off he flies, and we sing as he goes:
Bob-o'-link, bob-o'-link,
Spink, spank, spink;
When you can pipe that merry old strain,
Robert of Lincoln, come back again.
Chee, chee, chee.

William Cullen Bryant.

Wishing

Ring-Ting! I wish I were a Primrose,
A bright yellow Primrose, blowing in the spring!
The stooping boughs above me,
The wandering bee to love me,
The fern and moss to creep across,
And the Elm tree for our king!

Nay—stay! I wish I were an Elm tree,
A great, lofty Elm tree, with green leaves gay!
The winds would set them dancing,
The sun and moonshine glance in,
The birds would house among the boughs,
And sweetly sing.

Oh no! I wish I were a Robin,
A Robin or a little Wren, everywhere to go;
Through forest, field, or garden,
And ask no leave or pardon,
Till winter comes with icy thumbs
To ruffle up our wing!

Well—tell! Where should I fly to,
Where go to sleep in the dark wood or dell?
Before a day was over,
Home comes the rover,
For mother's kiss—sweeter this
Than any other thing.

William Allingham.

The Burial of Sir John Moore at Corunna

Not a drum was heard, not a funeral note,
As his corse to the rampart we hurried;
Not a soldier discharged his farewell shot
O'er the grave where our hero we buried.

We buried him darkly at dead of night,
The sods with our bayonets turning;
By struggling moonbeam's misty light,
And the lantern dimly burning.

No useless coffin enclosed his breast,
Nor in sheet nor in shroud we wound him;
But he lay like a warrior taking his rest,
With his martial cloak around him.

Few and short were the prayers we said,
And we spoke not a word of sorrow;
But we steadfastly gazed on the face of the dead,
And we bitterly thought of the morrow.

We thought, as we hollowed his narrow bed,
And smoothed down his lonely pillow,
That the foe and the stranger would tread o'er his head;
And we far away on the billow!

Lightly they'll talk of the spirit that's gone,
And o'er his cold ashes upbraid him;
But little he'll reck, if they let him sleep on
In the grave where a Briton has laid him.

But half of our heavy task was done,
When the clock tolled the hour for retiring;
And we heard the distant and random gun
That the foe was sullenly firing.

Slowly and sadly we laid him down,
From the field of his fame fresh and gory;
We carved not a line, and we raised not a stone,
But we left him alone with his glory!

Charles Wolfe.

How Many Seconds in a Minute?

How many seconds in a minute?
Sixty, and no more in it.

How many minutes in an hour?
Sixty for sun and shower.

How many hours in a day?
Twenty-four for work and play.

How many days in a week?
Seven both to hear and speak.

How many weeks in a month?
Four, as the swift moon runn'th.

How many months in a year?
Twelve, the almanack makes clear.

How many years in an age?
One hundred, says the sage.

How many ages in time?
No one knows the rhyme.

Christina G. Rossetti.

To-day

Here hath been dawning another blue day:
Think, wilt thou let it slip useless away?
Out of Eternity this new day was born;
Into Eternity, at night, will return.
Behold it aforetime no eye ever did;
So soon it forever from all eyes is hid.
Here hath been dawning another blue day:
Think, wilt thou let it slip useless away?

Thomas Carlyle.

The Wind and the Moon

Said the Wind to the Moon, "I will blow you out.
You stare
In the air
Like a ghost in a chair,
Always looking what I am about;
I hate to be watched—I will blow you out."

The Wind blew hard, and out went the Moon.
So deep,
On a heap
Of clouds, to sleep,
Down lay the Wind, and slumbered soon—
Muttering low, "I've done for that Moon."

He turned in his bed; she was there again!
On high
In the sky
With her one clear eye,
The Moon shone white and alive and plain.
Said the Wind—"I will blow you out again."

The Wind blew hard, and the Moon grew dim.
"With my sledge
And my wedge
I have knocked off her edge!
If only I blow right fierce and grim,
The creature will soon be dimmer than dim."

He blew and blew, and she thinned to a thread.
"One puff
More's enough
To blow her to snuff!
One good puff more where the last was bred,
And glimmer, glimmer, glum will go the thread!"

He blew a great blast, and the thread was gone;
In the air
Nowhere
Was a moonbeam bare;
Far off and harmless the shy stars shone;
Sure and certain the Moon was gone.

The Wind, he took to his revels once more;
On down
In town,
Like a merry-mad clown,
He leaped and halloed with whistle and roar,
"What's that?" The glimmering thread once more!

He flew in a rage—he danced and blew;
But in vain
Was the pain
Of his bursting brain;
For still the broader the Moon-scrap grew,
The broader he swelled his big cheeks and blew.

Slowly she grew—till she filled the night,
And shone
On her throne
In the sky alone,
A matchless, wonderful, silvery light,
Radiant and lovely, the Queen of the Night.

Said the Wind—"What a marvel of power am I!
With my breath,
Good faith!
I blew her to death—
First blew her away right out of the sky—
Then blew her in; what a strength have I!"

But the Moon, she knew nothing about the affair,
For, high
In the sky,
With her one white eye
Motionless, miles above the air,
She had never heard the great Wind blare. *George Macdonald.*

The Little Plant

In the heart of a seed,
Buried deep, so deep,
A dear little plant
Lay fast asleep!

"Wake!" said the sunshine,
"And creep to the light!"
"Wake!" said the voice
Of the raindrop bright.

The little plant heard
And it rose to see
What the wonderful
Outside world might be.
Kate L. Brown.

Paul Revere's Ride

Listen, my children, and you shall hear
Of the midnight ride of Paul Revere,
On the eighteenth of April, in Seventy-five;
Hardly a man is now alive
Who remembers that famous day and year.

He said to his friend, "If the British march
By land or sea from the town to-night,
Hang a lantern aloft in the belfry arch
Of the North Church tower, as a signal light,—
One, if by land, and two, if by sea;
And I on the opposite shore will be,
Ready to ride and spread the alarm
Through every Middlesex village and farm,
For the country folk to be up and to arm."

Then he said, "Good-night"; and with muffled oar
Silently rowed to the Charlestown shore,
Just as the moon rose over the bay,
Where, swinging wide at her moorings, lay
The Somerset, British man-of-war,
A phantom ship, with each mast and spar
Across the moon like a prison bar,
And a huge black hulk, that was magnified
By its own reflection in the tide.

Meanwhile, his friend through alley and street
Wanders and watches with eager ears,
Till, in the silence around him, he hears
The muster of men at the barrack door,
The sound of arms, and the tramp of feet,
And the measured tread of the grenadiers
Marching down to their boats on the shore.

Then he climbed to the tower of the old North Church,
By the wooden stairs, with stealthy tread,
To the belfry chamber overhead,
And startled the pigeons from their perch
On the sombre rafters, that round him made
Masses and moving shapes of shade;
By the trembling ladder, steep and tall,
To the highest window in the wall,
Where he paused to listen, and look down
A moment on the roofs of the town,
And the moonlight flowing over all.

Beneath, in the churchyard, lay the dead
In their night encampment on the hill,
Wrapped in silence so deep and still
That he could hear, like a sentinel's tread,
The watchful night wind, as it went,
Creeping along from tent to tent,
And seeming to whisper, "All is well!"
A moment only he feels the spell
Of the place and hour, and the secret dread
Of the lonely belfry and the dead,
For suddenly all his thoughts are bent
On a shadowy something far away,
Where the river widens to meet the bay,
A line of black, that bends and floats
On the rising tide, like a bridge of boats.

Meanwhile, impatient to mount and ride,
Booted and spurred, with a heavy stride
  On the opposite shore walked Paul Revere.
Now he patted his horse's side,
  Now gazed on the landscape far and near,
Then impetuous stamped the earth,
And turned and tightened his saddle girth;
But mostly he watched with eager search
The belfry tower of the old North Church,
As it rose above the graves on the hill,
Lonely and spectral, and sombre and still.
And lo! as he looks, on the belfry's height
A glimmer, and then a gleam of light!
  He springs to the saddle, the bridle he turns,
But lingers and gazes, till full on his sight
  A second lamp in the belfry burns.

A hurry of hoofs in a village street,
  A shape in the moonlight, a bulk in the dark,
  And beneath from the pebbles, in passing, a spark
Struck out by a steed flying fearless and fleet;
  That was all! And yet, through the gloom and the light,
  The fate of a nation was riding that night;
  And the spark struck out by that steed, in his flight,
Kindled the land into flame with its heat.
He has left the village and mounted the steep,
And beneath him, tranquil and broad and deep,
  Is the Mystic, meeting the ocean tides;
And under the alders, that skirt its edge,
Now soft on the sand, now loud on the ledge,
  Is heard the tramp of his steed as he rides.

It was twelve by the village clock
  When he crossed the bridge into Medford town.
He heard the crowing of the cock,
And the barking of the farmer's dog,
And felt the damp of the river fog,
  That rises after the sun goes down.

It was one by the village clock
  When he galloped into Lexington.
He saw the gilded weathercock
Swim in the moonlight as he passed,
  And the meeting house windows, blank and bare,
  Gaze at him with a spectral glare
As if they already stood aghast
  At the bloody work they would look upon.

It was two by the village clock
  When he came to the bridge in Concord town.
He heard the bleating of the flock,
And the twittering of birds among the trees,
And felt the breath of the morning breeze
  Blowing over the meadows brown.
And one was safe and asleep in his bed
  Who at the bridge would be first to fall,
Who that day would be lying dead,
  Pierced by a British musket ball.

You know the rest. In the books you
have read
How the British regulars fired and
fled—
How the farmers gave them ball for
ball,
From behind each fence and farmyard
wall,
Chasing the red coats down the lane,
Then crossing the fields to emerge
again
Under the trees at the turn of the road,
And only pausing to fire and load.

So through the night rode Paul Revere;
And so through the night went his
cry of alarm
To every Middlesex village and farm—
A cry of defiance, and not of fear—
A voice in the darkness, a knock at the
door,
And a word that shall echo forever-
more;
For borne on the night wind of the past,
Through all our history to the last,
In the hour of darkness and peril and
need,
The people will waken and listen to
hear
The hurrying hoof beats of that steed,
And the midnight message of Paul
Revere.

Henry W. Longfellow.

In Flanders Fields

In Flanders fields the poppies grow
Between the crosses, row on row,
That mark our place; and in the sky
The larks, still bravely singing, fly,
Scarce heard amid the guns below.

We are the dead. Short days ago
We lived, felt dawn, saw sunset glow,
Loved and were loved; and now we lie
In Flanders fields.

Take up our quarrel with the foe!
To you, from failing hands, we throw
The torch. Be yours to hold it high!
If ye break faith with us who die,
We shall not sleep, though poppies
blow
In Flanders fields.

John McCrae.

In Flanders Fields: An Answer

In Flanders fields the cannon boom
And fitful flashes light the gloom,
While up above, like eagles, fly
The fierce destroyers of the sky;
With stains the earth wherein you lie
Is redder than the poppy bloom,
In Flanders fields.

Sleep on, ye brave. The shrieking shell,
The quaking trench, the startled yell,
The fury of the battle hell
Shall wake you not; for all is well.
Sleep peacefully; for all is well.

Your flaming torch aloft we bear,
With burning heart an oath we swear
To keep the faith, to fight it through,
To crush the foe, or sleep with you
In Flanders fields.

C. B. Galbreath.

Little Boy Blue

The little toy dog is covered with dust,
But sturdy and stanch he stands;
And the little toy soldier is red with
rust,
And his musket moulds in his hands.
Time was when the little toy dog was
new
And the soldier was passing fair,
And that was the time when our Little
Boy Blue
Kissed them and put them there.

"Now, don't you go till I come," he said,
"And don't you make any noise!"
So toddling off to his trundle-bed
He dreamt of the pretty toys.
And as he was dreaming, an angel song
Awakened our Little Boy Blue,—
Oh, the years are many, the years are long,
But the little toy friends are true.

Ay, faithful to Little Boy Blue they stand,
Each in the same old place,
Awaiting the touch of a little hand,
The smile of a little face.
And they wonder, as waiting these long years through,
In the dust of that little chair,
What has become of our little Boy Blue
Since he kissed them and put them there.

Eugene Field.

Thanatopsis

To him who in the love of Nature holds
Communion with her visible forms, she speaks
A various language; for his gayer hours
She has a voice of gladness, and a smile
And eloquence of beauty, and she glides
Into his darker musings with a mild
And healing sympathy, that steals away
Their sharpness, ere he is aware. When thoughts
Of the last bitter hour come like a blight
Over thy spirit, and sad images
Of the stern agony, and shroud, and pall,
And breathless darkness, and the narrow house,
Make thee to shudder, and grow sick at heart;—
Go forth, under the open sky, and list
To Nature's teachings, while from all around—
Earth and her waters, and the depths of air,—
Comes a still voice—Yet a few days, and thee
The all-beholding sun shall see no more
In all his course; nor yet in the cold ground,
Where thy pale form was laid with many tears,
Nor in the embrace of ocean, shall exist
Thy image. Earth, that nourished thee, shall claim
Thy growth, to be resolved to earth again,
And, lost each human trace, surrendering up
Thine individual being, shalt thou go
To mix forever with the elements,
To be a brother to the insensible rock
And to the sluggish clod, which the rude swain
Turns with his share, and treads upon. The oak
Shall send his roots abroad, and pierce thy mould.
Yet not to thine eternal resting-place
Shalt thou retire alone—nor couldst thou wish
Couch more magnificent. Thou shalt lie down
With patriarchs of the infant world—with kings,
The powerful of the earth—the wise, the good,
Fair forms, and hoary seers of ages past,
All in one mighty sepulchre. The hills,
Rock-ribbed, and ancient as the sun,—the vales
Stretching in pensive quietness between;
The venerable woods—rivers that move
In majesty, and the complaining brooks

That make the meadows green; and, poured round all,
Old ocean's gray and melancholy waste,—
Are but the solemn decorations all
Of the great tomb of man. The golden sun,
The planets, all the infinite host of heaven,
Are shining on the sad abodes of death,
Through the still lapse of ages. All that tread
The globe are but a handful to the tribes
That slumber in its bosom. Take the wings
Of morning, pierce the Barcan wilderness,
Or lose thyself in the continuous woods
Where rolls the Oregon, and hears no sound,
Save his own dashings—yet, the dead are there;
And millions in those solitudes, since first
The flight of years began, have laid them down
In their last sleep—the dead reign there alone.
So shalt thou rest, and what if thou withdraw
In silence from the living, and no friend
Take note of thy departure? All that breathe
Will share thy destiny. The gay will laugh
When thou art gone, the solemn brood of care
Plod on, and each one as before will chase
His favorite phantom; yet all these shall leave
Their mirth and their employments, and shall come
And make their bed with thee. As the long train
Of ages glide away, the sons of men,—
The youth in life's green spring, and he who goes
In the full strength of years, matron, and maid,
And the sweet babe, and the gray-headed man,—
Shall one by one be gathered to thy side,
By those who in their turn shall follow them.

So live, that when thy summons comes to join
The innumerable caravan which moves
To the pale realms of shade, where each shall take
His chamber in the silent halls of death,
Thou go not, like the quarry-slave at night,
Scourged to his dungeon, but, sustained and soothed
By an unfaltering trust, approach thy grave
Like one who wraps the drapery of his couch
About him, and lies down to pleasant dreams. *William Cullen Bryant.*

The First Settler's Story

It ain't the funniest thing a man can do—
Existing in a country when it's new;
Nature, who moved in first—a good long while—
Has things already somewhat her own style,
And she don't want her woodland splendors battered,
Her rustic furniture broke up and scattered,
Her paintings, which long years ago were done
By that old splendid artist-king, the sun.

Torn down and dragged in civilization's gutter,
Or sold to purchase settlers' bread and butter.
She don't want things exposed from porch to closet,
And so she kind o' nags the man who does it.
She carries in her pockets bags of seeds,
As general agent of the thriftiest weeds;
She sends her blackbirds, in the early morn,
To superintend his fields of planted corn;
She gives him rain past any duck's desire—
Then maybe several weeks of quiet fire;
She sails mosquitoes—leeches perched on wings—
To poison him with blood-devouring stings;
She loves her ague-muscle to display,
And shake him up—say every other day;
With thoughtful, conscientious care she makes
Those travelin' poison-bottles, rattle-snakes;
She finds time, 'mongst her other family cares,
To keep in stock good wild-cats, wolves, and bears.

Well, when I first infested this retreat,
Things to my view looked frightful incomplete;
But I had come with heart-thrift in my song,
And brought my wife and plunder right along;
I hadn't a round trip ticket to go back,
And if I had there wasn't no railroad track;
And drivin' East was what I couldn't endure:
I hadn't started on a circular tour.

My girl-wife was as brave as she was good,
And helped me every blessed way she could;
She seemed to take to every rough old tree,
As sing'lar as when first she took to me.
She kep' our little log-house neat as wax,
And once I caught her fooling with my axe.
She learned a hundred masculine things to do:
She aimed a shot-gun pretty middlin' true,
Although in spite of my express desire,
She always shut her eyes before she'd fire.
She hadn't the muscle (though she *had* the heart)
In out-door work to take an active part;
Though in our firm of Duty and Endeavor
She wasn't no silent partner whatsoever.
When I was logging, burning, choppin' wood,
She'd linger round and help me all she could,
And keep me fresh-ambitious all the while,
And lifted tons just with her voice and smile.
With no desire my glory for to rob,
She used to stan' around and boss the job;
And when first-class success my hands befell,
Would proudly say, "*We* did that pretty well!"
She *was* delicious, both to hear and see—

That pretty wife-girl that kep' house
for me.

Well, neighborhoods meant counties in
those days;
The roads didn't have accommodating
ways;
And maybe weeks would pass before
she'd see—
And much less talk with—any one but
me.
The Indians sometimes showed their
sun-baked faces,
But they didn't teem with conversa-
tional graces;
Some ideas from the birds and trees she
stole,
But 'twasn't like talking with a human
soul;
And finally I thought that I could trace
A half heart-hunger peering from her
face.
Then she would drive it back and shut
the door;
Of course that only made me see it
more.
'Twas hard to see her give her life to
mine,
Making a steady effort not to pine;
'Twas hard to hear that laugh bloom
out each minute,
And recognize the seeds of sorrow in it.
No misery makes a close observer
mourn
Like hopeless grief with hopeful cour-
age borne;
There's nothing sets the sympathies to
paining
Like a complaining woman uncomplain-
ing.
It always draws my breath out into
sighs
To see a brave look in a woman's eyes.

Well, she went on, as plucky as could
be,
Fighting the foe she thought I did not
see,
And using her heart-horticultural pow-
ers
To turn that forest to a bed of flowers.
You cannot check an unadmitted sigh,
And so I had to soothe her on the sly,
And secretly to help her draw her load;
And soon it came to be an up-hill road.
Hard work bears hard upon the average
pulse,
Even with satisfactory results;
But when effects are scarce, the heavy
strain
Falls dead and solid on the heart and
brain.
And when we're bothered, it will oft
occur
We seek blame-timber; and I lit on
her;
And looked at her with daily lessening
favor,
For what I knew she couldn't help, to
save her.
And Discord, when he once had called
and seen us,
Came round quite often, and edged in
between us.

One night, when I came home unusual
late,
Too hungry and too tired to feel first-
rate,
Her supper struck me wrong (though
I'll allow
She hadn't much to strike with, any-
how);
And when I went to milk the cows, and
found
They'd wandered from their usual feed-
ing ground,
And maybe'd left a few long miles be-
hind 'em,
Which I must copy, if I meant to find
'em,

Flash-quick the stay-chains of my temper broke,
And in a trice these hot words I had spoke:
"You ought to've kept the animals in view,
And drove 'em in; you'd nothing else to do.
The heft of all our life on me must fall;
You just lie round and let me do it all."

That speech—it hadn't been gone a half a minute
Before I saw the cold black poison in it;
And I'd have given all I had, and more,
To've only safely got it back in-door.
I'm now what most folks "well-to-do" would call
I feel to-day as if I'd give it all,
Provided I through fifty years might reach
And kill and bury that half-minute speech.

She handed back no words, as I could hear;
She didn't frown; she didn't shed a tear;
Half proud, half crushed, she stood and looked me o'er,
Like some one she had never seen before!
But such a sudden anguish-lit surprise
I never viewed before in human eyes.
(I've seen it oft enough since in a dream;
It sometimes wakes me like a midnight scream.)

Next morning, when, stone-faced, but heavy-hearted,
With dinner pail and sharpened axe I started
Away for my day's work—she watched the door,
And followed me half way to it or more;
And I was just a-turning round at this,
And asking for my usual good-by kiss;
But on her lip I saw a proudish curve,
And in her eye a shadow of reserve;
And she had shown—perhaps half unawares—
Some little independent breakfast airs;
And so the usual parting didn't occur,
Although her eyes invited me to her;
Or rather half invited me, for she
Didn't advertise to furnish kisses free;
You always had—that is, I had—to pay
Full market price, and go more'n half the way.
So, with a short "Good-by," I shut the door,
And left her as I never had before.
But when at noon my lunch I came to eat,
Put up by her so delicately neat—
Choicer, somewhat, than yesterday's had been,
And some fresh, sweet-eyed pansies she'd put in—
"Tender and pleasant thoughts," I knew they meant—
It seemed as if her kiss with me she'd sent;
Then I became once more her humble lover,
And said, "To-night I'll ask forgiveness of her."

I went home over-early on that eve,
Having contrived to make myself believe,
By various signs I kind o' knew and guessed,
A thunder-storm was coming from the west.
('Tis strange, when one sly reason fills the heart,
How many honest ones will take its part:

A dozen first-class reasons said 'twas right
That I should strike home early on that night.)

Half out of breath, the cabin door I swung,
ith tender heart-words trembling on my tongue;
ut all within looked desolate and bare:
y house had lost its soul,—she was not there!
penciled note was on the table spread,
nd these are something like the words it said:
he cows have strayed away again, I fear;
watched them pretty close; don't scold me, dear.
d where they are, I think I *nearly* know:
eard the bell not very long ago. . . .
hunted for them all the afternoon;
try once more—I think I'll find them soon.
r, if a burden I have been to you,
l haven't helped you as I ought to do,
old-time memories my forgiveness plead;
e tried to do my best—I have indeed.
rling, piece out with love the strength I lack,
nd have kind words for me when I get back."

carce did I give this letter sight and tongue—
Some swift-blown rain-drops to the window clung,
And from the clouds a rough, deep growl proceeded:
My thunder-storm had come, now 'twasn't needed.
I rushed out-door. The air was stained with black:
Night had come early, on the storm-cloud's back:
And everything kept dimming to the sight,
Save when the clouds threw their electric light;
When for a flash, so clean-cut was the view,
I'd think I saw her—knowing 'twas not true.
Through my small clearing dashed wide sheets of spray,
As if the ocean waves had lost their way;
Scarcely a pause the thunder-battle made,
In the bold clamor of its cannonade.
And she, while I was sheltered, dry, and warm,
Was somewhere in the clutches of this storm!
She who, when storm-frights found her at her best,
Had always hid her white face on my breast!

My dog, who'd skirmished round me all the day,
Now crouched and whimpering, in a corner lay;
I dragged him by the collar to the wall,
I pressed his quivering muzzle to a shawl—
"Track her, old boy!" I shouted; and he whined,
Matched eyes with me, as if to read my mind,
Then with a yell went tearing through the wood.
I followed him, as faithful as I could.
No pleasure-trip was that, through flood and flame;

We raced with death: we hunted noble game.
All night we dragged the woods without avail;
The ground got drenched—we could not keep the trail.
Three times again my cabin home I found,
Half hoping she might be there, safe and sound;
But each time 'twas an unavailing care:
My house had lost its soul; she was not there!

When, climbing the wet trees, next morning-sun
Laughed at the ruin that the night had done,
Bleeding and drenched, by toil and sorrow bent,
Back to what used to be my home I went.
But as I neared our little clearing-ground—
Listen!—I heard the cow-bell's tinkling sound.
The cabin door was just a bit ajar;
It gleamed upon my glad eyes like a star.
"Brave heart," I said, "for such a fragile form!
She made them guide her homeward through the storm!"
Such pangs of joy I never felt before.
"You've come!" I shouted and rushed through the door.

Yes, she had come—and gone again. She lay
With all her young life crushed and wrenched away—
Lay, the heart-ruins of our home among,
Not far from where I killed her with my tongue.
The rain-drops glittered 'mid her hair's long strands,
The forest thorns had torn her feet and hands,
And 'midst the tears—brave tears—that one could trace
Upon the pale but sweetly resolute face,
I once again the mournful words could read,
"I have tried to do my best—I have, indeed."

And now I'm mostly done; my story's o'er;
Part of it never breathed the air before.
'Tisn't over-usual, it must be allowed,
To volunteer heart-history to a crowd,
And scatter 'mongst them confidential tears,
But you'll protect an old man with his years;
And wheresoe'er this story's voice can reach,
This is the sermon I would have it preach:

Boys flying kites haul in their white-winged birds:
You can't do that way when you're flying words.
"Careful with fire," is good advice we know:
"Careful with words," is ten times doubly so.
Thoughts unexpressed may sometimes fall back dead,
But God himself can't kill them when they're said!
You have my life-grief: do not think a minute
'Twas told to take up time. There's business in it.
It sheds advice: whoe'er will take and live it,
Is welcome to the pain it cost to give it.

Will Carleton.

Seein' Things

I ain't afeard uv snakes, or toads, or
bugs, or worms, or mice,
An' things 'at girls are skeered uv I
think are awful nice!
I'm pretty brave, I guess; an' yet I
hate to go to bed,
For, when I'm tucked up warm an'
snug an' when my prayers are said,
Mother tells me "Happy dreams!" and
takes away the light,
An' leaves me lying all alone an' seein'
things at night!

Sometimes they're in the corner, some-
times they're by the door,
Sometimes they're all a-standin' in the
middle uv the floor;
Sometimes they are a-sittin' down,
sometimes they're walkin' round
So softly an' so creepylike they never
make a sound!
Sometimes they are as black as ink, an'
other times they're white—
But the color ain't no difference when
you see things at night!

Once, when I licked a feller 'at had just
moved on our street,
An' father sent me up to bed without a
bite to eat,
I woke up in the dark an' saw things
standin' in a row,
A-lookin' at me cross-eyed an' p' intin'
at me—so!
Oh, my! I was so skeered that time I
never slep' a mite—
It's almost alluz when I'm bad I see
things at night!

Lucky thing I ain't a girl, or I'd be
skeered to death!
Bein' I'm a boy, I duck my head an'
hold my breath;
An' I am, oh! *so* sorry I'm a naughty
boy, an' then
I promise to be better an' I say my
prayers again!
Gran'ma tells me that's the only way to
make it right
When a feller has been wicked an' sees
things at night!

An' so, when other naughty boys would
coax me into sin,
I try to skwush the Tempter's voice 'at
urges me within;
An' when they's pie for supper, or cakes
'at's big an' nice,
I want to—but I do not pass my plate
f'r them things twice!
No, ruther let Starvation wipe me slow-
ly out o' sight
Than I should keep a-livin' on an' seein'
things at night!

Eugene Field.

The Raggedy Man

Oh, The Raggedy Man! He works fer
Pa;
An' he's the goodest man ever you saw!
He comes to our house every day,
An' waters the horses, an' feeds 'em
hay;
An' he opens the shed—an' we all ist
laugh
When he drives out our little old wob-
blely calf;
An' nen—ef our hired girl says he
can—
He milks the cows fer 'Lizabuth Ann.—
Ain't he a' awful good Raggedy
Man?
Raggedy! Raggedy! Raggedy Man!

W'y, The Raggedy Man—he's ist so
good,
He splits the kindlin' an' chops the
wood;
An' nen he spades in our garden, too,
An' does most things 'at *boys* can't
do.—

He clumbed clean up in our big tree
An' shooked a' apple down fer me—
An' 'nother 'n', too, fer 'Lizabuth Ann—
An' 'nother 'n', too, fer The Raggedy Man.—
Ain't he a' awful kind Raggedy Man?
Raggedy! Raggedy! Raggedy Man!

An' The Raggedy Man one time say he
Pick' roast' rambos from a' orchurd-tree,
An' et 'em—all ist roas' an' hot!
An' it's so, too!—'cause a corn-crib got
Afire one time an' all burn' down
On "The Smoot Farm," 'bout four mile from town—
On "The Smoot Farm"! Yes—an' the hired han'
'At worked there nen 'uz The Raggedy Man!
Ain't he the beanin'est Raggedy Man?
Raggedy! Raggedy! Raggedy Man!

The Raggedy Man's so good an' kind
He'll be our "horsey," an' "Haw" an' mind
Ever'thing 'at you make him do—
An' won't run off—'less you want him to!
I drived him wunst 'way down our lane
An' he got skeered, when it 'menced to rain,
An' ist rared up an' squealed and run
Purt' nigh away!—An' it's all in fun!
Nen he skeered ag'in at a' old tin can..
Whoa! y' old runaway Raggedy Man!
Raggedy! Raggedy! Raggedy Man!

An' The Raggedy Man, he knows most rhymes,
An' tells 'em, ef I be good, sometimes:
Knows 'bout Giunts, an' Griffuns, an' Elves,
An' the Squidgicum-Squees 'at swallers the'rselves!
An', wite by the pump in our pasture-lot,
He showed me the hole 'at the Wunks is got,
'At lives 'way deep in the ground, an' can
Turn into me, er 'Lizabuth Ann!
Er Ma, er Pa, er The Raggedy Man!
Ain't he a funny old Raggedy Man?
Raggedy! Raggedy! Raggedy Man!

An' wunst when The Raggedy Man come late,
An' pigs ist root' thue the garden-gate,
He 'tend like the pigs 'uz bears an' said,
"Old Bear-shooter'll shoot 'em dead!"
An' race' an' chase' em, an' they'd ist run
When he pint his hoe at 'em like it's a gun
An' go "Bang!—Bang!" nen 'tend he stan'
An' load up his gun ag'in! Raggedy Man!
He's an old Bear-Shooter Raggedy Man!
Raggedy! Raggedy! Raggedy Man!

An' sometimes The Raggedy Man lets on
We're little prince-children, an' old king's gone
To get more money, an' lef' us there—
And Robbers is ist thick ever'where;
An' nen—ef we all won't cry, fer shore—
The Raggedy Man he'll come and "splore
The Castul-halls," an' steal the "gold"—
And steal us, too, an' grab an' hold
An' pack us off to his old "Cave"!—An'
Haymow's the "Cave" o' The Raggedy Man!—
Raggedy! Raggedy! Raggedy Man!

The Raggedy Man—one time, when he
Wuz makin' a little bow-'n'-orry fer me,
Says "When you're big like your Pa is,
Air *you* go' to keep a fine store like
his—
An' be a rich merchunt—an' wear fine
clothes?—
Er what *air* you go' to be, goodness
knows?"
An' nen he laughed at 'Lizabuth Ann,
An' I says "'M go' to be a Raggedy
Man!—
I'm ist go' to be a nice Raggedy
Man!"
Raggedy! Raggedy! Raggedy Man!

James Whitcomb Riley.

Maud Muller

Maud Muller, on a summer's day,
Raked the meadow sweet with hay.

Beneath her torn hat glowed the wealth
Of simple beauty and rustic health.

Singing, she wrought, and her merry
glee
The mock-bird echoed from his tree.

But when she glanced to the far-off
town,
White from its hill-slope looking down,

The sweet song died, and a vague unrest
And a nameless longing filled her
breast,—

A wish, that she hardly dared to own,
For something better than she had
known.

The Judge rode slowly down the lane,
Smoothing his horse's chestnut mane.

He drew his bridle in the shade
Of the apple-trees, to greet the maid,

And asked a draught from the spring
that flowed
Through the meadow across the road.

She stooped where the cool spring bubbled up,
And filled for him her small tin cup,

And blushed as she gave it, looking
down
On her feet so bare, and her tattered
gown.

"Thanks!" said the Judge; "a sweeter draught
From a fairer hand was never quaffed."

He spoke of the grass and flowers and
trees,
Of the singing birds and the humming
bees;

Then talked of the haying, and wondered whether
The cloud in the west would bring foul
weather.

And Maud forgot her brier-torn gown,
And her graceful ankles bare and
brown;

And listened, while a pleased surprise
Looked from her long-lashed hazel eyes.

At last, like one who for delay
Seeks a vain excuse, he rode away.

Maud Muller looked and sighed: "Ah
me!
That I the Judge's bride might be!

"He would dress me up in silks so fine,
And praise and toast me at his wine.

"My father should wear a broadcloth
coat;
My brother should sail a painted boat.

"I'd dress my mother so grand and gay,
And the baby should have a new toy
each day.

"And I'd feed the hungry and clothe the poor,
And all should bless me who left our door."

The Judge looked back as he climbed the hill,
And saw Maud Muller standing still.

"A form more fair, a face more sweet,
Ne'er hath it been my lot to meet.

"And her modest answer and graceful air
Show her wise and good as she is fair.

"Would she were mine, and I to-day,
Like her, a harvester of hay:

"No doubtful balance of rights and wrongs
Nor weary lawyers with endless tongues,

"But low of cattle and song of birds,
And health and quiet and loving words."

But he thought of his sisters proud and cold,
And his mother vain of her rank and gold.

So, closing his heart, the Judge rode on,
And Maud was left in the field alone.

But the lawyers smiled that afternoon,
When he hummed in court an old love-tune;

And the young girl mused beside the well
Till the rain on the unraked clover fell.

He wedded a wife of richest dower,
Who lived for fashion, as he for power.

Yet oft, in his marble hearth's bright glow,
He watched a picture come and go;

And sweet Maud Muller's hazel eyes
Looked out in their innocent surprise.

Oft, when the wine in his glass was red,
He longed for the wayside well instead;

And closed his eyes on his garnished rooms
To dream of meadows and clover-blooms.

And the proud man sighed, with a secret pain,
"Ah, that I were free again!

"Free as when I rode that day,
Where the barefoot maiden raked her hay."

She wedded a man unlearned and poor,
And many children played round her door.

But care and sorrow, and childbirth pain,
Left their traces on heart and brain.

And oft, when the summer sun shone hot
On the new-mown hay in the meadow lot,

And she heard the little spring brook fall
Over the roadside, through the wall,

In the shade of the apple-tree again
She saw a rider draw his rein.

And, gazing down with timid grace,
She felt his pleased eyes read her face.

Sometimes her narrow kitchen walls
Stretched away into stately halls;

The weary wheel to a spinnet turned,
The tallow candle an astral burned,

And for him who sat by the chimney lug,
Dozing and grumbling o'er pipe and mug,

A manly form at her side she saw,
And joy was duty and love was law.

Then she took up her burden of life
again,
Saying only, "It might have been."

Alas for maiden, alas for Judge,
For rich repiner and household drudge!

God pity them both! and pity us all,
Who vainly the dreams of youth recall.

For of all sad words of tongue or pen,
The saddest are these: "It might have
been!"

Ah, well! for us all some sweet hope
lies
Deeply buried from human eyes;

And, in the hereafter, angels may
Roll the stone from its grave away!

John G. Whittier.

Sister and I

We were hunting for wintergreen
berries,
One May-day, long gone by,
Out on the rocky cliff's edge,
Little sister and I.
Sister had hair like the sunbeams;
Black as a crow's wing, mine;
Sister had blue, dove's eyes;
Wicked, black eyes are mine.
Why, see how my eyes are faded—
And my hair; it is white as snow!
And thin, too! don't you see it is?
I tear it sometimes; so!
There, don't hold my hands, Maggie,
I don't feel like tearing it now;
But—where was I in my story?
Oh, I was telling you how
We were looking for wintergreen
berries;
'Twas one bright morning in May,
And the moss-grown rocks were slip-
pery
With the rains of yesterday.
But I was cross that morning,
Though the sun shone ever so
bright—
And when sister found the most berries,
I was angry enough to fight!
And when she laughed at my pouting—
We were little things, you know—
I clinched my little fist up tight,
And struck her the biggest blow!
I struck her—I tell you—I struck her,
And she fell right over below—
There, there, Maggie, I won't rave now;
You needn't hold me so—
She went right over, I tell you,
Down, down to the depths below!
'Tis deep and dark and horrid
There where the waters flow!
She fell right over, moaning,
"Bessie, oh, Bessie!" so sad,
That, when I looked down affrighted,
It drove me *mad—mad!*
Only her golden hair streaming
Out on the rippling wave,
Only her little hand reaching
Up, for someone to save;
And she sank down in the darkness,
I never saw her again,
And this is a chaos of blackness
And darkness and grief since then.
No more playing together
Down on the pebbly strand;
Nor building our dolls stone castles
With halls and parlors grand;
No more fishing with bent pins,
In the little brook's clear waves;
No more holding funerals
O'er dead canaries' graves;
No more walking together
To the log schoolhouse each morn;
No more vexing the master
With putting his rules to scorn;
No more feeding of white lambs
With milk from the foaming pail;
No more playing "see-saw"
Over the fence of rail;

No more telling of stories
  After we've gone to bed;
Nor talking of ghosts and goblins
  Till we fairly shiver with dread;
No more whispering fearfully
  And hugging each other tight,
When the shutters shake and the dogs howl
  In the middle of the night;
No more saying "Our Father,"
  Kneeling by mother's knee—
For, Maggie, I *struck* sister!
  And mother is dead, you see.
Maggie, sister's an angel,
  Isn't she? Isn't it true?
For angels have golden tresses
  And eyes like sister's, blue?
Now *my* hair isn't golden,
  My eyes aren't blue, you see—
Now tell me, Maggie, if I were to die,
  Could they make an angel of me?
You say, "Oh, yes"; you think so?
  Well, then, when I come to die,
We'll play up there, in God's garden—
  We'll play there, sister and I.
Now, Maggie, you needn't eye me
  Because I'm talking so queer;
Because I'm talking so strangely;
  You needn't have the least fear.
Somehow I'm feeling to-night, Maggie,
  As I never felt before—
I'm sure, I'm sure of it, Maggie,
  I never shall rave any more.
Maggie, you know how these long years
  I've heard her calling, so sad,
"Bessie, oh, Bessie!" so mournful?
  It always drives me *mad!*
How the winter wind shrieks down the chimney,
  "Bessie, oh, Bessie!" oh! oh!
How the south wind wails at the casement,
  "Bessie, oh, Bessie!" so low.
But most of all when the May-days
  Come back, with the flowers and the sun,
How the night-bird, singing, all lonely,
  "Bessie, oh, Bessie!" doth moan;
You know how it sets me raving—
  For *she* moaned, "*Oh, Bessie!*" just so,
That time I *struck* little sister,
  On the May-day long ago!
Now, Maggie, I've something to tell you—
  You know May-day is here—
Well, this very morning, at sunrise,
  The robins chirped "Bessie!" so clear—
All day long the wee birds singing,
  Perched on the garden wall,
Called "Bessie, oh, Bessie!" so sweetly,
  I couldn't feel sorry at all.
Now, Maggie, I've something to tell you—
  Let me lean up to you close—
Do you see how the sunset has flooded
  The heavens with yellow and rose?
Do you see o'er the gilded cloud mountains
  Sister's golden hair streaming out?
Do you see her little hand beckoning?
  Do you hear her little voice calling out
"Bessie, oh, Bessie!" so gladly,
  "Bessie, oh, Bessie! Come, haste"?
Yes, sister, I'm coming; I'm coming,
  To play in God's garden at last!